D1556472

The HON Story

The HON Story

A History of HON INDUSTRIES 1944-1985

C. Maxwell Stanley
James H. Soltow

Iowa State University Press

⊗ This book is printed on acid-free paper in the United States of America

First edition, 1991

Library of Congress Cataloging-in-Publication Data

Stanley, C. Maxwell (Claude Maxwell)
    The HON story : a history of HON INDUSTRIES, 1944–1985 / C. Maxwell Stanley, James H. Soltow. — 1st ed.
        p.   cm.
    Includes index.
    ISBN 0-8138-0602-X (cloth). — ISBN 0-8138-0601-1 (pbk.)
    1. HON INDUSTRIES — History. 2. Office furniture industry — United States — History. 3. Conglomerate corporations — United States — History. 4. New business enterprises — United States — Case studies. 5. Entrepreneurship — United States — Case studies. 6. Success in business — United States — Case studies. I. Soltow, James H. II. Title. II. Title.
    HD9803.U64H667   1991
    338.7′6841′00973 — dc20   90-28715

C. Maxwell Stanley (1904–1984) was a founder of Stanley Consultants, Inc., and The Home-O-Nize Co. (eventually HON INDUSTRIES), both headquartered in Muscatine, Iowa.

James H. Soltow is Professor of History, Emeritus, Michigan State University.

Contents

Preface

Max Stanley's history of the company he founded provides an exceptionally frank and vivid account of his experiences and those of his many associates in that venture. At the time of his death in 1984, he had completed twelve chapters of *The HON Story,* covering the years from the conception of the enterprise in 1944 to 1965. He also was well along with a section of four chapters dealing with the period from 1966 to 1972. Notes that he left provided a general idea of his plan for writing about the years after 1972.

In 1986, Stanley M. Howe, chairman and president of HON INDUSTRIES Inc., invited me to undertake the editing of the manuscript left by Max Stanley, the completion of the chapters on the period from 1966 to 1972, and the writing of a section to bring *The HON Story* up to 1985.

In carrying out this assignment, I have had access to whatever corporate records I needed. Even more important, many current and retired officers and other HON members patiently explained the evolution of practices and policies in the areas with which they were most familiar. The following individuals talked fully and frankly about various aspects of the history of HON INDUSTRIES and its operating companies: James Arthur, Ralph Beals, Rex Bennett, Jerry Boulund, J. Harold Bragg, Clifford M. Brown, Robert L. Carl, Max A. Collins, Walter B. Conner, Arthur E. Dahl, R. Michael Derry, Philip Hecht, Stanley M. Howe, James Johnson, Edward E. Jones, Ronald L. Jones, Douglas McQuiggan, Clare A. Patterson, John Schaub, Mary Ann Stange, Jay Timmons, and L. Gene Waddell.

Richard E. Johnson, corporate planning manager of HON INDUSTRIES, assumed responsibility for moving the manuscript into production. Frank Kelly, senior writer, located and identified the pictures contained in the book. My warm thanks go to these and to all of the others at HON INDUSTRIES who helped to make possible the successful completion of my assignment.

Special thanks go to Robert L. Carl, secretary of HON INDUSTRIES, who served as liaison and guide. Drawing on his personal knowledge about the activities of the corporation and the location of sources of information, he uncovered answers to numerous questions for me, as he had done earlier for Max Stanley.

JAMES H. SOLTOW

Prologue

A Note on C. Maxwell Stanley

Max Stanley was born in Corning, Iowa, in 1904. After earning a bachelor's degree in general engineering and a master's degree in hydraulic engineering, both from the University of Iowa, he worked for several years for engineering firms in Chicago and in Dubuque.

Stanley arrived in Muscatine in 1932, at the depth of the Great Depression. With the knowledge that he had gained from his two degrees and six years of work experience, he became a partner in a small engineering firm. He then built this enterprise, which became Stanley Consultants, Incorporated, into a major international business involved in engineering, architecture, and planning. Becoming a leader in his profession, he wrote *The Consulting Engineer*, a definitive work on private consulting.

Most men would have been content with establishing one successful business, but Stanley was concerned that the veterans returning from World War II would need jobs. Many people at the time were predicting that the transition from the frantic pace of war production to a peacetime economy would result in a depression and large-scale unemployment. Stanley believed that businesspeople like himself could create jobs if they were willing to invest in new business firms. In addition, he would have an opportunity to implement some of the ideas that he had been developing about improved employer-employee relations in manufacturing plants.

Thus, Max Stanley determined to launch the business that would eventually become HON INDUSTRIES. Armed with an idea to make a line of steel kitchen cabinets with shelves that moved up and down at the touch of a switch, Stanley spearheaded the formation of The Home-O-Nize Co. in Muscatine in 1944.

Like most new entrants into the business world, Home-O-Nize encountered a multitude of unanticipated (and unanticipatable) problems, including fire and flood. But Stanley was persistent in guiding the young firm through the perils. He was willing to put his own financial resources and business reputation on the line by investing and persuading others to invest in what was then perceived as a highly speculative venture. Above all, he had to demonstrate a great deal of flexibility and ingenuity to take advantage of the opportunities that presented themselves. When a severe steel shortage after World War II prevented implementation of the original plan to manufacture kitchen cabinets, Home-O-Nize turned to contracting work to keep the company alive. At a crucial point, the acquisition of Prime-Mover brought much needed business and financing.

However, it was the scrap barrel that pointed the young company toward its niche in the business world—the manufac-

C. Maxwell Stanley (1904– 1984), launched The Home-O-Nize Co. in 1944 with Clement T. Hanson and H. Wood Miller. By 1985, Home-O-Nize had become HON INDUS- TRIES, a diverse and national Fortune 500 business.

ture of products for the office. Starting with card file boxes made from scrap aluminum left over from its jobbing business, Home-O-Nize added combination filing-storage cabinets and then nonsuspension and suspension filing cabinets.

Filing cabinets dominated the sales of Home-O-Nize's office furniture in the early years of its participation in the industry. Other products were soon introduced—desks, bookcases, and chairs. The company pioneered in the use of nylon rollers for drawer operation, first in filing cabinets and then in other products, with favorable results in terms of both performance and consumer acceptance. After establishing dominance in the middle market for office furniture, HON INDUSTRIES moved in the 1970s toward establishing a position in the contract segment of the industry.

Max Stanley, by himself, carried much of the burden of running Home-O-Nize in the early years, although he was also managing partner of Stanley Consultants, a major consulting engineering firm with headquarters in Muscatine. He served as chairman and president from the incorporation of the company in 1944 until 1964, when he relinquished the presidency. Stanley as chairman continued to participate in major policy decisions until the day of his death in 1984.

As successful as he was in business, Max Stanley played an active and important role in other areas of life. For many years, he held a strong interest in finding alternatives to the use of force in conflict resolution among nations of the world. To this end, he and his wife, Betty, founded and generously endowed the Stanley Foundation in 1956 to encourage and support research and education in the field of foreign relations. Stanley chaired many international conferences and authored two books—*Waging Peace* and *Managing Global Problems: A Guide to Survival*—as

well as numerous articles and papers on foreign policy. He served as president of *World Press Review,* a New York–based monthly magazine that published excerpts from foreign newspapers and interviews with specialists in international affairs.

Stanley also held an interest in higher education, serving as chairman of the board of trustees of Iowa Wesleyan College and president of the University of Iowa Foundation. Stanley was a major donor to his alma mater, the University of Iowa. In addition, Max and Betty gave their valuable collection of African art to the university's Museum of Art. He received honorary doctoral degrees from Iowa Wesleyan College, Augustana College, and the University of Manila, and was made an honorary rector at the University of Dubuque. The C. Maxwell Stanley Professorship in Production Management was created at the University of Iowa College of Business Administration in his honor.

Although Max Stanley well deserved to be called a "citizen of the world," he never forgot that he was a citizen of Muscatine as well. Reflecting his concern about local economic development, particularly job creation, Stanley played a major role in the formation of the Muscatine Industrial Development Commission in 1957. For many years, he served as chairman of this organization, which hoped to bring new industries to the community. Max and Betty donated the Stanley Gallery to the Muscatine Art Center in 1976. Among other organizations to which he gave enthusiastic support were the United Methodist Church and the Boy Scouts.

A former mayor of Muscatine said of Max Stanley: "He was a tremendous business man, but he was also a very humble man. He was soft spoken and dedicated to his profession and his family. His accomplishments could not be measured."

PART ONE

THE PERILS OF LAUNCHING A NEW ENTERPRISE, 1943-1950

The Home-O-Nize Co.—which became HON INDUSTRIES—was conceived in a backyard in June 1943. Almost four years of preparations followed before the company even made its first products. During those years, many changes had to be made in the plans of the founders—Stanley, Hanson, and Miller—as we learned the lessons about launching a new enterprise into the business world.

Even after starting production in 1947, there was no assurance that Home-O-Nize would survive. For three-and-a-half years, we faced peril after peril. At times, there seemed to be little logic to our continued existence as a business. However, we were determined to succeed, and I was fortunate to find the funds to keep the company alive. Finally, a fortuitous acquisition—that of a piece of material-handling equipment—brought badly needed financing and business to assure the survival of The Home-O-Nize Co.

CHAPTER ONE

Birth of an Enterprise

For every new venture, there must be a point of departure—a moment when talk and speculation give way to decision and action. That moment, for what is now HON INDUSTRIES Incorporated, came on a pleasant Sunday afternoon in June of 1943. Clem Hanson and I were relaxing in the backyard of Hanson's Moline, Illinois, home, where our families had gathered for a meal and a visit. We had known each other since college days, having courted, and later married, sisters. As was customary at our family gatherings, the kids were playing, the sisters were chatting and clearing the remains of a hearty meal, and Clem and I were solving the world's problems. Our discussions ranged broadly. We talked about the progress of World War II, the nation's political and economic challenges, and anticipated postwar problems. We returned, inevitably, to a topic of common interest. We had often observed with disdain the mediocrity of management in many manufacturing companies, particularly the management of corporate relationships with employees, customers, and communities.

The Founders

Clement T. Hanson, then 42, a 1925 graduate of the College of Commerce at the University of Iowa, was an advertising executive and an able professional in the field. He was a keen observer and competent analyst of communications, human and public relations, and marketing. Following initial employment as a reporter for the *Des Moines Register,* Hanson became associated with the Hendrickson Agency of Davenport, Iowa. There, he acquired broad skills in all phases of advertising. After 10 years with Hendrickson, Hanson moved to the Tri-City Blue Print Company of Moline to take charge of sales for a new printing process called planograph, later a universally used offset process.

Clem was married to Sylvia Holthues, my wife's sister; their sons James and Thomas were then 10 and 5. I was married to Elizabeth M. Holthues. Our son David was then 15; our other son Richard, 11; and our daughter Jane, 7.

My background was quite different from Clem's. Graduating in 1926 from the College of Engineering at the University of Iowa, I spent a year with Byllesby Engineering and Management Corporation in Chicago. A year of graduate study in Iowa City led next to an M.S. degree, after which I worked in Dubuque and Chicago for the Management and Engineering Corporation. One jump ahead of a Depression pink slip, I purchased a half interest in a small consulting practice in Muscatine, Iowa, in 1932.

Before Pearl Harbor, that small consulting practice, by then known as the Stan-

When this photo was taken, Stanley had every reason to look serious. He and his partners had a dream of a company making a timely product and treating its people with dignity and respect. But they were also coping with the harsh realities of being desperately undercapitalized.

Clem Hanson was Stanley's brother-in-law and the first person on the payroll. His duties encompassed almost everything.

ley Engineering Company, had grown from a staff of three to one of about 70 and was on its way to becoming a sizable, multidisciplinary organization. During the early war years, we had been heavily involved in the design and construction of air bases and other military facilities. At age 39, I had developed strong confidence in my talents, not only in engineering, but also in organization and management.

Over the years, Clem and I had discovered many common opinions on public policy, business organization, and industrial management. We shared similar ideas about human relations. We both believed that there was a need in our country for more enlightened approaches to employer-employee relations. We joined others in criticizing many industries for an all-too-prevalent "public-be-damned" attitude toward consumers of their products. We had often expressed the egotistical belief that we could do better. Clem and I were worried, as many people then were, that employment would be a major problem when, at war's end, the country converted to a peacetime economy.

During our conversation that Sunday afternoon, I remarked, "Clem, what do you think about starting a manufacturing enterprise of some kind when peace comes?" Hanson reacted immediately and favorably. We then enumerated the skills that the two of us could contribute to the venture: organization, administration, engineering, marketing, sales, and advertising abilities. Hanson suggested that we invite a mutual friend, Wood Miller, to join us and add his product ideas and design experience to our venture. Our conversations that afternoon concluded with talk about the basic policies, ethical standards, and human relations that we wanted to build into the structure of our dream company.

Graphics and industrial design were the skills that H. Wood Miller brought to our enterprise. After high school, Miller had spent six years at the Art Institute of Chicago, where he took a design course of study. Miller, at 42, was serving a number of industrial clients through the H. Wood Miller Company. He had been employed previously at the Hendrickson Agency do-

ing layout and art work. There, Hanson and Miller had become good friends.

Miller was married to Irma Begg; their daughters Joann and Jerry were then 15 and 13. The Hanson and Miller families were well-acquainted, and the Stanleys had visited with them occasionally. I found that Miller and I had many common concerns and beliefs, including that of the importance of offering sound, attractive, and useful products.

As we anticipated, Miller's response was positive and enthusiastic; he was ready to join us in the venture. Thus, a triumvirate was formed. A crucial decision had been made.

From that day on, we set out boldly, but cautiously, to create a manufacturing company to start operation soon after the war ended. Because the end of World War II seemed distant, we agreed on a steady, but deliberate, pace. The mighty American military power was only beginning to influence the course of war. Most of the people we would later recruit as staff for our venture were then a part of our country's military forces.

Motivations

Not one, but several, motivations impelled our decision. One was a shared desire to structure a company that handled relations between employer and employee well. The three of us believed that good personal relations were fundamental to success and that they could be achieved. We concurred in the idea that employees, as fellow human beings, should be treated with dignity and fairness, not exploited in the interest of profits. The validity of these concepts has been tested and proved by the continuing success of the company that became HON INDUSTRIES.

A second motivation was a desire to share in the opportunity and responsibility of preventing the massive unemployment that was widely predicted. We would start a business and thereby provide jobs for returning veterans. Although widespread unemployment did not materialize as expected, we thought at the time that we could contribute in a positive way to the transition of the country's economy from war to peace.

The very challenge that lay in creating and managing a manufacturing company was a third important motivation. Our self-confidence was abundant. We believed that we were as intelligent and able, if not more intelligent and more able, than most of the executives and managers we knew. Miller had design concepts he wanted to develop; Hanson had marketing approaches and customer service concepts he wanted to implement; and I had management ideas I thought would work. We were eager for a chance to prove our abilities.

No doubt other motivations were present. Neither Miller nor Hanson was overly satisfied with his employment at that time. Although neither was intensely money-oriented, I am sure that both expected our proposed venture to offer greater rewards, both financial and personal, than their then-current employment. I felt that I had some time on my hands. Wartime construction work was largely complete, and the Stanley Engineering Co. staff was small. It did not appear likely that I would enter military service. Hence, I viewed the venture as a stimulating avocation and challenge, a new world to conquer.

Whatever our motivations, the decision was made in Hanson's backyard that Sunday afternoon. With Miller's concurrence, we were on our way. We didn't know what we would manufacture, but we were going to have a company. The small seed had been planted from which the now blooming HON INDUSTRIES would eventually grow. Our confident enthusiasm was matched only by our considerable naivete. Little did we understand the difficult problems and obstacles that new enterprises usually encounter. But this was as it should be. Had we foreseen the hurdles, we might never have ventured.

Initial Steps

The crucial backyard decision was only a beginning. We had much to do before we would have an operating en-

terprise, let alone a profitable one. We obviously needed to select our general field of manufacture and pinpoint initial product offerings. We needed a name and a corporate entity. We required detailed designs and working models before we could test the initial product and explore the market. How would we manufacture and market our goods? How could we finance our operations?

We moved ahead on all of these fronts during the balance of 1943 and most of 1944. The magnitude of the task became evident to me, and I'm sure to my associates, only as we began to grapple actively, but not urgently, with preliminary preparations.

Choosing a Product.   Hanson, Miller, and I promptly began examining various product lines. Rather quickly we focused on the home market, particularly the kitchen. We foresaw a gigantic postwar building boom to relieve the dearth of housing. Miller was full of ideas. He had done some preliminary work on home freezer units. The prewar trend toward the use of frozen foods seemed likely to continue. In our view, the home unit was going to replace rental lockers and supplement the limited freezer capacity of refrigerators. Miller also advanced some exciting kitchen cabinet concepts. He proposed electrically operated upper cabinets that could be raised or lowered for the homemaker's convenience. The cabinets would be highly styled, easily installed, and have readily extendable modular units.

We decided to go in this direction. We would enter the home appliance field with home freezers, followed by kitchen cabi-

Wood Miller, a mutual friend and gifted designer, developed the concept and design for the kitchen cabinets that launched the new enterprise.

The promise of a postwar housing boom gave the new business the hope of success.

Every home would have a kitchen, and frozen food would be an important part of postwar housekeeping. The trio planned to sell kitchen cabinets to the new homeowners along with a home freezer.

Hanson and Miller designed the fledgling company's first logo when the kitchen was thought to be the destination of Home-O-Nize products.

gestions, looking for one that created a desirable image and had potential as a marketing tool. We quickly discarded the use of our own names or geographic locations. Hanson emphasized a market-related coined name, with his proposal for "Home-O-Matic" giving way to "Home-O-Nize." With a nice verbal ring, the name offered significant opportunities as a sales tool. Its first syllable suggested the ultimate destination of the products that we were planning to offer. The third syllable would rhyme well. "Nize" could be used in such slogans as "Economize with Home-O-Nize" or "Modernize with Home-O-Nize." A dealer could be a "Home-O-Nizer." For visual impact, Hanson and Miller designed a neat logo with two musical notes placed within the capital O. Home-O-Nize was happily adopted. Of course, we had no premonition of the future difficulties that this ingenious name would create.

Manufacturing Arrangements

Recognizing that neither Hanson, Miller, nor I had actual production experience, we began a search for a person or an association to bring skills in sheet metal fabrication to our company. Miller's wide acquaintance in the Quad Cities area was helpful in this search. We conferred with Dale Hermes, then employed by the Herman Nelson Division of the American Air Filter Company, based in Moline. His advice was helpful, but no relationship was developed. Our contact with him, however, later led to an association of great benefit to Home-O-Nize.

Miller also put us in touch with Albert F. Uchtorff, president and principal owner of the Uchtorff Company in Davenport. The "Uchtorff diversion," as we later labeled the relationship, turned out to be a frustrating experience. The Uchtorff Co. was a job shop, manufacturing a wide variety of sheet metal products, including conventional square-cornered kitchen cabinets. Uchtorff's response was prompt and positive. He expressed a desire to join our venture, pointing out that his plant could manufacture products for Home-O-Nize, at least initially. This was an attractive ar-

nets, and then perhaps other appliances. This would take advantage of Miller's experience as chief consulting designer for the manufacturers of Universal and Tappan gas and electric ranges. The product options seemed wide open. Happy with the initial decision, we forged ahead, completely unaware that we would never produce or sell a single freezer or kitchen cabinet.

Choosing a Name.   Hanson took the lead on a name. We examined many of his sug-

rangement because production and sales could advance while major investments in plant and equipment were deferred. So, the three of us decided to become a foursome.

In November 1943, the four of us signed a partnership agreement to establish an organization for the design, manufacture, and sale of home appliances and other apparatus. The agreement contemplated the later formation of a corporation. In the meantime, we were to share alike in the organization, make equal financial contributions, and receive an equal division of profits. Each of us would continue his present employment, promising to make comparable contributions to the venture without initially receiving a salary. In the agreement, we indicated our desire to arrange a suitable manufacturing contract between the new organization and the Uchtorff Co. We were to proceed expeditiously to develop designs, construct models, complete the business organization, develop a sales program, and take the other steps necessary to begin business operations at as early a date as practicable.

Incorporation

When we were ready to incorporate, I retained Matthew Westrate, a Muscatine lawyer who had provided services to the Stanley Engineering Co. He was later to be a judge on the District Court of Iowa and is now deceased. Under his guidance, The Home-O-Nize Co. was incorporated in Iowa. The authorized capital of the corporation consisted of 500 shares of common stock without par value and 500 shares of preferred stock with $100 par value. Hanson, Miller, Uchtorff, and I were the incorporators and directors. Officers were Stanley, president; Uchtorff and Miller, vice presidents; and Hanson, secretary-treasurer. Davenport, Iowa, was established as the principal place of business. On January 6, 1944, we signed the Articles of Incorporation, and, in due time, a Certificate of Incorporation was issued by the secretary of state. Bylaws were adopted at the first annual meeting of the stockholders on March 15, 1944.

Meanwhile, in December 1943, the fledgling company's headquarters had been established in Miller's office over the Wagner Printery at 315½ West Fourth Street, Davenport. Home-O-Nize agreed to pay the princely sum of $10 per month for its share of rent. The door sign read: THE HOME-O-NIZE CO. — MAKERS OF HOME APPLIANCES.

By early January, we needed money. Hanson, Miller, and I had contributed a nominal $20 earlier, but it had been spent. On January 6, 1944, the four directors each subscribed to purchase, for $1,000, 10 shares of stock within three weeks.

On the same date, I prepared an operational plan, a 10-page document titled "Scheduled Procedure — The Home-O-Nize Co." Development, engineering, purchasing, production, service, sales, and office departments were outlined, and departmental functions were defined. Objectives for a four-month "immediate" period were a part of the document, as were the responsibilities assigned to each of the four of us. Finally, an approach to "future planning" beyond the immediate period was presented.

Product Development

Product development continued during 1944. Miller produced sketches of a deep-freeze unit; I obtained a compressor unit; and Uchtorff built a model that was transported to my garage for a consumer test. Miller continued the conceptual designing of the kitchen cabinets. His ideas were exciting, but we needed to determine how well they worked in practice and how they could be constructed. At the Davenport office, Hanson and Miller established the model shop required to perform these functions. Hand-forming equipment, benches, and tools were soon assembled. William Booth, an experienced sheet metal worker, began on a part-time basis shearing, punching, welding, buffing, and painting under the part-time supervision of Hanson and Miller. Gradually, working models emerged for examination and testing.

Iowa Charter Asked by Home Appliance Concern

Articles of incorporation were filed with the Iowa secretary of State in Des Moines today by the Home-O-Nize company of Davenport. The firm is capitalized at $50,000 and will design and manufacture household appliances, according to a United Press dispatch.

Officers are C. Maxwell Stanley, Muscatine, president; Albert F. Uchtorff, Davenport, vice president; H. Wood Miller, Davenport, vice president, and C. T. Hanson, Moline, secretary-treasurer.

An Iowa charter is granted to Home-O-Nize. (Rock Island Argus, January 14, 1944)

Three key elements distinguished the new company's cabinets from other designs and styles of the 1940s. The quick erector frame allowed appliance dealers to install custom kitchen cabinets; a drop-down mechanism enabled housewives to see the contents of the top shelf; and drawers replaced doors so that pots, pans, canned goods, and appliances could be easily stowed and retrieved. These photos of the prototype show the upper shelves in place and lowered. The artist's rendering shows the cabinet as it would appear.

By the middle of 1944, the work load and supervisory requirements had grown too demanding to be handled on a part-time basis. We had previously developed a retainer arrangement with Miller. He would devote part of his time to Home-O-Nize while his own firm, H. Wood Miller Company, would continue to provide service to his other clients. Hanson, with some trepidation, agreed to resign his position at Tri-City Blue Print Company in order to become the first full-time employee of Home-O-Nize, at a salary of $400 per month. He supervised the model shop, accelerated exploration of the market, and developed a set of marketing programs.

Our four-man board of directors met frequently during 1944. Minutes show that we dealt with a variety of topics. At one time, we seriously considered designing

and manufacturing sheet metal housings for service station greasing equipment produced by the Montgomery Elevator Company. We authorized a contract, but nothing came of it. In September, we decided to have Uchtorff produce "ready for market, prewar kitchen cabinets" with suitable modifications, to be marketed as Home-O-Nize products. These cabinets, we thought, would accelerate our entry into the market, making it easier to obtain and hold dealers and jobbers. We also decided to move our office within the next few months to remodeled quarters at the Uchtorff plant, to be rented for $25 per month. C. A. Patterson was employed during this time to produce, under Miller's supervision, detailed designs for the modernized Home-O-Nize line of kitchen cabinets.

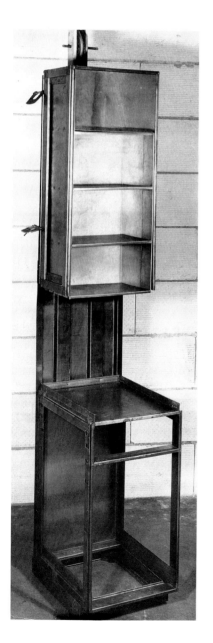

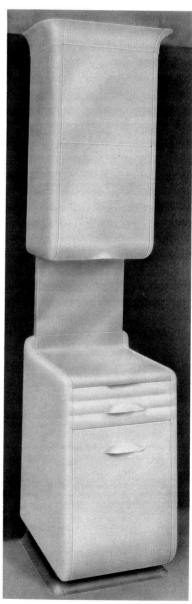

In October, the outlook was optimistic enough that we acted to discontinue the design services that Miller had been performing for outside clients. We had continued this service in order to improve our cash flow. Uchtorff was then given drawings of the new base cabinets and asked to estimate tooling, die, and production costs for 10,000 units. Our hopes at the moment were far from small. About the same time, however, we decided to assign a lower priority to the production of home freezers in order to concentrate on the kitchen cabinets.

While design and model making were just getting under way, Hanson was starting to develop plans to build a dealer organization and to prepare sales literature. Early in 1944, Hanson and I visited with G. W. Timmerman of Midwest Timmerman, a large Davenport distributor of home appliances. Because our models were not ready, we could only describe our products and show him sketches and renderings. That was enough to win his wholehearted support. He was willing to take on the Home-O-Nize line once we could produce. In the months ahead, Timmerman's advice was valuable, and his enthusiasm spurred us on. By the fall of 1944, Hanson had developed sales procedures and an organization as well as samples of sales literature for our approval.

The Lyric and the Duet. By late November, Home-O-Nize was ready to present its unique kitchen cabinets. Working models had been prepared featuring our initial lines, the Lyric and the Duet, which were steel modular units of various widths for field assembly. The Lyric's upper and lower cabinets were attached to a vertical quick erector frame. Upper cabinets provided ceiling-high storage space with either stationary or moving shelves. An optional feature was easy accessibility, accomplished through motor-driven upper shelves that lowered with push-button control. Lower cabinets had full-depth drawers (no doors), with numerous possible arrangements for various storage functions. Optional features included pull-out countertops, bread-boards, knife racks, and corner units for L- or U-shaped installations. The Duet was a lower cabinet with various widths and a double sink. Both lines were attractively styled with soft corners, molded end panels, and ceiling and base covers.

The Home-O-Nize cabinets were of outstanding, advanced design, undoubtedly superior to anything on the market at that time. We were ready for a full-scale test of dealer reaction to our product. Timmerman graciously volunteered to invite some Midwest area distributors to Davenport for our sales pitch and a viewing and testing of working models of the cabinets. The date was set for December 9, 1944. Invitations were extended, and arrangements for the presentation were made.

Scuttling the Manufacturing Plan

Before the presentation date arrived, however, a disturbing and frustrating event completely altered Home-O-Nize's approach to manufacturing and financing. Uchtorff pulled out, ending that association.

We had not been caught entirely off guard. Relations with Uchtorff had become more and more difficult. Although we asked him in December 1943 to prepare a detailed manufacturing contract between his company and Home-O-Nize, he had not done so by September 1944. Shortly thereafter, I drafted a contract and forwarded it to Uchtorff, who did not respond.

Uchtorff was stalling because he was increasingly disenchanted with the direction that Hanson, Miller, and I wanted to go. He did not like the highly styled, ingeniously designed kitchen cabinets that we proposed. He was negative toward plans to tap so large a market that Home-O-Nize would ultimately need a plant of its own. In short, he seemed determined to limit Home-O-Nize's production to cabinets of the modified, prewar type that he had manufactured and to hold production to levels compatible with the capacity of his own plant. A venture of this type would have been profitable to Uchtorff, but it was not acceptable to Hanson, Miller, and myself. Unable to get his way, Uchtorff became less accessible, missing many formal and informal meetings.

Sometime in November 1944, Uchtorff approached Hanson with a proposal: "Why do you want to monkey around setting up a new company? Home-O-Nize will never get anywhere. Come along with me. We have plant, equipment, and everything." Hanson loyally rejected the proffer, but he was deeply distressed. Just when our progress was real, Uchtorff was pulling the rug out from under us.

When Uchtorff failed to appear at a board meeting on November 30, the blow-up became official. Because the treasurer's report revealed that funds in our bank account were now reduced to $850, the three directors present agreed to call on each director of the corporation to make an additional purchase of 10 shares of stock for $1,000. Soon after, Uchtorff indicated his unwillingness to buy more stock. Instead, he stated his readiness to sell the 10 shares that he had. With board approval, I purchased Uchtorff's stock. Wanting nothing to do with our triumvirate, Uchtorff withdrew from Home-O-Nize's board of directors.

Our planned approach to manufacturing had been scuttled. We were compelled for the first time, but not for the last, to deal with adversity, rise above abject disappointment, and move ahead, albeit on an altered course. The experience was traumatic, particularly for Hanson. With such great uncertainty about the future, he began to have doubts about the wisdom of his decision to give up secure employment to work full time with Home-O-Nize. The experience was less troubling to Miller and to myself because each of us still had a company of his own.

In retrospect, I am convinced that the parting of ways with Uchtorff was not only inevitable but beneficial, at least in the long run. His interests and objectives were obviously different from those of the three founders. In fact, our attitudes and approaches were so different that cooperation and harmony would have been extremely difficult, if not impossible. At the time, however, his precipitous departure caused serious consternation and frustrated our carefully prepared plans.

Clem Hanson in the model shop after it was moved from Davenport to the company's newly organized manufacturing facility in Muscatine.

CHAPTER TWO

Preparations for Production

With Uchtorff's departure, our alternatives were limited: find another manufacturing source for early production, or promptly establish a Home-O-Nize manufacturing facility. The first alternative was not promising, because we had carefully surveyed potential manufacturing sources before going with Uchtorff. Moving more rapidly with our own plant seemed the logical answer, particularly as the outcome of World War II was then quite predictable. Only the timing of our victory in Europe and the Far East was uncertain.

A Set of Goals

In spite of the major shift that we had to make in our plans, we held the product presentation planned for December 9, 1944, and it gave us a needed shot in the arm. As he predicted, Timmerman's endorsement of our invitation brought a number of important distributors to Davenport. Following the luncheon, we unveiled a working model of the Home-O-Nize kitchen cabinet with power-operated upper shelves. Hanson presented data targeting a huge potential market: the more than 18 million families in the United States with annual incomes of over $2,500 in 1944. The uniquely designed Home-O-Nize units were packaged items, not tailor-made or built-in cabinets. They could be stocked, installed, and moved just like a range or a refrigerator.

We had assembled the nucleus of a product distribution system consisting of well-known and established firms. Our confidence in the market potential of the Home-O-Nize kitchen cabinets had been reinforced. A terse excerpt from my logbook conveys my reaction to the presentation: "Showing of cabinets to distributors. All were enthusiastic: reception exceeded our fondest hopes!" All of this was the result of a $50 lunch!

With strengthened determination, the three founders decided to pursue several goals simultaneously: 1) to arrange financing for our venture; 2) to establish by purchase or construction a suitable manufacturing plant and equip it to produce kitchen cabinets; 3) to complete detailed cabinet designs for production; 4) to recruit staff for production, sales, and management; and 5) to develop production and marketing programs for kitchen cabinets.

Arranging sources for steel and other production materials was viewed as a secondary, less demanding task. Unfortunately, we later discovered that procurement of steel would be a major stumbling block, precipitating many traumatic decisions. Quite unaware of this eventuality, we accelerated our efforts to attain the objectives that we had formulated. We expected Home-O-Nize kitchen cabinets to roll off the assembly line within the first quarter of 1947.

11

Early Financing Efforts

Although purchase of common stock by the founders funded our preliminary operations through 1944, I had been continually studying alternatives for further financing. The time for action had arrived because the founders lacked the financial resources to foot the bills for plant, equipment, tools, dies, and working capital. Sale of additional stock seemed to be an appropriate preliminary to debt financing.

A Failed Financing Package.   Accordingly, I consulted with Claude A. Edmonds, president of the Central State Bank in Muscatine to which we had transferred the Home-O-Nize account. We developed a proposed program for increasing the equity of the company. In March 1945, we increased to 1,000 the number of authorized shares of common stock; granted Hanson, Miller, and myself an option to purchase an aggregate of 500 shares of common stock; and established dividends of $5 per share on the previously authorized preferred stock. We planned to offer a package consisting of one share of common and one share of preferred stock at a price of $200 per unit. Iowa law permitted private sale to a limited number of shareholders without approval from the State Commissioner of Insurance.

This carefully designed financing package failed miserably. Investors were not clamoring to buy units of stock in a paper corporation. In fact, 18 months later, the stock register revealed only one new shareholder. Thanks to Clem Hanson's power of persuasion, J. F. Gatrell had purchased five units.

Our preparations to manufacture kitchen cabinets continued only because the founders were exercising their common stock purchase options. By early 1946, Hanson's holdings had increased to 60, Miller's to 36, and mine to 380, bringing our aggregate close to the 500-share limit.

Manna from Heaven.   In February 1946, we applied to a federal agency, the Smaller War Plants Corporation,[1] for a loan of $100,000 to be handled through the Central State Bank. With some able assistance from Edmonds, our application was approved. By September, we had drawn down the proceeds of the loan. These funds, as welcome as manna from heaven, enabled us to exercise an option to purchase a plant that we had already leased. The funds also partially covered the cost of equipment. We were able to continue preparations for production.

A Successful Sale of Stock.   With the loan proceeds in hand, we needed to make a second and, we hoped, more fruitful effort to increase equity holdings. I continued discussions with Edmonds, but I also solicited help from Robert L. Roach of Muscatine, who introduced me to John Quail of Quail & Company, investment bankers and brokers in Davenport. Efforts with Quail to arrange a public offering on terms acceptable to us were unsuccessful. Home-O-Nize still appeared to be too much of a pig in a poke.

Concluding that no simple and easy financing approach would be forthcoming, we reluctantly organized a do-it-yourself program. Stockholder meetings in September and November of 1946 set the stage for this new effort. The number of authorized shares of common stock was increased to 2,500, with the aggregate option to Hanson, Miller, and myself expanded to 1,000 shares. An earlier application to the Iowa Commissioner of Insurance led to a certificate authorizing Home-O-Nize to sell 1,000 shares of common stock at $100 per share to the general public. The certification required that the proceeds of the sale be deposited in an escrow account until they amounted to $50,000. At that time, the entire proceeds could be released to the company.

We employed William C. Newsom as an agent to assist in stock sales and as a

1. The Smaller War Plants Corporation (SWPC), created in 1942, was terminated by executive order on December 27, 1945. When Home-O-Nize applied for a loan in February 1946, the lending functions of SWPC were in the process of being transferred to the Reconstruction Finance Corporation, another government agency that had been founded in 1932.

potential sales manager. Newsom, a former salesman with the Newhouse Paper Company of Moline, had recently returned from military service. Obtaining a stock salesman's license, he embarked on the tough assignment that we had given him. Home-O-Nize was not yet operational, let alone profitable. Any investment in Home-O-Nize was highly speculative, so much so that the Commissioner of Insurance required each stock certificate to be stamped SPECULATIVE STOCK. As directors and officers, we had no proven track record of managing a manufacturing corporation. Moreover, Muscatine, the primary target for stock sales, had previously witnessed public promotions of stock sales for ventures that turned out to be unsuccessful.

Newsom proved equal to the task. Working tirelessly, he contacted a long list of prospective shareholders. His courteous approach, friendly personality, and keen intellect generated confidence. By January 10, 1947, escrowed funds in excess of $50,000 were released to Home-O-Nize. By the end of March 1947, 998 shares of the common stock that we were authorized to sell had been subscribed and paid for. Newsom, with occasional assists from Hanson and myself, was largely responsible for bringing $99,800 into our treasury. The 500 shares purchased by the founders (Hanson 98, Miller 36, and Stanley 366) had produced another $25,000. (We paid only $50 a share for the first 500 shares in lieu of any compensation for organizing the company.) The $124,800 of equity enabled us to move toward actual production. Authorized public sale of common stock continued during the balance of 1947 and into 1948.

We enthusiastically took the successful stock sale in stride, but I have often wondered how it was accomplished. Why did successful business and professional people invest in an unproven venture? Perhaps it was because the Home-O-Nize concept of kitchen cabinets was exciting. Undoubtedly, it had something to do with the fact that most of our new shareholders were acquainted with me or one of the other founders. In addition, the many Muscatine investors were concerned about local

employment, as the community's major employers, the pearl button and the sash and door industries, were on the decline. But certainly Newsom's effective sales effort was an important factor. I am deeply thankful that those who risked their money in 1946, at least partly because they had confidence in me, were ultimately very well rewarded.

Origins of the Oak Street Plant

Even before the successful stock sale had been initiated, a plant site had been selected. Long before Uchtorff's withdrawal, we had searched the Davenport area for a building that might be leased or purchased as a manufacturing plant. We found nothing appropriate or appealing.

An Old Button Factory. As the next phase of preparation began, I looked around Muscatine. The most appealing prospect, or perhaps I should say the least unappealing, proved to be the plant of the U.S. Button Company at Third and Oak Streets. It was vacant, except for a third floor stockroom partially filled with pearl button products, and it was available for lease or purchase. This two- and three-story

The empty factory of the U.S. Button Company became the manufacturing facility and office for the new enterprise.

building, with total floor space of 18,000 square feet, was located on three lots, making it possible to construct an 18,700-square-foot, one-story addition. Negotiations regarding the lease of the building, with an option to buy, were completed in late September 1945. We took possession in October. A year later, in September 1946, we purchased the building, using the proceeds of our $100,000 loan.

The building initially housed the Boepple Button Company. John F. Boepple, an immigrant from Germany, pioneered the once-booming pearl button industry in Muscatine. Interestingly, this was the first of four deserted pearl button plants that Home-O-Nize (and later, HON INDUSTRIES) would purchase over the years. It marked a milestone in Muscatine's transition from dependence on pearl buttons and sash and door products to a highly diversified industrial base in the years after World War II.

Rehabilitation and extension of the plant got under way in November 1945, when R. E. (Ed) Doonan, then city engineer of Waverly, Iowa, joined Home-O-Nize to help with the initial planning and to supervise construction, and then to become plant superintendent. In November 1946, Doonan became a member of our board of directors. I had high regard for Doonan's integrity and competence, having worked with him on Stanley Engineering Co. projects in Waverly. Doonan and I developed the general plan for plant arrangement as well as lists and specifications for equipment. We consulted with Dale Hermes and Louis H. York, both of the Herman Nelson Division of the American Air Filter Co. York, within a year, would become Home-O-Nize's first plant foreman. In March 1946, Doonan and I contracted for the finishing system. With this major commitment behind us, Stanley Engineering Co. was retained in April to prepare detailed plans and specifications for the building and electrical work.

The ground floor of the old building was selected for the parts fabrication department, to be equipped with shears, press brakes, punch presses, and related equipment. The wood floor, except for the

office on the corner of Third and Oak Streets, was removed; the basement was filled with sand and a new concrete floor poured. A new conveyorized finishing system dictated the layout of the new addition. It included six-stage washing, dry-off, two paint booths, and high-temperature baking ovens. (In 1985, this original system was still in use at The HON Company's Oak Street Plant.) The concrete block and frame addition built around the finishing and painting system included areas for assembly, warehouse, and shipping and receiving docks. Except for new electrical and mechanical systems, rehabilitation of the existing building was held to a minimum.

A Willing but Inexperienced Construction Crew.

Knowing that we would exercise the option to purchase the building, construction was started in May 1946. Home-O-Nize elected to be its own contractor. We recruited a construction crew of about a dozen people, most of them recently returned veterans. Many of this group, staying on with Home-O-Nize as we went into production, would have long careers with the company. They included Lyle B. McCullough, who had been employed earlier in the model shop and soon became purchasing agent of the Oak Street Plant; Harold (Bud) Barton, who ultimately became maintenance supervisor of the Geneva Plant; Ray Shellabarger, later assistant plant supervisor of the Oak Street Plant; Edmund (Tiny) Metz, a utility person at the Division Street department or partition department of the Geneva Plant; and Raymond Wichers, who became production superintendent of the Geneva Plant. All of these men served HON until their retirement in the late 1970s or early 1980s.

This small group constituted a willing, if somewhat inexperienced, construction crew that was quite capable, under Doonan's guidance, of surmounting all difficulties. To obtain roof beams, they dismantled large pallets used for shipping army tanks—pallets that we had bought at a bargain price. When the subcontractor's masons walked off the job during an area strike, McCullough mixed mortar while

Doonan and Barton finished the concrete block wall. Despite, or perhaps because of, numerous pranks played on one another, the esprit de corps developed among these early members long continued to help Home-O-Nize through difficult times.

While construction progressed, Doonan and I selected and purchased the remaining production equipment, some of it new but much of it used. A brochure prepared in December 1945 stated that the "continuous type painting and finishing equipment with Bonderite apparatus, spray booths, ovens, and conveyers" was ready for operation. It further stated that the building alterations and extensions, plus "five heavy-duty punch presses, two squaring shears, one roll former, three 200-ton press brakes, and eleven spot welders" would be ready for full-scale production in January 1947.

Designing Kitchen Cabinets

Detailed design of kitchen cabinets continued while we arranged financing and organized production facilities. The beginnings of a product engineering department were established in May 1945, when Elmer (Duke) Cossman was employed to work with Miller and Hanson in Davenport. In September, Cossman moved to a makeshift arrangement on the third floor of the Third Street wing of our Muscatine plant. Later, a temporary draftsman was added.

Using his dilapidated Ford Model A truck, Bill Booth moved the model shop from Davenport to Muscatine. He continued as our model maker, commuting daily from Davenport. McCullough, the first Home-O-Nize employee hired in Muscatine, began work in November as a helper to Booth in the model shop located on the second floor of the new building. Hanson and Miller traveled periodically from the Quad Cities to supervise model and design work.

I set up a small office on the third floor close to the design and model work and used it on a part-time basis. This first president's office had an old oak desk, a wobbly swivel chair, and a folding chair for visitors.

The most extraordinary feature was the door. An eye-level knothole about three inches in diameter in one of the top panels allowed almost anyone to look through at me. The door was poorly painted, unpleasant, and uninviting. This ostensible lack of class disturbed my associates, but our resources were so limited that I resisted their pleas to upgrade the office. Instead, I concentrated my efforts on keeping the enterprise afloat, in the firm belief that elegance should follow profits.

Despite our crude facilities and grave financial situation, we forged ahead. Additional working models were built and tested; detailed designs were formulated; drawings and specifications of parts were prepared. By early 1946, product designs were sufficiently advanced to indicate the appropriate fabrication processes and to determine the equipment needed to produce them.

As construction got under way in May 1946, we began ordering tools and dies from the Swan Engineering & Machine Company of the Quad Cities. As the building neared completion in December, and as shears, punch presses, and press brakes were being installed, we received the tools and dies from Swan, ready for tryout.

Our patent attorney had obtained registration of the Home-O-Nize trademark in July 1945. By the end of 1946, design and appearance patents on the kitchen cabinets had been granted by the U.S. Patent Office, and mechanical patents had been applied for.

New Wysong & Miles shears in place. In the early years, the company usually purchased used factory equipment, largely because of the long waiting period for delivery of new machine tools and the shortage of cash.

Machinery Arriving for New Home-O-Nize Firm

Construction work in preparation for the introduction of a new Muscatine product upon the market early next year is preceeding according to schedule at the manufacturing plant being completed by the Home-O-Nize co. at East Third and Oak streets, it is announced by C. M. Stanley, president.

The firm will produce metal kitchen cabinets and is expected to furnish employment to approximately 100 persons when the plant is in full production.

Equipment and machinery ordered last summer is now starting to arrive at the factory and installation is in progress. In the stage of erection at present is the gas fired finishing oven and paint spray equipment which R. G. Doonan, plant manager, reports is the most up to date to be installed anywhere and will assure a baked enamel finish of the highest quality to be found in the home appliance industry upon Home-O-Nize kitchen cabinets.

Arrangements for the distribution of Home-O-Nize metal kitchen cabinets have been made with leading appliance wholesale firms which will absorb the firm's entire production for the first several years of operation. Acceptance of the Home-O-Nize line of cabinets is reported by sales personnel to be extremely satisfactory.

Advertising and promotion plans have crystallized under the direction of C. T. Hanson, vice president, and W. C. Newsom, sales manager.

Home-O-Nize co. officials plan to be ready for production around the first of the year at which time personnel will be added to the force as required until the required complement has been reached.

Present personnel includes, in addition to the construction crew, red Winn, Jr., auditor, Elmer ossman and Arthur Dahl in the anning department, and Lyle Cullough, Ray Zeidler, Bob gren, Ray Shellabarger and old Barton, who are enrolled a GI training program for men and junior plant executives.

C. M. STANLEY

Progress in establishing the Oak Street Plant was closely followed by the local press. (Muscatine Journal, November 19, 1946)

Expansion of Management

While construction was under way, we were recruiting the first members of our management staff in addition to Doonan and Newsom. Fred S. Winn, after returning from military service as a captain in the Quartermaster Corps, joined us as bookkeeper and chief clerk. Fred was a graduate of the University of Illinois, with a major in accounting, and he had several years of experience in accounting before military service. Winn would later serve as secretary-treasurer.

In October 1946, Arthur E. Dahl left Stanley Engineering Co., where he was a draftsman, to join the expanding Home-O-Nize staff. Before military service, Art had attended Augustana College. His original assignments were related to design and preparation for production of the kitchen cabinets. Later, he headed production control and planning, moved to the management of the Prime-Mover operation, and then became senior vice president of HON INDUSTRIES.

To supplement the management staff, we planned to transfer members of our construction crew to supervisory and office positions as well as to production and maintenance jobs. Thus, by the end of 1946, a skeletal operating organization was in place. Our staff numbered about 16 or 18 (original rosters have not been found). Applications for jobs were numerous, as the word spread around Muscatine about the opening of a new factory.

A Production Plan

Production and marketing programs were also well advanced by the end of 1946. In June, I had prepared a "production directive" for 1947 that ambitiously called for initial production of 800 of the simplest model—an 18-inch stationary cabinet—to take place in February 1947. Monthly schedules called for an increase to a level of 4,000 units by August, projecting a yearly output of 33,200 kitchen cabinets. This plan included initial production of sink cabinets—the Duet—in April and the first motorized upper cabinets in August. In retrospect, this seems like an impossibly tight start-up schedule, given the inexperience of the Home-O-Nize organization. Had it been accomplished, it might well still stand as a challenge to today's experienced management of HON INDUSTRIES. Undoubtedly, we were quite naive, but fortunately, our naivete was matched by our determination to succeed.

McCullough, our newly appointed purchasing agent, began ordering against this schedule—bearings, paint, and other purchased parts for the kitchen cabinets. We contracted with the St. Louis Terminal Warehouse Company to establish a bonded warehouse within the plant. Materials from vendors stored in this warehouse would serve as collateral for money borrowed from the bank to ease our cash flow.

We were staffed. I would oversee production. Doonan would serve as plant superintendent. York would join us in February to supervise the production operations. The Veterans Administration had approved an on-the-job training program. Barton, McCullough, Shellabarger, Robert Nygren, and Raymond Zeidler would participate under York's tutelage in this program, which emphasized sheet metal fabrication. The marketing program seemed simple. Newsom would become sales manager on the conclusion of his work as a securities salesman. Hanson would oversee the marketing operation and handle the advertising.

Distributors were eager to receive our product. In October, Midwest Timmerman Co. gave us an order for 50 carloads of kitchen cabinets. (At approximately 150 units per car, this meant 7,500 cabinets.)

Meanwhile, an attractive, duotone sales brochure rolled off the printing press. Prepared by Hanson, it announced the offering of "Kitchen Cabinets for Modern Kitchens." This first, and sadly last, kitchen cabinet brochure was mailed to the distributors who had attended the presentation in December 1944, as well as to other prospects. It produced a series of favorable responses. Distributors requested quantities of brochures for their sales forces and showrooms, as they indicated a readiness to place firm purchase orders for cabinets whenever we could specify delivery schedules. One dealer stated his enthusiasm as follows:

> The new model which you have shown me is, in my opinion, all that could be desired in the finished product. I am particularly enthusiastic about the "QUICK ERECTOR CONNECTOR" which makes the installation so simple that the best merchandisers will be attracted to this product because of the simplicity of its installation. In my opinion, it is the only kitchen cabinet that will be enthusiastically received by furniture dealers, department stores, and large installment sales stores since it will require no service installation.

Impact of the Steel Shortage

Alas, The Home-O-Nize Co. had a serious problem, quite beyond its control. We were stymied by a steel shortage, which we had not at all foreseen. For months, Hanson had been in contact with steel manufacturers, trying to order mill deliveries of cold rolled sheet steel. We could buy small quantities from warehouses for

Art Dahl, head of the planning division for the company, at work in 1947 in what had been a carding and sorting room for U.S. Button Company. The assembly line system design is shown on the chalkboard.

The Bonderite finishing system, shown here almost complete, cleaned and etched the metal's surface and applied a coat of phosphorus in preparation for painting.

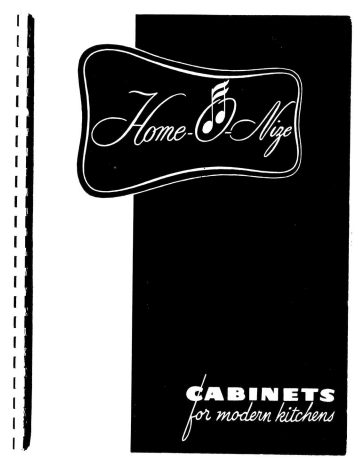

The primary sales literature used in securing dealers and distributors.

The bootstrap approach to securing factory orders. (Des Moines Register, February 9, 1947)

terest in processing such applications.

We tried numerous approaches, beginning in early 1946. Hanson contacted sales representatives of many companies and personally visited steel producers in the Chicago and St. Louis areas. He communicated with the Civilian Production Administration of the U.S. government as well as with Edwin Martin, then chairman of the U.S. Senate Subcommittee on Steel. We came upon a reprint of a speech by Benjamin Fairless, then president of the U.S. Steel Company. He talked about the economic benefits of the free enterprise system and how it provided opportunities for people (like us) to establish new businesses, make jobs, expand the economy, and fill consumer needs. Impressed by his remarks, we wrote a letter to him suggesting that he could help our new enterprise move ahead by supplying desperately needed steel. He responded graciously with a letter, but we received no steel.

Our application to the Special Assistance Division of the Civilian Production Administration finally produced results. A telegram from them, dated November 22, 1946, gave us a priority rating for the first quarter of 1947—43 tons of the 55 tons of sheet steel that we had requested for the first two months of production. But the rating proved ineffective, for no steel was delivered until late 1948.

model work, but production called for substantial quantities at mill prices. We needed 443 tons per month for manufacture of the 4,000 units scheduled for August 1947. The response of the several steel companies that we contacted was uniform: "Sorry, we can't sell steel to you unless you have a quota."

Satisfying the strong pent-up demand for automobiles, home appliances, and other consumer durable goods consumed enormous quantities of cold rolled steel. Producers in the United States could not turn out enough steel to go around, and no foreign steel was then available. Steel had to be rationed through a quota system based on a user's purchases in the years immediately preceding World War II. Home-O-Nize wasn't even a dream then, so we were out in the cold. Warehouse steel was out of the question; available quantities were inadequate, and prices were too high. The government had established procedures for a new company to obtain a quota, but the procedures were so complex that steel companies had little in-

Going into Contract Work

As 1946 ran its course, we were nearing readiness for production. It appeared certain, however, that initial manufacture of kitchen cabinets would have to be deferred, perhaps for a considerable period. What a dilemma: Home-O-Nize was "all dressed up, with no place to go."

Our options were limited. We could wait out the steel shortage, which would require severe staff reductions and penny-pinching control of expenditures to protect our marginal cash position. This course of action would have brought us face-to-face with indefinite, frustrating uncertainty. Design of an alternative product line was no answer because time was too short. The only sensible option was to seek work under contract from other manufacturers, compatible with our plant capability. If such work could be found, we could start operations, maintain staff, produce income, meet loan amortization payments, and, with some luck, generate margins over direct costs. Meanwhile, development of the kitchen cabinets could continue until mill shipments of steel became available.

Stampings, Incorporated. At this time, our initial contact with Dale Hermes made in 1943 paid off. Hermes had left the Herman Nelson Division of the American Air Filter Co. to manage Stampings, Inc., a new corporation formed by Stanley and James Leach of Bettendorf, who were in the bottled gas business. Stampings had developed and planned to market hoods, bases, and other accessories for residential, farm, and commercial installations of bottled gas. By happy coincidence, Hermes was using office space adjacent to Miller at 315½ West Fourth Street in Davenport. He knew that we were looking for work.

When production requirements were examined, it appeared that our equipment was adequate for all operations except the drawing of 8-inch-deep hoods from aluminum blanks. After some scurrying about, we located in a plant in La Porte, Indiana, a used 150-ton hydraulic press that we could purchase for this purpose. The Swan Engineering & Machine Co., fabricators of the draw dies, could produce the hoods until the press could be installed in our plant. Specially constructed wood and metal skids would be needed to facilitate the transfer of these hoods to Muscatine.

These arrangements were satisfactory to Stampings, so we signed a contract on November 28, 1946, just in time to avoid serious staff reduction. My logbook notes: "Closed deal with Stampings, Inc. for work for Home-O-Nize. Will aggregate $88,500 in 1947 on estimated schedule. This means production and revenue soon!" An $88,500 order may seem paltry today, from the perspective of the total annual sales of HON INDUSTRIES, but it was a lifesaver for us then.

As construction and equipment installation were completed, attention shifted to the organization of production for Stampings. York, whom we had previously selected as shop foreman, joined Home-O-Nize in February 1947. Barton, Nygren, Shellabarger, Metz, Wichers, Zeidler, and others of the construction crew became the nucleus of Home-O-Nize's production work force—Barton as a foreman, Zeidler on maintenance, and the others as press operators and assemblers.

Several other members were recruited. We shifted Gene Fuller, initially employed on construction, to the office; he later became a buyer at the Oak Street Plant. Dale Shellady was hired as a press operator in March 1947; he continued employment, much of it on the big hydraulic press, until his retirement in 1969. Clayton Welsch started in March as a setup man, the only early employee with any sheet metal experience other than York; when he retired in 1977, he was equipment engineer. Other March recruits included Leonard Luedtka, who served as storekeeper for the Oak Street Plant until retirement in 1974; Jasper S. Thompson, who was a steel department planner for the Oak Street Plant when he retired in 1980; and Rex Feustal, who was a maintenance man at the Oak Street Plant for about 11 years.

Spot welder stations ready for business.

CHAPTER THREE

Struggle for Survival

O n April 5, 1947, the first products made under contract left the plant. It was a great day. The skids, ordered for transporting the aluminum hoods from Swan's to Muscatine, had been completed. As these were delivered to Stampings, Fred Winn wrote the first invoice to a customer. A trickle of revenue from sales began. At long last, after nearly four years, Home-O-Nize was operating.

Even though the first shipment to Stampings provided cause for celebration, Home-O-Nize was operating in a most precarious manner. The indefinite postponement of kitchen cabinet production rendered our substantial investment of time and money in developing, designing, tooling, and marketing of no immediate value. The Stampings contract, while most welcome, only partially loaded the plant, and it made little use of our newly installed, expensive finishing system. Constructing and equipping the plant, together with the development costs for kitchen cabinets, had depleted much of our cash. There was little chance of substantial equity or debt financing until we achieved profitability. Moreover, Home-O-Nize was totally dependent on Stampings for even a limited volume of production. We were thus completely vulnerable to any decline in their sales.

Working for Stampings

Successful production of bottled gas housings for Stampings obviously had to be our first priority. Under York's capable supervision, our work force expanded, our output increased, and our costs declined. The on-the-job training program, financed by the Veterans Administration and administered by York, helped strengthen our supervisory staff. By mid-April 1947, we were producing 540 units per workday. An entry in my log, dated May 20, reads: "Closed April books with only $370 loss. Should be in black in May."

The huge 150-ton hydraulic press arrived. The movers edged it through a hole in the wall to its position in the pressroom where it became our most prestigious machine. Draw dies were received from Swan and, with the help of Oscar Fauser of Stampings, they were installed in the hydraulic press as Dale Shellady took charge of the press. The entire Stampings operation was in place in what we now call the Oak Street Plant Number 1.

Stampings became confident that Home-O-Nize would meet the schedules and quality standards that were imposed, at mutually acceptable costs. Moving their warehouse to Muscatine, Stampings relied solely on us for their bottled gas housing requirements. When our production soon outstripped the needs of Stampings, we had to slow down our delivery schedules. This reduced our total sales for 1947, but it was only a temporary setback. Our first manufacturing contract grew into a fine association extending over many years.

Establishing a Personnel Policy

From the beginning, we developed programs and policies to carry out the philosophy of human relations that had impelled us to start the company. In 1947, Clem Hanson and I drafted a statement titled "How The Home-O-Nize Co. Plans to Conduct Its Plant." It set forth the basic beliefs on which the personnel policies of The Home-O-Nize Co. would be built:

1. Every worker is a person and so is entitled to the treatment and consideration granted to human beings.

2. The welfare of the workers and the welfare of the company are interdependent; neither can prosper unless the other likewise prospers.

3. The customer who buys is the final judge of our products. Honest effort and maximum output mean good merchandise at a fair price. Both contribute greatly to the success of the company and the welfare of the workers.

4. Maximum productivity and its fruits can be attained only by a wholesome, happy relationship between workers and management.

5. Finally, the first interest of the worker, of the company, and of the buying public will be best served by the dependability, productivity, and responsibility of all.

As Clem Hanson and I were preparing our first crude personnel manual, he suggested, "Why not use the word 'member,' instead of 'worker' or 'employee,' to designate everyone in the Home-O-Nize organization, whether in the office or in the shop?" Hanson's suggestion prompted the practice that we still use at HON INDUSTRIES. The word *member* projects a greater sense of belonging and participation. Its use is compatible with the open and informal pattern of human relations that the or-

Aluminum hoods ready for cleaning in the Bonderizer are shown in the background. The Stampings contract for bottled gas hoods, like those shown here, enabled the company to start manufacturing operations.

ganization has achieved over the years.

In February 1947, even before we started production, we employed John Van Lent as personnel director. According to the conventional wisdom prevailing then, the small size of our work force did not warrant a personnel director. Van Lent was given other duties, but his priorities were oriented toward personnel. With the anticipated growth of Home-O-Nize's work force, Van Lent would have responsibility for recruiting, counseling, and handling of grievances. He would also assist me in developing personnel policies, position descriptions, job classifications, wage and salary scales, and member insurance programs.

Even in the early days, we maintained wage and salary levels comfortably above the median of local practice. In October 1947, when our operation was barely under way, we established an automatic cost-of-living adjustment keyed to the Cost-of-Living Index. Our program was initiated even before General Motors and other large corporations implemented cost-of-living adjustments under union pressure. From the beginning, modern personnel practices reflecting an enlightened approach to human relations helped us develop good internal relationships at Home-O-Nize.

The Home-O-Nize Co. made components for bottled gas units for Stampings, Inc.

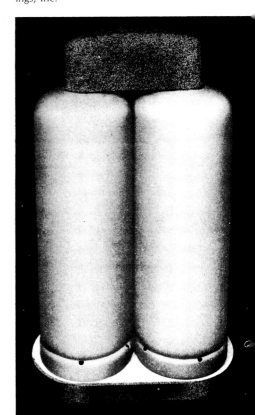

Dale Shellady (foreground) and Butch Ziedler at punch presses.

These coasters were made from the drop-off of pieces for the Stampings contract. They were the first products to bear the Home-O-Nize name.

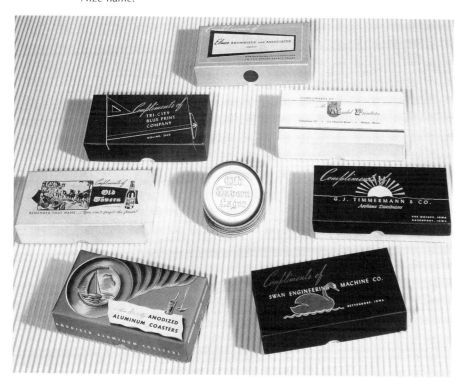

Entry into Office Products

Unexpectedly, the Stampings contract contributed to Home-O-Nize's entry into the office products field. Cutting blanks for the deep-drawn hoods from aluminum coil stock left considerable drop-off, originally sold as scrap at a much lower price per pound than we paid for the coiled stock. From the beginning of production, we discussed possible uses for this drop-off. Within a few weeks, we were making anodized aluminum coasters for beverage glasses and marketing them to business organizations for use as gifts. Then, Hanson, a rose fancier, came up with another product constructed of two pieces of drop-off punched from the aluminum posts we fabricated to support aluminum hoods. Using these two pieces, we manufactured ground markers for use in gardens to identify roses or other plants. They were marketed under the trade name of Flower Names Limited. Originally, these ingenious markers were offered with silk-screened rose names. Later, as we became aware of the numerous rose varieties, we packaged the markers with black crayon for individual naming. With these humble offerings, Home-O-Nize began merchandising its own products to bring in a few dollars.

Meanwhile, serious attention was given to the design and production, from the aluminum drop-off, of a 3-by-5-inch deep-drawn card file, with rounded corners, piano hinges, and baked-on enamel finish. Neither records nor recollections reveal whose idea this was, but it caught on, particularly with the discovery that steel index card files were in short supply. Prototypes were quickly made and tested, and dies were purchased.

Production of our first office products was started in September 1947. With more card files than money, Hanson and Newsom traveled to Chicago to attend the National Stationers Show. Avoiding door guards and registration desks, they displayed the card files at the booth of the Amberg File and Index Company. Soon, we selected Elmer Krumweide & Associates of Chicago to represent us in the sale of this product. An entry in my log during November 1947 reads: "Card index file going nicely on sales and promotion."

Amazingly, sales of our own products in 1947—largely card files—amounted to about $20,000.

A Historic Decision. Pleased with the market's reception of card files and disappointed with our continuing inability to purchase steel with which to make kitchen cabinets, our thinking began to focus more on the office products field. The board of directors at a meeting on March 30, 1948, resolved that "Home-O-Nize's efforts in sales, advertising, and product development should be directed to the office supply and equipment field."

Accordingly, we doubled our product line in May 1948 with the addition of 4-by-6-inch aluminum card files.

Over the years, this historic decision has been recited often in the telling of HON's early story. Our line of office products was further extended a few months later with offerings of calling card files and recipe files, the latter painted red and white and full of printed helps to the homemaker. Another version of this card file was painted black and red and sold in large quantities to the Sunbeam Company for use as premiums.

The Deere Contract

In the meantime, we continued to search for additional contract work to load our plant more fully. Hanson, Miller, and I were all on the alert. Near misses included a newly patented window sash holder for an eastern company, parts fabrication for the Amana Refrigeration Company, and several others.

Finally, Hanson unearthed a solid prospect, temporarily ending our pursuit of will-o'-the-wisps. He had contacted John Deffenbaugh, then manager of Deere's Harvester Works in Moline. Postwar demand for farm equipment was exceeding Deere's manufacturing capacity, giving rise to the company's decision to subcontract some work. Hanson convinced Deffenbaugh to consider us. How Clem and I persuaded him to take such a risk on Home-O-

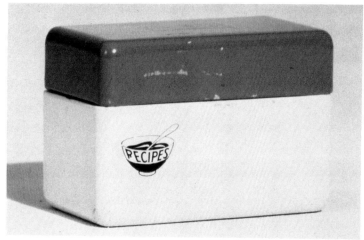

Nize's unproven ability to perform, I do not know. But persuade we did, and on August 26, 1947, we signed a contract to manufacture pickup attachments for grain combines.

This order, with tight delivery schedules, thoroughly challenged our fledgling organization. The loyal Home-O-Nize outfit rose to the occasion, maintaining quality standards, meeting delivery schedules, and keeping costs within estimates. A profitable operation was assured. Again, great credit is due York for his supervision of manufacturing, training of personnel, and maintenance of quality without benefit of inspectors or a formal quality control program.

The recipe box was made from aluminum. Home-O-Nize simply used the scrap from the liquified petroleum gas tank hoods, applying deep-draw technology. They were sold complete with index tabs. Painting them green turned the recipe box for the kitchen into a card file for the office.

Stanley and Hanson persuaded John Deere & Company to give Home-O Nize a contract to manufacture pickup attachments for combines, despite the new company's lack of a track record.

*Shipping day. The crew
that built the shipping
dock stayed on to run the
factory. Fridays were exciting because Fred Winn
could generally beat the
payroll checks to the bank
with receipts from the day's
shipments.*

*The maintenance shop had
a temporary quality to it
until the company was
much better established.*

The contract work for Deere and Stampings, along with card files, kept us reasonably busy through the latter part of 1947. By the end of the year, we had some 27 people employed on direct and indirect production, plus a minimal office and managerial staff. A roster of shop personnel for December 1947 reveals hourly wages ranging from $0.70 for a beginning packager to $1.20 for a setup man. (What a difference from the 1980s!)

Within the year, two people who would become long-time members started work. Robert L. Carl, later secretary of HON INDUSTRIES, began with Home-O-Nize as a clerk. Helen Martin, soon to marry Tiny Metz, another early member, became our first female production worker.

Financial Pressures

Sales volume for 1947 was about $90,000, covering the months from early April, when we went into actual production. Operating losses for 1946 and 1947 combined, including start-up but not development costs for the kitchen cabinets, amounted to $30,100.

Our cash deficiency was severe. Stock sales continued, but they provided only $41,400 from May through December. Newsom's efforts produced $21,400. Hanson invested $2,500; I invested $7,000; the mother, brother, and sister of our wives bought $7,500 of preferred stock; and my parents purchased another $3,000 of common stock. The aggregate amount was inadequate to cover the combined losses of 1946 and 1947 plus development costs for the kitchen cabinets and the remaining construction costs.

Our working capital was grossly inadequate. Winn quickly became skilled at holding off creditors. He learned how to take advantage of the "float" on checks, and he frequently hand-carried invoices to Stampings and to Deere in order to wait for checks to be prepared. Some accounts were settled with stock. James P. Conley and Ralph C. Stromer, then partners in the Ioway-Record Printing Company of Muscatine, each took one share of common stock in payment of a bill for $200. Conley later said that his only regret was that Home-O-Nize had not been more in debt to Ioway-Record Printing at the time.

Efforts to obtain mill steel for kitchen cabinets continued throughout 1947. Newsom, inadequately challenged by the management of sales of card files and with the stock sale nearing its end, helped Hanson contact steel companies. But their endeavors were to no avail.

Organizational Structure

At the annual meeting in March 1948, we expanded the size of the board of directors to five. In order to add a director representing local investors, we selected A. J. Whitsitt, then manager of the Batterson Store of Muscatine, as our new director, joining Hanson, Miller, Doonan, and myself.

As our hopes of producing kitchen cabinets seemed far removed, the roles played by the founders began to change. Miller concentrated more and more on his own design service. Hanson laid the groundwork for the Clement T. Hanson Advertising Agency, devoting most of his time to that project. Both served Home-O-Nize, however, whenever there was need for their help. I continued as chief executive officer, working on a part-time basis without compensation.

The organizational structure at the end of 1947 included Doonan as plant superintendent, York as foreman, Newsom as sales manager, Winn as office manager, McCullough as purchasing agent, Van Lent as personnel director, and Dahl in charge of a group of services that included production planning and control as well as engineering.

The plant was humming as we entered 1948, and it continued doing so through the first eight months of the year, thanks to Stampings and Deere. Nevertheless, austerity was the rule. Hanson and Newsom, concerned with our public image, painted the dingy first floor office interior a fresh green. They removed ragged shades from the windows and turned them upside down and inside out. They failed, however, to convince me to spend the money re-

quired to level the sloping floor or to replace the potbellied stove that heated the office. Even McCullough's request for paint to give his upstairs office a face-lift was denied.

Early in February 1948, Stanley M. Howe joined Home-O-Nize as an assistant to Dahl in his broad scope of responsibility. With a degree in general engineering from Iowa State University, Howe went on to complete the two-year M.B.A. program at the Harvard Graduate School of Business Administration. During the previous Christmas holidays in the newly repainted office, I had persuaded him to join Home-O-Nize, an act that still stands as one of my major contributions to the organization. Stan had numerous opportunities to go elsewhere, but he feared that corporate responsibility would come only coincidentally with gray

Harold "Peewee" Whisler (left) and Ray Shellabarger at work assembling components for the flower markers.

hair. I assured him that responsibility would come quickly at Home-O-Nize.

Others beginning long-time careers in 1948 included Raymond Meyn, employed as a spot welder; William Brendel, a press operator who was continuously employed until his death in 1971; and Elmer Boldt, an assembler who retired in 1965. LeVern Greer was first employed in 1948, worked for a few years, left the company, and returned in 1956 to become a production supervisor at Home-O-Nize.

A most disappointing event was Doonan's resignation during the summer of 1948. This marked the end of a difficult period for both of us. Doonan had performed well during planning and construction, but once production started, he had difficulty adjusting to his intended role as plant superintendent. Despite repeated counseling, he was not providing satisfactory leadership. His relationships with people were not what they should have been. After several months of discussion, we agreed on his resignation as plant superintendent and his withdrawal from the board.

I had faced, for the first time but not the last, the difficult decision to terminate a manager who, despite demonstrated loyalty and effort, did not fit. The task was particularly trying because I liked Ed Doonan, considered him a friend, and had encouraged him to leave a good position to join unproven Home-O-Nize. But after leaving Home-O-Nize, he soon found a position as a county engineer, where his talents were better matched to the job requirements.

How often executives must encounter the unpleasant task of terminating a loyal and dedicated manager whose aptitudes simply do not fit. How frequently executives procrastinate, even though the evidence is clear that termination is required. Over the years, I have observed that failure to deal directly, positively, but kindly with such situations is always a disservice to the organization and to its other members. Moreover, it is usually a disservice to the individual involved. Dealing frankly with such situations often allows that person to redirect his or her career objectives along more satisfactory lines.

Deere Contract Not Renewed

Another disappointing event of 1948 was Deere's decision not to renew our contract for the manufacture of pickup attachments for the following season. Months before the scheduled completion of our contract for the 1948 season, it became doubtful that the contract would be renewed, despite Deere's satisfaction with our performance. Deere had purchased a former defense plant near Ankeny, Iowa. This large facility was being rehabilitated to manufacture implements, including the pickup attachments. Deffenbaugh did extend our contract to include pickup attachments adapted for the harvesting of sunflower seeds. Although disappointed by Deere's decision, we remained indebted to Deffenbaugh for the opportunity that he had given us at a crucial moment. Some years later, after Deffenbaugh had retired, we produced aluminum parts for a bird feeder that he had designed and was marketing.

The End of Kitchen Cabinets

Out of necessity, not desire, we reluctantly abandoned our intended production of kitchen cabinets and appliances. We had not found a supply source for mill steel despite all our efforts. Even the 43 tons of steel authorized by the Civilian Production Administration in November 1946 had not been received from the Granite City Steel Company.

In August 1948, after months of deliberation, the board of directors authorized the officers to dispose of materials, tooling, and equipment assembled specifically for the manufacture of kitchen cabinets and, if possible, to sell the design and patent applications. Established manufacturers with access to mill steel had already introduced new lines of steel kitchen cabinets. Thus, even if Home-O-Nize could eventually purchase steel at mill prices, the company would have the disadvantage of being a late entrant into the market.

Our capsuled assessment was that we had missed the moment of opportunity because of the unavailability of steel. In retrospect, this may have been in our best interests. Our kitchen cabinet designs may have been too avant-garde to have been marketed in quantity in a competitive market. So we abandoned our dreams and sought better uses for our limited resources. Significantly, no manufacturer has yet developed and sold large numbers of motorized upper kitchen cabinets that could be stocked, installed, and moved as appliances.

More Financial Headaches

Home-O-Nize had a profitable year in 1948. Sales aggregating $419,700 produced a net profit of $39,900, even after a write-off of $21,000 on kitchen cabinets and after paying, for the first time, federal income tax in the amount of $1,537. However, Home-O-Nize still was sadly underfinanced. Working capital requirements for accounts receivable and inventory had increased proportionately with sales. Loan amortization payments of $10,000 in principal plus annual interest had to be met. Creditors who had been held in abeyance had to be paid.

During the year, we developed with the Central State Bank a do-it-yourself arrangement for factoring accounts receivable on sales of office products. In June, with five profitable months behind us, I obtained from Byron McKee at the Muscatine Bank and Trust Company a tentative commitment for a substantial loan on favorable terms.

By the end of 1948, our cash position became more difficult. We were receiving no more revenues from Deere. At the same time, we needed cash for inventory and start-up costs in connection with a contract that we had signed in July to manufacture corn pickers.

Our last hope for appreciable relief faded when McKee told me in December that his loan committee had overruled his earlier commitment to give Home-O-Nize a term loan. As a result of this disappointing decision, we were reluctant to do business with that institution for many years. It made me more cognizant than ever of the intense competitive spirit between the two Muscatine banks.

Sale of stock brought in only $25,600 in 1948—far short of what was needed to provide adequate working capital. Of this amount, only $7,500 was sold to outsiders. Our new director, Whitsitt, bought $3,000 worth of stock. Shares worth $2,600 went to members of the organization, partially in lieu of salaries. The remaining amounts were $3,000 from the Hansons, $2,000 from my parents, and $8,000 from me. In addition, I made a loan of $16,000 to the company, without security. Fred Winn continued to have trouble keeping creditors happy.

CHAPTER FOUR

Darkness Before the Light

CORN PICKERS AND PRIME-MOVERS

Even though Home-O-Nize had earned a profit in 1948, we were still in grave danger of becoming just another statistic contributing to the high mortality rate for new business ventures. Not until the end of 1950—three-and-one-half years later—would we clearly see the light at the end of the tunnel. Until then, collapse was rumored on more than one occasion, and quite frankly, at times I was afraid the rumors might prove to be true. These years were the most prolonged period of frustration, tension, and challenge of my entire professional and business career. I lay awake many nights searching for answers to problems that seemed to be beyond solution. Even close associates, believing the task to be hopeless, urged us to give up the struggle.

Year of the Corn Picker

Home-O-Nize badly needed more contract work. Therefore, we responded promptly to overtures from Associated Manufacturers, Incorporated, of Waterloo, Iowa. This company was seeking a contractor to produce a newly designed corn picker for direct attachment to the front end of a tractor. Because of our successful production of pickup attachments for Deere, we were confident—perhaps overly so—about our ability to manufacture corn pickers. In July 1948, Dahl and I went to Waterloo to

sign a contract for $450,000 to produce pickers in quantity for the 1949 market season. Despite our joy at the time, with this contract we had inadvertently exposed ourselves to the greatest fiasco in the history of Home-O-Nize.

As the Deere contract for pickup attachments closed out in August 1948, we rushed to prepare for the production of corn pickers. Parts fabrication and assembly were set up at the Oak Street Plant, with the first shipments targeted for early 1949. Again, the Home-O-Nize organization responded grandly to the challenge, with leadership supplied by Art Dahl, Louis York, and others. Units, fabricated to the designs provided by Associated, were ready for testing in December.

The test, held in a cornfield near Muscatine, was observed by Associated officials, a number of Home-O-Nize members, and McKee, president of the Muscatine Bank and Trust Co. The picker failed after one pass of the field. Obviously, there were bugs in the design, which Richard Shore, an Associated engineer, worked diligently to correct. (Perhaps, McKee's witnessing of the failed test had something to do with his bank's decision not to make the term loan to Home-O-Nize as earlier promised.)

A Fiasco Unfolds. Despite this failure and continuing financial pressures, we ap-

28

proached 1949 with great expectations. It would be the "year of the corn picker." However, our anticipation of profitable progress was soon smashed.

Although the basic concept of the corn picker appeared to be sound, the condition of Associated Manufacturers was not. First, as we should have deduced from the field test, Associated's detailed design proved to be full of bugs. Second, as we should have discovered through more thorough investigation, Associated was grossly underfinanced—perhaps being even weaker financially than Home-O-Nize. Third, partly because of these deficiencies, Associated lacked a dealer organization capable of moving the quantity of pickers that we had contracted to manufacture.

During January and February of 1949, we produced 38 corn pickers under great handicaps. Numerous design changes to overcome the flaws revealed in the field test slowed and later stopped production. Even in the early months of this contract, payment on invoices was repeatedly delayed, despite efforts by Winn and Dahl to collect. Continuing controversy arose over extra charges for the design changes. By the end of February, assembly had been all but discontinued, making it necessary for us to reduce personnel.

Four months of conferences and negotiations with Associated led to a contract amendment, made on July 1, aimed at permitting resumption of production. Our discussions with Paul R. Christiansen, Associated's new manager, generated confidence that production of the corn pickers could be resumed. Eleven units were produced in July, and 72 more in August. With more space needed for production, we leased three 40-by-100-foot Quonset huts and a small office building on Sampson Street in South Muscatine. We transferred the corn picker assembly operation and some of the parts fabrication during September. Production of corn pickers stood at 76 units in September and 69 in October.

Unfortunately, our troubles with Associated were not over. Design changes seemed to be unceasing. Collection of invoices remained laborious. Discord be-

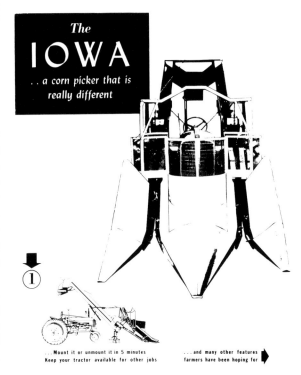

A contract to make a corn picker looked promising at the outset, but it nearly destroyed the company financially.

tween Associated and its primary distributor—Irwin Equipment, Incorporated, of Omaha—arose over the poor performance of the corn pickers. By late October, the Irwin controversy was in the hands of attorneys. Production stopped. An entry in my log for October 31, 1949, reads: "Looks like corn picker sales for the year are through. Leaves us out on a limb. Drastic staff reductions needed."

That marked the end of corn picker production, but not the end of the corn picker fiasco. Sporadic conferences with Associated continued until October 1950. An entry in my log for October 24, 1950, reads: "Settlement agreement signed with Associated. If they perform, we come out whole." But Associated didn't perform. Instead, they defaulted, entered into bankruptcy, and then went out of business. Finally, in 1951, after salvaging what we could from inventory, we wrote off a loss of $52,541 on the corn pickers.

 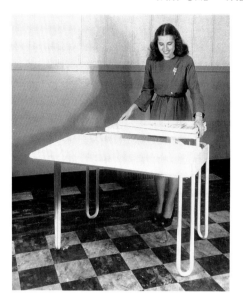 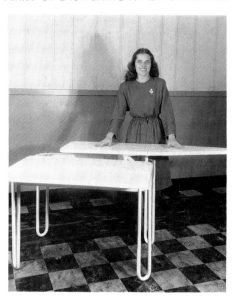

The scramble for manufacturing contracts brought all sorts of business through the door, including this hideaway ironing board.

A Critical Time

As the prospects for corn pickers faded, we scrambled to keep the reduced work force busy through the balance of 1949. Work for Stampings continued, although a generally soft economy resulted in a smaller volume than we had expected. We supplemented this with a number of contracts with other manufacturers. Metal connector parts were fabricated for a local manufacturer, Peter Products, for use in movable walls that they were assembling for the Johns-Manville Company. Signs were manufactured for the Red Jacket Pump Company, and pump bases for the Carver Pump Company. Cabinets were constructed for Collins Radio Company. We also developed and manufactured an ironing board for G. W. Timmerman, the staunch supporter of our kitchen cabinets. But none of these contracts was sizable.

Production and sale of card files continued. Finally, in late 1948, we received from the Granite City Steel Company about one-half of our original order for mill steel; the other half followed later. With this steel, we designed and started production of storage cabinets, 66 inches high. These were painted white and were offered through local outlets as household units. Soon we discovered that with olive paint they could be offered as storage cabinets for the office at a higher net price to us.

Despite this modest enlargement of our office product line, a recession in the general economy contributed to a decline of sales, from $79,000 in 1948 to $41,000 in 1949. However, the strong commitment to the office product field made in the board's historic decision of 1948 led us to consider the purchase of the Dependable Chair Company of Omaha. Had these negotiations succeeded, we would have added office chairs and stools to our product line in 1949.

The corn picker fiasco set Home-O-Nize back severely. The company's total sales in 1949 dropped by more than $100,000 to a level of $322,900. Losses amounted to $29,700, including a final write-off of $2,300 on kitchen cabinets. Beyond this recorded loss, we had at the end of 1949 more than $64,000 tied up in inventory, work in process, and uncollectible receivables for the corn picker. Home-O-Nize's cash position, diminished by more than $100,000 within the year, was at the worst level ever experienced—or ever to be experienced.

The situation was dismal. Revenues from contract work, principally Stampings, together with those from factoring accounts receivable on office products, did not cover expenses. Because Home-O-Nize lacked credit, suppliers were beginning to ship materials only on a COD basis.

York, Carl, and others from the office would join our members on the Stampings assembly line on Friday afternoons to increase the week's production. Winn hovered by with paper and pen in hand to prepare the invoice that he would hand-carry to Stampings' Davenport office in order to secure funds to cover our payroll. Even so, pay checks were often delayed, and Winn was busy fending off creditors. The Central State Bank, understandably, would not factor accounts receivable for corn pickers.

Sale of stock to outsiders was out of the question, given the rumors of imminent shutdown. The Hansons invested another $1,200 in common stock. I recall Clem saying, "Max, this is the last I can do." In fact, during the latter part of 1949, Hanson, in deep despair—an unusual attitude—was ready to call it quits.

Keeping Home-O-Nize Alive

But calling it quits was something that I would not do. Too many people had invested in Home-O-Nize because they had confidence in me. Even if I had reconciled myself to personal financial loss, I could not let others down.

Having exhausted my personal funds, I went to my partners in Stanley Engineering Co. with a proposition to borrow from the firm, with my partnership interest serving as security for the loan. With reluctance, they agreed. I came back again and again, and their concerns became intense. Some stormy sessions resulted. Nevertheless, this aid enabled me to buy stock worth $30,500 as well as to make loans to Home-O-Nize during 1949. This is why the doors of Home-O-Nize remained open. It took me until 1956 to repay, with interest, those loans from Stanley Engineering.

As Home-O-Nize's struggle for survival drew to a close at the end of 1950, there were 117 shareholders. The outstanding stock had been qualified by the State of Iowa. We thus had become a publicly owned corporation, even though some 44 percent of the common stock was held by myself and members of my family. I had not planned, nor even contemplated, a personal holding of this size. It resulted from

my efforts to carry Home-O-Nize over the shoals of bankruptcy. This situation did present some temptation to increase Stanley holdings to a level over 50 percent in order to assure absolute control. The temptation was a fleeting one, however, because, in the long run, neither Home-O-Nize nor I would have benefited. Future financing by common stock would have been sharply curtailed, as the Stanleys were not likely to have the resources to make further substantial equity investment in Home-O-Nize.

The Bell Prime-Mover

Late in 1949, a welcome opportunity to expand our offering of products came about as the result of my personal acquaintance with Gen. George H. Olmsted of Des Moines. Olmsted, a West Point graduate, had been active in the insurance business before World War II. After returning from the service, he became a director of the Equity Corporation of New York and the Bell Aircraft Corporation, in which Equity held a controlling interest. Our acquaintance was the result of United World Federalist activities. My son David, then executive director of the Iowa Federalists, introduced us.

Because Olmsted was a skillful financial manager, I shared some of Home-O-Nize's problems with him. In response to his suggestion, I prepared and sent to him data regarding our situation. Just before the end of 1949, he asked me if Home-O-Nize would be interested in acquiring a product—the Bell Prime-Mover—then manufactured and sold by Bell Aircraft.

Larry Bell, president of the company, had encouraged the development of the Prime-Mover, an engine-powered wheelbarrow with a capacity of 1,000 pounds, as a hedge against the postwar conversion from a military to a civilian economy. By 1949, two facts had become evident. First, Bell was still busy with military contracts. Second, the Bell Prime-Mover was not producing the anticipated magnitude of sales and profits. A market survey that had forecast annual sales of 25,000 units was proving to be unrealistic. Hence, Equity's direc-

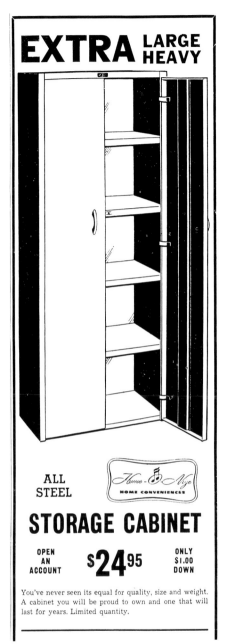

Just by painting the storage cabinet green like the card files, it was suitable for office use and brought in more money.

tors on the Bell board were pressing for divestment.

The Bell Prime-Mover Model 343, designed by aeronautical engineers, was being produced in an aircraft plant accustomed to the high overheads characteristic of cost-plus military contracts. Such a piece of construction equipment was obviously misplaced in those surroundings. However, a simplified, more ruggedly designed machine manufactured in a cost-oriented plant might succeed.

We responded favorably. I traveled first to Des Moines to discuss the Prime-Mover deal with Olmsted and then to Niagara Falls to explore the opportunity with Bell officials. Bell's secretary, Leston Faneuf, and vice president, Harvey Gaylord, visited Muscatine to look us over. All of this led to a contract, approved first by the Home-O-Nize board and then by the Bell board. We thereby acquired on March 2, 1950, a "business constituting the production, distribution, and sale of a material handling device known as the Bell Prime-Mover."

The contract to buy the Prime-Mover product from Bell Aircraft Corporation would mean steady cash income and ultimately would save The Home-O-Nize Co.

A Good Deal for Us. Our first wholly owned subsidiary, The Prime-Mover Co., was incorporated to operate this new business. Under the terms of the contract, we acquired all patents, trademarks, tools, dies, fixtures, patterns, records, and sales materials as well as inventories of parts, accessories, and some finished Model 343s. Parts were in sufficient quantity to assemble enough units of the Model 343 to meet market needs through the remainder of 1950. Bell agreed to lend certain Prime-Mover technical personnel for a limited time and to provide engineering data on the design of an improved model.

The complex financial arrangements were tailored to fit our strained situation. Bell made a loan of $125,000 to The Prime-Mover Co. to cover the cost of the purchased items, to be drawn down as inventory, and other items were delivered. Maturities for repayment ran from $2,500 in December 1950 to $22,500 in December 1956 with interest at 4 percent. Bell also loaned Home-O-Nize $25,000 at the same rate, to be repaid in 1956 and 1957, on the condition that I subordinate a $49,893 note covering the loans that I had made to Home-O-Nize in 1948 and 1949. The Prime-Mover Co. was further required to pay Bell a royalty of 2.7 percent on each of the first 25,000 chassis sold to distributors and one of 3 percent on accessories and spare parts.

It was a good deal for us, and Bell seemed to be pleased. One Bell officer expressed satisfaction that this prodigy would now be lodged where it belonged—in our Sampson Street Quonset huts rather than in an aircraft plant.

An Organization for Prime-Mover. The contract provided that Bell would name two directors to the board of The Prime-Mover Co. until we had paid off all financial obligations. The initial Prime-Mover board included Olmsted and Gaylord, as the Bell representatives, along with Hanson, Miller, and myself. Initial officers were Stanley, president; Hanson, vice president; and Winn, secretary-treasurer.

Art Dahl was the logical person to head the Prime-Mover organization as vice president and sales manager. His talents and interests flowed along these lines. To assist Dahl in sales promotion, we employed R. Howard Worst. After many years with Prime-Mover, Worst became a copywriter in corporate advertising before his retirement in 1979. Ralph Heckathorne, loaned by Bell for several months, assumed service responsibilities. Richard Andrews, an Iowa State graduate in mechanical engineering with several years of experience, was employed as product designer. George Pedersen, an experienced industrial engineer educated at the University of Iowa, was engaged to handle quality control. Despite satisfactory performance, neither Andrews nor Pedersen remained with us for long. To round out the administrative staff, Gene Fuller was transferred from Home-O-Nize to assist in production control and purchasing. Hazel Derrick was employed as a stenographer and later served for many years as secretary to Dahl.

The Prime-Mover organization undertook sales, collections, product design, purchasing, and servicing, and owned inventories and accounts receivable. Home-O-Nize contracted with The Prime-Mover Co. to provide certain materials and all labor required for the fabrication of parts and final assembly of the units. With little delay, the corn picker was happily cleared out of the Sampson Street Quonsets, and the Prime-Mover operation was moved in.

Model 343 units, accessories, and spare parts were sold through the rest of 1950. Meanwhile, Dahl and Andrews busied themselves with the design and testing of a larger and more rugged model (capacity of 1,500 pounds) with a four-cycle, rather than a two-cycle, engine. In June, the board of directors viewed an experimental unit. Testing of a prototype began in August, tooling was nearly completed by the end of December, and fabrication of parts was started. Dealers who viewed the experimental model were enthusiastic and were ready to place orders when the Model 15 was introduced in early 1951.

Home-O-Nize Moves Ahead

Prime-Mover was the major focus of our attention during much of 1950, but

R. G. Ervin, Jr. (left), a representative of Bell Aircraft Corporation, with Harold Barton (center) and Art Dahl of The Prime-Mover Co., in April of 1950. This photo was taken right after production of Prime-Movers was moved to Muscatine.

considerable progress was also being made in other areas. Volume from Stampings was steady throughout the year. We continued to perform contract work for a number of other companies as well, of which the sizable volume for Herman Nelson was the most important. New opportunities for military-related contract work increased because of the Korean War. At year's end, we were involved in several negotiations, including one for a major subcontract from Bell Aircraft.

Sales of office products reached $70,000 in 1950, up from $41,000 in 1949, as we continued to enlarge our product line. The product line included the 3-by-5- and 4-by-6-inch card files and the business card files, along with seven models of combination cabinets (containing file drawers and storage space), a two-drawer nonsuspension file, and a storage cabinet with a height of 66 inches. A four-page flier was produced with photographs and descriptive information about the office products that we offered. (It included the Home-O-Nize logo with two musical notes in the "O.")

When Dahl took charge of Prime-Mover, Howe assumed all of the planning responsibilities for Home-O-Nize, including product design, industrial engineering, and production control. In just over a year of employment, Howe had clearly demonstrated his readiness to assume these re-

Prime-Movers would require additional manufacturing space, which became available in these Quonset huts in South Muscatine.

sponsibilities. To enlarge Howe's staff on office product design, we employed Philip A. Temple, a mechanical engineer just graduating from the University of Iowa. Temple later became vice president, seating group, with our Corry Jamestown subsidiary. Lyndon K. Fisher, later administrative services manager at the Richmond Plant of The HON Company, joined Home-O-Nize in 1950 as a clerk. At the annual meeting in March, Kenneth Fairall, a Muscatine businessman, was elected as a director, to replace A. J. Whitsitt, who had purchased a business of his own.

As the year progressed, the work force at the Oak Street Plant grew. The Prime-Mover operation had increased our load substantially. A number of new recruits began long careers with our organization. Norman Marshall, model maker for The HON Company until retirement, joined Home-O-Nize in late 1949 as a toolroom machinist. Donald Hammond, Richard Noble, Clarence Lick, Fred Bodman, and Leonard McEvoy were all employed in 1950. Bodman retired in 1968 and Noble in 1973. Hammond, starting as an operator on the primitive equipment of 1950, went on to be an operator of complicated tape-controlled machines in the Prime-Mover Plant. McEvoy was a spot welder at The HON Company's Oak Street Plant. Lick began working for Luedtka in the warehouse; he later became supervisor of the finished

goods warehouse at The HON Company Geneva Plant.

The Financial Picture at the End of 1950

Financial progress during 1950 was modest, but most encouraging. Having hit bottom the previous year, where could we go but up? The combined sales of Home-O-Nize and Prime-Mover totaled more than $600,000, appearing to foretell a healthy outlook for the future.

Although Home-O-Nize's sales of office products and contract work in 1950 were down slightly ($311,000 versus $329,000 the previous year), we achieved a profit of $10,500 versus the loss of $29,700 in 1949. Our cash position was no longer eroding. We had not calculated the final amount of the write-off related to the corn picker fiasco, but we still hoped to collect some of the substantial sum locked up in inventory and receivables for that doomed product.

With only a partial year of production, Prime-Mover had accounted for an additional $298,200 in sales, with a recorded loss of $34,100. This loss was about as expected. We had expended $14,900 to transfer the operation from Niagara Falls to Muscatine and $18,700 on the development of the Model 15 Prime-Mover.

As the holiday season of 1950 approached, our spirits were more relaxed than they had been for several years. With Prime-Mover operations well under way, the volume of office products growing, and good prospects for contracts, we confidently looked ahead to a profitable 1951. We had weathered some tough storms. Home-O-Nize would be a survivor!

This country's treasured private enterprise system allows entrepreneurs to venture, but it does not guarantee success. It demands of entrepreneurs the dedication to overcome difficulties as well as the financial resources to see the new venture through to profitability. Finding the funds required to carry Home-O-Nize through 1949 had strengthened my determination to carry on. Even in those dark days, I was sure that Home-O-Nize would eventually succeed.

A demonstration of the Prime-Mover in a concrete pouring exercise outside the Quonset hut. A young Dick Stanley is shown at right. He would later serve on the board of directors.

PART TWO

Operation Independence, 1951-1955

With the survival of The Home-O-Nize Co. reasonably assured, we turned our attention toward expanding sales and improving profitability. When we had to delay manufacture of kitchen cabinets, necessity rather than choice had launched us into contract work. We were grateful for the contracts from Stampings, Deere, Herman Nelson, Bell Aircraft, and others. But experience had taught us the uncertainties of performing work under contract for other manufacturers. We had become convinced that we could not attain our goals of greater sales volume and increased profitability as long as we were tied so firmly to contract work.

In 1951, we launched Operation Independence, the goal of which was to expand our Prime-Mover and office product businesses even as we sought more contract work for the short term. We viewed Prime-Movers and office products as twin opportunities to gain our independence. Prime-Mover, with sales of $298,000

in 1950, seemed the most promising vehicle for early takeoff. Office products, with but $70,000 in sales in 1950, appeared to offer a more difficult path to self-sustaining and profitable growth.

During the five-year period of Operation Independence, from 1951 through 1955, we saw our basic objectives realized. By 1953, total consolidated sales of The Home-O-Nize Co. passed the $1 million milestone; two years later, they exceeded $2 million. Profitability resumed in 1952, to start what has now become more than three decades of uninterrupted profits for The Home-O-Nize Co. (and later HON INDUSTRIES Inc.). Net profits stood at more than $100,000 at the end of Operation Independence. Our financial situation was greatly improved.

As a result of Operation Independence, Home-O-Nize made a transition from what was primarily a job shop doing contract work for other companies to a manufacturer of its own product lines. Contract work declined from nearly 40 percent of our total sales to just a bit more than 20 percent, with its end in sight. Prime-Mover, while experiencing slower growth than anticipated, played a special role in Operation Independence, providing an added volume of work for the Home-O-Nize production force. The pleasant surprise, and the truly dynamic element of Operation Independence, turned out to be the rapidly expanding sales of office products, with the emergence of Home-O-Nize as a factor in the office furniture industry. By the end of this period, it was clear that office furniture was destined to be the company's core business.

This impressive story is best told in segments. Chapter 5 discusses marketing and product development in the contract work and Prime-Mover areas of the company's operations. The following chapter deals with these same subjects for Home-O-Nize's rapidly growing office products business. Chapter 7 treats the important topics of production, management, human relations, and finance. Because the organization was small during this period, the chronicles of progress overlap at times.

CHAPTER FIVE

The Role of Contract Work and Prime-Mover

Contract work remained vital to the success of Operation Independence, at least in the short run. It was the speediest path to the enlarged volume needed to achieve greater profitability. We needed increased earnings to get Prime-Mover on its feet and to expand the development, production, and sale of our office products and Prime-Movers.

Making Prime-Mover sound and profitable was also an important objective of Operation Independence. Prime-Mover had to generate profits to liquidate the sizable amounts due to Bell in connection with the purchase of the operation. Beyond that, we expected Prime-Mover to become a lucrative, growing part of our total operation. Unfortunately, achieving growth and profitability proved to be slower and more difficult than we had expected.

Expanding Our Contract Work

Our contract with Stampings, Inc., received first priority—a bird in the hand being worth several in the bush. Our association was now nearly five years old. With no production facilities of their own, Stampings looked to us as their sole manufacturing source. The operation, although not as large as we might have wished, was steady and profitable. By attending carefully to quality and schedules, and by cooperating closely with Stampings' staff, we

maintained a fine relationship throughout the years of Operation Independence and beyond. In addition to the various models of bottled gas housings, we produced for a time Cargo Guards—truck heaters fueled by bottled gas—until they were dropped for lack of success.

In January 1951, we negotiated a contract with the Herman Nelson Division of the American Air Filter Co., which provided a substantial volume of work in 1951 and 1952, along with some minor amounts in 1953 and 1954. We produced intake louvers for the Herman Nelson air conditioning units designed for schools. We also produced storage cabinets, some with doors and some open, to be installed in classrooms alongside the air conditioning units. The experience with these cabinets was useful to us in developing our own lines of storage cabinets and bookcases for the office.

Military Contracts. After the slowdown following the end of World War II, U.S. production of military equipment was again on the upswing after the outbreak of the Korean War. The Pentagon was pressing prime contractors who had converted from civilian to military work during World War II to make that conversion again. However, many manufacturers wanted to maintain production of civilian goods while meeting the demands of the Pentagon. This was all part of the "guns and butter" pattern of production prevailing in the early 1950s. But this situation offered opportunities for Home-O-Nize to become a subcontractor.

During the last quarter of 1950, Herman Nelson Division, Red Jacket Pump Manufacturing Company, Carver Pump Company, and Collins Radio Company subcontracted some defense work to us. My report to the annual meeting of shareholders in March 1951 anticipated a "large volume of military subcontract work" for the immediate future.

Our relationship with Bell Aircraft, arising out of our purchase of Prime-Mover, stood us in good stead for gaining military work. Bell gave us a contract involving design of containers for shipping Tarzan bombs. We did considerable work on this during 1951, only to have the contract terminated in early 1952 because Bell had not been authorized to proceed with actual production of the bombs.

Our major military work was production of fairings to be used on engine nacelles of the B-47 bomber. We worked for Bell Aircraft, which was a subcontractor to Boeing Aircraft Company. This was a most attractive opportunity, as the volume was substantial and the work extended over several years. We produced these fairings at a comfortable profit, even after renegotiation of our prices for tooling and manufacture. Work for Bell, including other products in addition to the fairings, accounted for 17 percent of Home-O-Nize's total sales in 1951 and 27 percent in 1952.

Even before we received the order for fairing production, Bill Hammon, who became our sales manager in May 1951, was pursuing other military contracts. He was successful in negotiating contracts with Magic Chef, General Motors, and others. Of these, only the contract with Magic Chef for production of tank bulkheads for B-47 bomber subassemblies produced appreciable volume. Our experience with this subcontract was not a happy one. We fell behind in our delivery schedule, so Magic Chef canceled the contract in September 1952.

Prime-Mover's Role in Operation Independence

From the time of its acquisition, Prime-Mover had helped Home-O-Nize by providing work load and revenues through the intercompany "contract" for parts fabrication and assembly. This work accounted for 16.2 percent of Home-O-Nize's total revenues in 1951 and 13 percent in 1952, helping to keep the Oak Street Plant busy in the years before sales of office products began to accelerate. The acquisition of Prime-Mover contributed in other ways as well—Bell's loan of $25,000 to Home-O-Nize and the subcontracts from Bell for military work.

Management. Prime-Mover's board of directors functioned separately from that of its owner, The Home-O-Nize Co. Hanson, Miller, and I continued to serve during these years. Olmsted represented Bell throughout this period. Leston Faneuf replaced Harvey Gaylord as the other Bell

These components, like all other items made at the plant, had to follow close tolerances. The equipment was old, but the work was good.

representative in February 1951, and W. G. Gisel replaced Faneuf in February 1955.

Prime-Mover officers throughout the period were Stanley, president; Dahl, vice president; and Winn, secretary-treasurer. Vice President Dahl participated in product design decisions, supervised Prime-Mover sales, and purchased component parts. Production—including parts fabrication and assembly, production control, and scheduling—was performed by The Home-O-Nize Co. under Stan Howe's direction. A common engineering department, reporting to me but coordinated by Howe, handled product design for both Prime-Mover and office products until a separate Prime-Mover engineering department was created in 1955, to report to Dahl. Dick Andrews was involved in Prime-Mover product design through most of 1954. A common staff, supervised by Fred Winn, handled financial and accounting matters for both companies.

Product Development. By early 1951, we had sold all the units of the Model 343 that could be assembled with the parts purchased from Bell. Contractors and other users welcomed this model, particularly when equipped with a dump bucket to move concrete from mixers to points of placement, or when equipped with a platform to move other materials around a construction site or within an industrial plant. However, the Model 343 proved to be too small and delicate to perform heavy duties.

With Bell's concurrence, we designed the Model 15 as a more rugged machine with greater capacity (1,500 pounds) and a purchased four-cycle engine replacing the temperamental two-cycle one on the 343. Accessories offered for use with this chassis included a dump bucket, a platform, a blade for snow removal or light grading, and dual front wheels for soft ground.

With production of this new model just starting in the fall of 1951, orders for almost 100 units were already on hand. Despite a slow start and setbacks caused by fire and flood (to be discussed in a later chapter), we completed and shipped 621 of the new Model 15 Prime-Movers during 1951. The Model 15 continued to gain acceptance, forming the backbone of Prime-Mover's business in construction equipment into the 1980s.

Although Prime-Mover dominated the domestic market for concrete buggies, we soon discovered the limitations of that market. A sales target of only 2,500 units per year—just 10 percent of the early Bell forecast—was a goal that could not be attained with a unit similar to Bell's Model 343 or our Model 15. We fought a stubborn battle to increase sales of the Model 15 from the level of the 621 units shipped in 1951. After down, up, and down years, we reached a volume of 803 chassis in 1955—representing a sales volume of $475,000, up from the $420,000 of four years earlier. Experience proved to be a tough master. It appeared that we had to lower our sights.

The principal limitation to increased sales was the market's appraisal of uses for the Prime-Mover. Larry Bell's concept of a motorized wheelbarrow had been an exciting one, quite in tune with the postwar rush to engine-powered lawn mowers and snowplows. Undoubtedly, he visualized the homeowner, along with the farmer, the manufacturer, and the contractor, as a major source of demand for his new product. However, the Model 343 as designed by Bell's engineers was not well-suited to this market. Its 1,000-pound capacity was too large for most household uses, and its list price of $495 was too high for widespread purchase as a powered wheelbarrow. As a piece of material-handling equipment for use in construction or industry, it had to compete in the market with many other products.

With engineering changes introduced by Home-O-Nize, the new models of the Prime-Mover designed in ensuing years turned out to be safer and more versatile machines with greater capacity.

The mason tender broadened the product line and increased sales potential for The Prime-Mover Co.

Strenuous efforts to promote the Prime-Mover for uses other than construction proved very disappointing during these years. With a platform, it could not compete effectively with a pickup truck or a forklift. A Prime-Mover with a blade could not perform as well as a tractor, jeep, or a bulldozer with a blade. We searched aggressively for special uses—as, for example, a Prime-Mover equipped as a rig to service industrial maintenance crews or a fleet of earth movers—but to no avail. In short, the Model 15 Prime-Mover was well-accepted as a concrete buggy, but it found only limited functions in other areas.

With but a single product and some accessories, the need to expand the Prime-Mover product line became increasingly evident. As early as January 1951, the board was considering the addition of smaller models of "power buggies," with a capacity of 500 to 900 pounds. Miller was authorized to prepare design concept studies, but no acceptable product resulted. Projected manufacturing costs indicated that retail prices would have to be too high to appeal to a mass market. For several years, therefore, we focused our limited product development capability on developing accessories for the Model 15 and examining special applications that could lead to substantial volumes.

Gradually, we came to believe that our best hope for success would be to expand our line of products for the construction market rather than to create a new model of Prime-Mover. Accordingly, in 1953, I outlined, and the board approved, a set of criteria for new products for 1954. The product, for distribution through our current sales organization, should meet an already existing need and use. The tooling and development of the product should require a minimum amount of time and a small outlay of capital.

Following these criteria, we investigated masonry saws, both the stationary type to cut concrete blocks or bricks and the mobile type to cut slots in concrete slabs. Even though these saws met fully the criteria that we had established, we dropped the idea after about eight months of study, primarily because we encountered firmly entrenched competition. Then we studied rotary concrete finishers used by masonry and concrete contractors, but again we backed away because of competition in that market.

Our reluctance to confront established competitors prevented us from adding product lines that could have moved through an expanding group of distributors of construction equipment. Thus, Prime-Mover's product expansion was retarded through these years. This undoubtedly accounts for Prime-Mover's slow growth in contrast to the rapid expansion of Home-O-Nize in the office product field, where we confronted stiff competition boldly and successfully. The preoccupation of management with our rapidly expanding business in office products was another factor contributing to the retardation of Prime-Mover's growth.

Finally, with the employment of Waldo Rodler as chief engineer in late 1954, The Prime-Mover Co. launched a three-pronged program of product development. First, the Model 15 would be improved, to be offered as the Model 15A. This was accomplished in May 1955. Second, a front-end loader for attachment to the Model 15A chassis would be designed. This would lead later to the Model L-812, a counterbalanced masonry tender, and then to the lower-cost and more maneuverable Models L-31 and L-36 mason tenders.

Third, the design of a larger, rider-type Prime-Mover was planned. Although initially conceived as a 3,000-pound unit, the final result was a 2,000-pound capacity unit—the M-20, using the power drive line of the M-15A. The M-20 was put into production in March 1956.

Spare Parts.   The spare parts business, we discovered in those early years, was a profitable one, as spare parts and accessories carried a higher markup than did chassis. Moreover, provision of spare parts to dealers servicing Prime-Movers created a steady and growing sales volume. This proved to be true even though the more rugged design of the M-15 required less replacement of parts than had been true of the more delicate Model 343.

Rebuilding the Prime-Mover Distribution System

With the acquisition of the Prime-Mover, we inherited from Bell what at first appeared to be an imposing distribution system. Many of the distributors, particularly those overseas, had been selected because they were selling or servicing helicopters, Bell's chief product for the civilian market.

The U.S. Market.   Within the United States, most of the distributors were stronger in the industrial field than in construction. Of all the dealers that we inherited, no more than a dozen produced appreciable sales for the Model 15 during the early 1950s.

Thus, Prime-Mover had to rebuild its distribution system quickly. This became Art Dahl's major assignment during the years of Operation Independence. Dahl sought to find dealers who served the construction industry and who would take a real interest in retailing equipment with a relatively low unit price. Caterpillar and other large-volume dealers in heavy construction equipment were seldom motivated to promote the Prime-Mover aggressively. Dahl did a fine job of revamping the domestic segment of Prime-Mover's distribution system. By 1955, some 80 dealers were active.

The European Market.   Bell had enjoyed significant sales of Prime-Movers in Europe while the Marshall Plan was aiding reconstruction there. But as the financial assistance from the United States declined, sales in Europe fell off sharply. Thus, most of our European dealers, who had been appointed by Bell, lost interest in the Prime-Mover.

During my visits with dealers in several European countries in 1954 and 1955, I found the obstacles to expanding sales of Prime-Movers there to be many and frustrating: tariffs and shipping costs priced our equipment out of the market; competition was stiff with equipment designed and built with lower labor costs in Europe; construction techniques often were not adaptable to the use of the Prime-Mover; and markets were fragmented among many relatively small nations.

Last but not least was an instance of design piracy committed by the Fenwick firm, our distributor in France. When I visited Fenwick in 1955, I was surprised to see in the Paris shop a familiar-looking concrete buggy with the label "Made in France." It was obvious that Fenwick had copied this unit and some 50 others directly from our Model 15. The only difference was that square corners on the sides, engine housing, and bucket had been substituted for Prime-Mover's smooth curves, probably because form dies were expensive. Needless to say, the number of Prime-Mover dealers was reduced by one after my visit.

Sales of the Model 15 in Europe never achieved the level and pace enjoyed by the Model 343. It soon became apparent that to service a European market required manufacturing there—a concept we later explored.

For a while, the Marshall Plan helped to provide great marketing opportunities for The Prime-Mover Co. in Europe. Here, a group of optimistic Frenchmen toast the success of the Prime-Mover at a trade show in Lyons.

From left to right, Howard Worst, Henry Faron, Fred Winn, and Art Dahl examine a Prime-Mover in Muscatine. Faron represented Fenwick S.A., of Paris, France, an organization that later turned out be design pirates.

Organization of Sales. After the Model 343 had been out of production for several years, we tried to stimulate sales of the Model 15 by means of a trade-in offer. This was part of a planned program to de-emphasize Prime-Mover's former relationship with an aircraft manufacturer. We believed that image to be of doubtful value in the construction equipment business, so we gradually eliminated the word Bell from the Prime-Mover logo and sales literature.

During these years, we operated with a minimal sales organization. Art Dahl was responsible not only for overall sales but also for primary contacts with dealers and distributors. He was assisted by Howard Worst. Harwell Peterson was added to the staff in 1954, providing further help.

Despite the slow growth of Prime-Mover's sales volume, we achieved an acceptable profit margin by 1955. Although we did increase prices toward the end of the period, the major contribution to an improvement of earnings at Prime-Mover was the implementation of an effective cost-reduction program—to be discussed in a later chapter. Our product was gaining acceptance as Prime-Mover was being increasingly recognized as an important producer of concrete buggies, thereby adapting to a niche in the overall market for construction equipment. We had succeeded in stabilizing the operation of our first acquisition. Prime-Mover, although smaller than we had hoped, was prepared to continue on a profitable basis during the years ahead. Thus, The Prime-Mover Co. contributed to the success of Operation Independence.

CHAPTER SIX

From Specialty Office Products to Office Furniture

Sales of office products rose dramatically from 1951 to 1955, to stand in excess of $1 million in 1955. The office accounted for almost two-thirds of Home-O-Nize's total revenues in that year. We had expected that an expansion of our business in this highly competitive market would be slow and difficult. Almost before we knew it, however, sales of office products were expanding more rapidly and were becoming more profitable than those of Prime-Movers.

In mid-1952, when it was apparent that sales of office products would grow to nearly double those of the previous year, I prepared a comprehensive plan for emphasizing this part of our business. The goal of Operation Independence was now to make office products the core business that would sustain the growth of The Home-O-Nize Co. We were greatly encouraged by the market's acceptance of our limited line of office products as well as by the good margins. Equipping the modern American office seemed to be the wave of the future. Expansion of business in this market appeared to be the best way to break away from contract work completely.

Expansion of our office products business offered another advantage. We could now use effectively the building and equipment we had installed for the manufacture of kitchen cabinets. Office products required the fabrication of sheet steel with

the use of the shears, press brakes, punch presses, spot welders, and finishing system that we had already installed. Thus, the office appeared to offer us a viable substitute for the kitchen that we had earlier planned to equip.

Table 6.1. The Home-O-Nize Company: Sales of Office Products, 1950–1955

Year	Office Products Sales ($)	Annual Increase (%)	% of Total Company Sales
1950	70,000		11
1951	110,000	59	19
1952	205,000	86	35
1953	333,000	62	33
1954	649,000	95	49
1955	1,061,000	64	64

Product Development

We structured Operation Independence to move along several lines simultaneously to achieve the goal of making office furniture our principal business: to design and introduce new lines, to strengthen marketing efforts, and to increase both the capacity and efficiency of production. With only 12 specialty items, Home-O-Nize's product offerings in 1951 barely scratched the surface. Thus, our choice of new products was almost unlimited. As the result of a quick succession of

The nonsuspension file was the first standard office file produced by the company. It was introduced as a two-drawer model and was quickly followed by a four-drawer model, as well as three- and five-drawer models two years later.

new product introductions, we were offering 42 items by the end of 1953, and 93 by September 1955.

Two-drawer and four-drawer non-suspension files, 26½ inches deep, were put on the market in 1952. These files used drawer tracks, drawer fronts, hardware, and other parts already developed for our combination cabinets. They were produced with and without plunger locks and in both letter and legal size. In 1954, three-drawer and five-drawer models were added.

Steel supply was still a problem in 1952. Stan Howe, on a flying trip to a government agency in Kansas City, was greatly surprised to learn that, for the first time, our requested allotment of steel was being granted in full. This happy turn of events led him to design a line of bookcases, capitalizing on our experience in producing similar units under contract for the Herman Nelson Division. These units, 34½ inches wide, either open-faced or with steel or glass doors, were offered in both 30- and 48-inch heights, with the 30-inch height offered in two depths. Along with the bookcases, we introduced the Model 30D duplicator cabinet, which was a bookcase with a bracket-supported drop leaf and with steel doors. These attractive products with a "waterfall" front edge were well-received.

With the addition of a drop-down shelf, the standard bookcase became another product—this mimeograph stand.

In 1953, we concentrated on combination cabinets. Quality was improved; features were added; and a new name—Unifiles—was created. Unifiles were made unique by the Unilock feature, by which one keyed handle operated plungers to lock the door and all drawers. An optional interior security compartment with a combination dial lock was added. The 38-inch-high Unifiles were offered with both letter- and legal-sized drawers. With these design changes and options, the Unifile line included 14 models; two earlier introductions brought the combination cabinet total to 16 items. With the basic frame of the 38-inch Unifile, a few modifications brought about the 38E and 38F storage cabinets, one open and the other with doors. Sales of the popular combination cabinets were greatly stimulated by these changes.

The Model 200 Series.

The transition from specialty office products to basic office furniture undoubtedly began with the introduction of the Model 200 series of full-suspension filing cabinets. These files—letter-sized and legal-sized, with two, three, four, and five drawers—featured triple-tied cradles with 10 roller bearings, cam-operated drawer followers, side wall stiffeners, full bottom trays, thumb latches on all drawers, and heavy steel torque plates in the four corners of the base. Sales literature proclaimed: "Soundly engineered H-O-N construction and design formed the foundation for this sturdy, full-suspension file. In addition, heavier metal and strategic reinforcements are used at certain points to obtain a rigid framework that provides smooth, firm, full-suspension action."

Bill Hammon, sales manager from 1951 to 1954, deserves credit for prompting our decision to produce full-suspension files. Working with dealers, he developed the specifications for a file that filled a gap in the offerings of the industry. Our 200 series files, with thumb latches, were of superior quality, but they were priced below the so-called Grade A files then on the market. Later, we pioneered nylon rollers, which were quieter, longer lasting, and lower cost than ball bearings. Gradually, as the market recognized their superiority, ny-

The Unifile, popular at home or office, has remained a steady seller from its introduction in 1953 to today.

Modern and attractive in its time, the Home-O-Nize home office suite included the company's first effort at making desks.

These hairpin leg desks were sold as components that dealers could assemble as left-, right-, or double-pedestal desks.

Garment racks and costumers represented great income opportunities for the company. In fact, at a list price of $95.00, the 72-inch Streamliner with a four-tier hat rack was the most expensive item in the 1955 catalog.

lon rollers replaced ball bearings in all of our major products.

The Model 200 full-suspension files helped catapult Home-O-Nize into the office furniture business. They proved to be the foundation for the numerous models developed in subsequent years. Other product introductions during the period included our first single-pedestal desk with a Panelyte top, hairpin legs, and matching tables. The Home Suite—our first attempt to reach the home market—comprised a version of this first desk, made with a narrower top and a matched pair of combination cabinets, all assembled with different hardware and painted in pastel colors. A five-drawer transfer file rounded out the new products designed by Home-O-Nize during these years.

Our offerings were augmented in May 1954 by our first acquisition in the office product line. The Essington Company manufactured a line of costumers and garment racks. For less than $15,000, we purchased this small company's assets, consisting of designs, tools, and dies for 22 different models fabricated from aluminum.

The catalog of office equipment that we issued in September 1955 consisted of 20 pages bound in a cover. The Model 204 four-drawer, letter-sized, full-suspension file listed at $62.95 in 1955. Thirty years later, the similar Model 214 was priced at $264. In 1955, the 32ADU Unifile was offered for $56.95. The comparable model listed at $323 in 1985. Such was the effect of inflation!

The decision-making criteria used for new product introductions during Operation Independence greatly influenced the future of Home-O-Nize. Stan Howe and I made very pragmatic choices. We solicited suggestions from our sales manager and sales representatives. However, their ideas were often far beyond the limits of our immediate resources. We had to choose products that 1) required minimal time and cost to develop, 2) could be manufactured without new processes or equipment, 3) used common parts of products already manufactured, and 4) augmented the marketability of products already offered to our dealers. These low-risk criteria proved sound. In fact, they remain, in modified form, as part of the decision-making process on new products at HON INDUSTRIES and its operating units.

Marketing

Early decisions about product quality and pricing determined the direction of Home-O-Nize's increasingly strong move into the broad, chaotic office furniture market. In the early 1950s, more than 160 companies were manufacturing steel office furniture, with offerings ranging from a broad line of Grade A, upper-level products to a few inexpensive, lower-priced items.

Seeking the Middle Market. Grade A manufacturers—such as Steelcase, General Fireproofing, Art Metal, Shaw-Walker, Corry Jamestown, Yawman and Erbe, Columbia, and Globe-Wernicke—offered complete lines, mostly produced of heavy-gauge steel with attention to fine finishing. These companies generally sold through franchised dealers, but, in some cases, they sold directly to national accounts. Many of these manufacturers maintained heavy advertising programs, some being directed to consumers. Home-O-Nize had neither the broad line nor the prestige required to enter this field.

Our collective sense of taste and propriety, as well as sound business judgment, steered us away from the bottom segment of the office furniture market. Entry into this area would have been shortsighted and self-defeating.

Avoiding both the top and bottom levels, we focused on the middle market, where products were sold on the basis of a combination of function, quality, and price. We viewed Cole and Allsteel as the strongest companies in this segment of the market. We determined to broaden our line gradually and also to maintain good quality and a pricing policy to compete effectively with them.

Sales Organization

The years of Operation Independence started without a sales manager. William Newsom, our first sales manager, found other employment during the dark days when our very survival was in doubt. After his departure, sales functions were performed by John Van Lent and the office staff, with guidance from Clem Hanson and overall supervision from me.

Meanwhile, my search for a sales manager led to another Bill, this time, the incredible William Hammon. My secretary at Stanley Engineering Co., Charlene Hilton, knowing that I was looking for a sales manager for Home-O-Nize, mentioned that Hammon, her sister's husband, was looking for employment. She described him as an active, go-getter type. An interview was arranged. Hammon proved to be a buoyant extrovert with sales experience, so I offered him the job. He assumed management of office product sales in May 1951, reporting directly to me. He also aided me with negotiations for the B-47 fairing contract, and he independently obtained several other small military contracts during 1951. From 1952 to the end of 1954, Hammon's time was devoted exclusively to promoting Home-O-Nize office products.

By changing executive responsibilities, the appointment of a sales manager at this time encouraged creation of the divisional structure that would prevail for many years. Sales Manager Hammon headed what would become first the H-O-N Division and later The HON Company. His responsibilities included management of sales and providing advice on new product selection. Hanson continued to serve in an advisory capacity on marketing, with his agency handling our advertising.

During his three-and-one-half years with Home-O-Nize, Hammon greatly enlarged and improved our core of manufacturers' representatives. In 1951, Home-O-Nize had only a handful of manufacturers' representatives, including Elmer Krumweide of Chicago, Len Jacobs of Los Angeles, Dick Nowels & Co. of Denver, and L. A. Roark of Dallas. These representatives had been selected by Hanson and Newsom primarily for their ability to move card files. As we expanded our line, we found that few of these individuals were well-suited to handle our entire product line. Hammon set about to restructure and enlarge our group of manufacturers' repre-

Home-O-Nize eventually was abbreviated to H-O-N so that it would seem more appropriate for office equipment. In this 1955 catalog, a four-drawer full-suspension file had a list price of $62.95.

sentatives, providing more intensive and extensive coverage of the entire United States. This group included two of our finest representatives, Ernie Stewart of Texas and Robert Cleary of Chicago, the last to be replaced by company sales staff.

Hammon nurtured our association with the Wholesale Office Equipment Company, a stocking manufacturers' representative with warehouses in San Francisco, Los Angeles, Seattle, and Denver. This association brought us into contact with colorful Sib Smith, the dynamic head of Wholesale Office Equipment, whose advice on marketing and product selection proved to be very valuable.

While Hammon made a substantial contribution to the growth of Home-O-Nize's sales, it became evident that he was more of a promoter than a manager. Perhaps, he had promoted me. For one thing, his tastes were too extravagant for that period of austerity. Although Hanson and I counseled repeatedly with Hammon, we had little success in changing his mode of operation.

By 1954, it was obvious that Hammon and Home-O-Nize needed to part. His natural flamboyancy was straining relationships with associates in the company and with some of our representatives and dealers. Hammon's resignation on December 29 of that year was neither unexpected nor fully voluntary. But it was a relief.

To fill the gap, we selected our third Bill as sales manager—William Duval, Jr., formerly a regional sales manager with the Oscar Mayer Company. Duval responded to our advertisement in April 1955. We liked him, and he welcomed the challenge that Home-O-Nize offered in switching from sausage to hard goods. In June 1955, he started work as sales manager, with duties similar to those previously held by Hammon. Duval promptly began to improve our relations with manufacturers' representatives and dealers and generally continued to strengthen our distribution system. He would later make significant contributions to the progress of Home-O-Nize's office furniture, including initiation of the marketing of our products through wholesalers.

Advertising Our Wares.   We started to advertise our office products nationally in 1952. Under Hanson's guidance, small ads were inserted in *Geyer's Topics* and in *Office Products*. These ads were intended to support our sales representatives by bringing our products to the attention of dealers. This dealer-oriented type of advertising continued to prevail in the early 1980s, as The HON Company had not by that time been able to justify extensive advertising aimed directly at the consumer.

Also giving Home-O-Nize greater exposure, our initial product exhibit occurred in October 1952. We set up a small booth at the meeting of the National Stationers and Office Equipment Association (now the National Office Products Association), held at the Stevens Hotel in Chicago. Reaction to our products was gratifying. We continued to participate in such conventions, which were also frequently used as a means of assembling our manufacturers' representatives for an annual sales conference.

Emergence of the H-O-N Division

One important development of Operation Independence was the change that we made in our public image. The Home-O-Nize label with two musical notes inserted was obviously an unsatisfactory logo for office products. We discussed the matter of corporate and product names at length. Finally, we decided on a compromise.

The corporate name would remain Home-O-Nize. However, office products would be labeled H-O-N, and they would be offered by the H-O-N Division of The Home-O-Nize Co. While we expected H-O-N to be pronounced in three syllables, the trade failed to read our minds or heed our intentions. Most of those in the trade promptly began to pronounce it HON, in one syllable. The origin of the current HON INDUSTRIES, the corporate name, and of The HON Company, its principal profit center, was that simple. The change from reference to office supplies to office equipment to office furniture came naturally as our product line expanded.

CHAPTER SEVEN

People and Machines at Work

The strong forward thrust of Home-O-Nize was evident in the marketplace, as our material-handling equipment and, especially, our office products came to the attention of more and more people. The success of Operation Independence, however, rested on significant internal changes within Home-O-Nize. Progress in the marketplace resulted basically from our ability to produce goods when needed and at acceptable costs. Much of our success in low-cost mass production depended, in turn, on the efforts of a loyal and motivated work force. Neither production nor marketing would have succeeded unless our financial situation had shown marked improvement. Management, by ably coordinating product development, production, marketing, and financing, laid the groundwork for continued growth.

Production: Contract Work

With more than three years of experience, the manufacture of products for Stampings was running smoothly. Except for the B-47 fairings, our contract work was similar to the sheet metal fabrication that we did for office products. All of this type of production was performed in the Oak Street Plant.

Production of the fairings involved, for us, new materials and new processes. Each fairing consisted of an outer skin, a sheet of magnesium, about 30-by-24 inches, formed to the compound curves of the nacelle, backed by aluminum reinforcing members and fitted with catches and locking devices. We purchased the magnesium sheets formed to the curves and trimmed them to size. We fabricated most of the other parts. The skin and parts of each fairing were assembled on precision fixtures. Numerous holes were drilled for the rivets holding the assembly together. Each fairing assembly required many hours of labor, much of it by hand. Tolerances were small, quality specifications were tight, and inspection and testing were rigid.

On receiving the contract, we set up an assembly area in the Sampson Street Quonsets, but most of the parts were fabricated in the Oak Street Plant. Considerable time was required to build tools, dies, jigs, and fixtures, and to assemble materials. Typical of military work, frequent design changes handed down from the prime contractor to Bell and then relayed to us delayed the production.

Once again, our staff and work force rose to the challenge of a completely different type of manufacturing. We moved quickly up the learning curve, so that we soon achieved a profitable margin. We succeeded in satisfying Bell by keeping schedules and maintaining quality.

For Home-O-Nize, making
parts for the B-47 bomber
involved working with new
materials and new proc-
esses and required meeting
close tolerances (UPI/
Bettmann Newsphotos).

Bookcases were easily
made with the technology
used in the production of
storage cabinets for the
Herman Nelson Division.
They proved consistent
sellers.

Production: Prime-Mover

With the introduction of the Model 15, production at The Prime-Mover Co. was more difficult. We encountered all of the problems normally associated with the introduction of a new product involving new processes. Start-up involved designing, building or purchasing, and testing tools and dies for sheet metal parts and jigs and fixtures for machining castings. It was also necessary to purchase major components such as engines, tires, and wheels; to contract for outside production of gears, shafts, and similar items for which we did not have the necessary machine tools; and to construct the fixtures needed for assembly of the units. This was more complicated than the assembly of the Model 343 with parts purchased from Bell.

Slow delivery of purchased parts, particularly gears and other transmission elements, was most troublesome. When this continued to be a headache, we explored alternative sources. I traveled twice to Detroit to discuss with the Transmission and Gear Company the manufacture of complete transmissions. Several other companies with gear-cutting capabilities were contacted as potential suppliers. Finally, we concluded that if we wanted the Prime-Mover to be a viable and profitable product, we would have to equip ourselves to cut gears and to assemble the transmissions within our own plant. Thus, we gradually installed the required equipment, hiring Harry Fuhlman as supervisor of the operators running it.

Because sales of Prime-Movers increased only slowly during the next few years (from 621 units in 1951 to 803 in 1955), production capacity at Prime-Mover remained adequate for the five-year period, except for the gradual addition of the machining operation.

Cost Reduction. As Prime-Mover production slowly began to improve, we directed increasing attention to cost reduction. We needed greater profitability without increasing the selling price of our units. In activating a cost reduction program, we sought minor changes in design, better tools and dies, improved methods of manufacture, a larger volume of purchases of materials and parts from better sources, and more in-house production rather than outside purchase of parts and components. Records do not reveal the unit cost of the Model 15 chassis at the initiation of the cost-reduction program; however, it stood at $355 in April 1954 and $328 in August 1954. Our target for 1955 was $280. These efforts allowed us to avoid a price increase until late 1955.

The objective of our cost-reduction program was to achieve lower manufacturing costs without sacrificing quality and performance. Indeed, our experience demonstrated that effective cost reduction would usually improve quality and performance. Time after time in the years ahead, we applied these lessons to the manufacture of both office products and material-handling equipment.

Production: Office Products

Manufacture of office products posed no particular problems in 1951 and 1952, as the added sales consisted mostly of the card files and combination cabinets that we were already making. Increased production of each of these items could easily be handled with the rather primitive production methods we were then using.

However, as office product sales came to account for one-third or more of the total sales volume of Home-O-Nize in 1953, production capacity had to be expanded. Initially, space was provided by cutting back miscellaneous contract work and shifting fabrication of some Prime-Mover parts to Sampson Street. The Oak Street Plant was well-suited to cutting, shaping, bending, welding, and painting the sheet metal that constituted most of the office products added during Operation Independence. The cabinet assembly line was improved by adding more stations, more spot welders, and better assembly fixtures.

Throughout most of the years of Operation Independence, capital expenditures were largely limited to minor items: spot welders, additional punch presses, improved tools and dies, and second-hand machine tools. Little more was needed, and the cash position of Home-O-Nize was still tight.

But the expanding sales of office furniture altered our needs. In 1955, we took a bold step with our first purchase of an automatic drawer welder for $16,000. The excitement was great as the machine was installed, the parts were placed in the fixture, and the button was pushed. The table holding the fixture moved to a series of stops, and sparks flew as the automatic spot welders went into action. Assembled drawers were lifted from the table and banked on inclined storage racks within reach of an operator loading them onto the paint line. The machine not only broke the bottleneck of drawer assembly, but it also assured the fabrication of drawers with uniform dimensions. The automatic drawer welder was so efficient that only 10 months of savings in labor costs paid for the investment. Now more than three decades old, this welder, with careful maintenance and many modifications, still operates in The HON Company's Oak Street Plant Number 1.

When sheet steel became available, it was cut into smaller pieces and then formed into components. This photo shows (from left to right) Otto Grothe (partially obscured by the shears at left), Clarence Nolan, Jr., Bill Brendel, and Leonard Luedtka.

Expanded sales of office products permitted longer runs of the popular items. This, in turn, warranted installation of more sophisticated tooling and time-saving methods.

By 1953, an intensive cost-reduction program was organized. New products were designed and earlier ones modified to reduce labor content. The assembly line was rearranged to reduce material handling, particularly of bulky, easily damaged sheet metal parts. Commonality of parts was adopted wherever practicable. Time studies and work simplification programs were initiated. Controls were established to govern the flow of purchased items to reduce the inventory of work in process as well as to avoid delays and confusion.

Careful attention to cost reduction, carried out under the supervision of Stan Howe, was one of the major accomplishments during Operation Independence. Production of office products was rapidly elevated from a job shop operation to bulk production on an assembly line basis. The result was to raise capacity from 40 files per day to 40 files per hour.

Origins of the Geneva Plant

Our need to make exceptionally efficient use of floor space served us well. Austerity had taught us how to increase output per square foot to a high level. By 1955, however, knowing that we needed to add production space, we began to look for it. We also wanted to phase out the Sampson Street Quonsets in favor of more satisfactory working quarters.

The availability of an unfinished warehouse along old Highway 61 (now Route 22) about two miles east of the Muscatine city limits came to our attention. Construction on the building had been halted when the Gobble Grocery Company, the expected occupant, decided to abandon the wholesale business. Negotiations with Carl Paetz of Gobble, the Whiting Construction Company (of Iowa City), builders, and financiers led to a long-term lease. We reached an agreement that the 40,000-square-foot building, with the addition of an office building, would be completed for occupancy in 1956.

The new building was labeled the Geneva Plant—recognizing the township, a nearby creek, and a country school by that name. More than doubling our floor space, it would become the new home of Prime-Mover, the B-47 fairing assembly, and small office products. Space in the Oak Street Plant would be released for manufacture of file cabinets and other office products. The Sampson Street Quonsets would be abandoned.

Perils of Flood and Fire

Adding to the normal problems that we had to deal with, Mother Nature threw us a few curves. The normally peaceful Mississippi River went on a rampage in April 1951 and again in April 1952, both times shutting down the Oak Street Plant, located just three blocks from its banks. As our supervisors tried to hold back the rising water with sandbags, the work force elevated the electrical and other apparatus within the plant likely to be damaged by water. The floor leaked and eventually had to be flooded to prevent uplift from hydraulic pressure. At the height of the flood, with three feet of water standing in the plant, boats were used for access. On each occasion, several weeks of production were lost as we battled the flood and then restored the plant to operation. Sampson Street production, too, was interrupted when the supply of Prime-Mover parts could not be delivered from the Oak Street Plant.

Then, early on a cold December morning in 1951, I learned that the Sampson Street Plant was aflame. Fortunately, the fire resistance of the metal Quonset huts limited the damage to the contents, and our substantial losses were largely covered by insurance. But again, several weeks of production were lost.

Management and Staff

By necessity, delegation of managerial authority and responsibility was practiced from the earliest days of The Home-O-Nize Co. Clem Hanson worked full time for several years to get the company started,

even while he was organizing the Clement T. Hanson Advertising Agency. This agency became his career, although he continued as vice president and director of The Home-O-Nize Co. Miller, with neither interest nor experience in corporate management, played no role beyond serving as a director (until 1958) and handling a few industrial design assignments. The H. Wood Miller Co. remained his primary career.

The automatic drawer welder paid for itself in added production capacity within a year after it was installed.

Making drawer fronts for filing cabinets. By the time this photo was taken, more cash was available for such things as painting the walls and marking the floors. Press operators, from right to left, are Elmer Boldt, Fred Bodman, Edmund Metz, and Bill Brendel. The man in the checkered shirt is Kenneth Rummery.

The Geneva Plant, a 40,000-square-foot structure planned as a wholesale grocery warehouse, provided needed space for the manufacture of Prime-Movers and small office products.

Floods in 1951 and 1952 stopped production, cut off needed revenue, and represented a real hardship for members, some of whom suffered flood damage of their own.

My duties as senior partner of the rapidly growing Stanley Engineering Co. were those of a chief executive officer. I was also project manager on contracts with several major clients. Yet, the often burdensome and time-consuming executive responsibilities at Home-O-Nize were largely mine— necessarily on a part-time basis. Thus, my long work weeks were devoted to responsibilities at Stanley Engineering and at Home-O-Nize, together with continuing public service and community activities. However, at no time did I harbor the idea of withdrawing from Stanley Engineering to become a full-time president of Home-O-Nize.

This personal situation strengthened my philosophical belief in the principle of delegation of authority commensurate with responsibility. I viewed my role as one of planning and establishing objectives, along with monitoring progress, counseling, and coping with the all-too-numerous trouble spots. Implementation and direction of established programs became the responsibility of the managers of Home-O-Nize.

Accordingly, throughout my tenure as president, I adopted a rather loose style of management, with the intention of allowing executives to develop their full capabilities. I could not observe closely their day-to-day actions. I could only assess their accomplishments, summarized on the "bottom lines" of their respective operations. Thus, circumstances and philosophy combined to create a results-oriented style of management that would contribute significantly to the effectiveness of the decision-making process at all levels right up to the present day.

Stan Howe's appointment as vice president, production, in 1954 formalized the role that he had already assumed in directing Home-O-Nize's manufacturing operations. The broadly defined production functions for which he was responsible included product design, industrial engineering, plant engineering, purchasing, production control, cost accounting, and personnel, as well as the actual manufacture of products. The Production Division, expanding at a pace consistent with our sales growth, employed nearly 95 percent of our members.

As responsibility for planning and coordination of production grew, so did the need for an experienced supervisor. A search led us to Rex Bennett, then with the J. I. Case Company. When he was employed in 1955, many of the functions related to production were placed under his supervision, thus relieving Howe from some of his day-to-day responsibilities.

York was superintendent of the Oak Street Plant throughout the years of Operation Independence. His principal assistant was Ray Shellabarger. Frank Newton and George Butler, both employed as production workers in 1951, soon became lead men and later supervisors. Newton continued with Home-O-Nize until 1967; Butler served as second-shift superintendent at Oak Street until his death in 1973. James Hawley, hired as an inspector in 1952, moved into quality-control work, in which he served until retirement in 1985. Others joining Home-O-Nize in this period and later assuming supervisory roles included Ervin Easterla (1952), a toolmaker and later supervisor of the Oak Street toolroom until his death in 1976; Richard Duggan (1952), a plant worker and later stores supervisor for Prime-Mover; and William Lee (1954), who advanced from toolroom apprentice to senior tool design engineer (before transfer to Corry Jamestown).

Throughout these years, McCullough served as Home-O-Nize's purchasing agent. Bernard (Beanie) Wheeler, employed in 1951 as a clerk, soon mastered cost accounting and served as cost accounting supervisor until he retired in 1978. Willard Huggins, an engineer, was with the company from 1955 until 1963. Ilene Boldt joined Home-O-Nize in 1955; she retired as a materials control clerk-typist in 1982.

When Rodler became head of the Prime-Mover engineering department, Robert Mangels was employed as a draftsman-designer. Mangels, after many years as a product engineer in The Prime-Mover Co., retired from The HON Company's product engineering department in 1985. Orville Emrick, a draftsman, left Stanley Engineering in 1952 to join Home-O-Nize to work on product design until he retired

in 1972 as assistant to the vice president of product engineering. LeVern Greer and Norman Marshall, both employed earlier, were model shop operators for Prime-Mover and office products, respectively.

The production of Prime-Movers at the Sampson Street Quonsets was principally an assembly operation, initially under Harold "Bud" Barton's supervision. As the in-house production of gears and other parts replaced purchase from outside suppliers, the need for an experienced machine shop foreman became evident. Harry Fuhlman, employed in 1952, filled the spot so well that he remained a supervisor of this work for The Prime-Mover Co. until his retirement in 1979. Later, as we struggled to reduce the production costs of Prime-Movers, we felt the need for a superintendent with extensive machine shop experience. Our search led to Stratton (Stub) Fillingham, an orchid buff, who had been with us for two years and had earlier worked for J. I. Case as a master mechanic for some years. In 1956, Fillingham took over the supervision of all Prime-Mover production operations as superintendent of the Geneva Plant, a position he held until retirement in 1970.

Toolmakers such as Ervin Easterla kept the aging equipment operating at close tolerances.

Recognition dinners for service have always been an important part of member relations. The third time they were held, 10-year awards went to (from left to right) Ray Meyn, Allie Bell, Stan Howe, John Schmoldt, Helen Metz, Bob Carl, and Ed Bennett. These people signed up when a regular paycheck wasn't always regular.

A Strong Human Relations Program

By the end of Operation Independence, the work force at Home-O-Nize, including Prime-Mover, totaled more than 165. With Home-O-Nize increasingly recognized as a good place to work, our personnel director always had more than enough applicants for jobs. Turnover was low, as a member who passed the probationary period of 90 days rarely left the company. Many of those first employed in the early years made Home-O-Nize their lifetime career.

This record of employment continuity has been in large part due to our recognition that fair treatment is crucial to attracting and holding the right kind of people at all levels. We knew that competent, cooperative, loyal, and motivated people promote success, just as unqualified, uncooperative, disloyal, and indifferent people lead to failure.

Even as Home-O-Nize was struggling to survive, the company was implementing a forward-looking set of personnel practices. During the years of Operation Independence, we formalized and expanded some of the programs that we had initiated in earlier years. Right from the start, we shared information with all members. In March 1947, Van Lent initiated the publication of a monthly house organ—two pages, 8½-by-11 inches—called *Notes*. This little sheet, displaying the two quarter notes in the *O* of the Home-O-Nize logo, was a first effort to keep members informed.

Meetings of management and members provided another means of communication at Home-O-Nize. In 1949, the first such meeting occurred, with our members gathering on a few benches in the warehouse of the Oak Street Plant. The agenda included presentation of the same report that I had made at the annual meeting of shareholders, followed by questions and answers. As the organization grew, we developed other formats for member meetings, holding them quarterly and expanding the opportunities for two-way communication between management and the work force.

A General Policy Committee was another early innovation that strengthened two-way communication between members and management. Initially, the committee consisted of five or six people elected by members representing different departments. Chaired by the president, this committee met periodically to discuss matters affecting members.

Three other committees were created in the late 1940s. Louis York and Art Dahl were on a Safety Committee that implemented safety procedures and stimulated company-wide attention to accident prevention. An Activities Committee, consisting of Clem Hanson, Ray Shellabarger, Gene Fuller, and Tiny Metz, planned and managed the first company picnic, held at Wildcat Den State Park in August 1947. A Health Committee (membership not recorded) worked with management to develop our early health and insurance programs.

Financial Participation. We established in the early years another basic element of the company's pattern of member relationships—the opportunity to participate financially. Indeed, members participated in the very first profits ever earned by The Home-O-Nize Co. As Home-O-Nize became a regularly profitable enterprise during the years of Operation Independence, opportunities for financial participation became truly meaningful.

The initial announcement of profit sharing, made in 1949, led to the stormiest annual meeting of shareholders in our history. (The setting for the meeting in February 1949 was stormy in another way as well. As Clem Hanson called the meeting to order, Betty and I were being towed out of a ditch in the midst of ice and snow some 100 miles west of Muscatine.) Much disturbed about the profit-sharing plan, inasmuch as no dividends had yet been paid, several shareholders vigorously voiced their opposition. Particularly vocal was the widow of one substantial early purchaser of Home-O-Nize stock. Hanson and the other directors pacified the shareholders who, within a few years, came to realize the significant benefits of profit sharing.

Profit sharing began as a cash distribution to eligible members—those employed for more than one year—in proportion to their base compensation. Initially, an arbitrary amount was allocated to profit sharing. Later, a formula was worked out by which members received $1.00 for every $3.00 available for dividends and for retained earnings to finance expansion. Using this formula, combined with corporate dividend policies, the amount of profit sharing has exceeded dividend payments every year. As the profit-sharing kitty grew, payments to members were divided between semiannual cash distributions and a contribution to each member's Profit-Sharing Retirement Trust account.

Member ownership of Home-O-Nize shares was encouraged from the beginning, with the stock register recording holdings by a number of members at the beginning of Operation Independence. During the days of cash stringency, some members had been paid partially in stock, with their approval, of course. Subsequently, in the 1960s, stock offerings were made that periodically gave members an opportunity to purchase shares at 10 percent below the market price.

ISSUED EVERY MONTH BY AND FOR THE MEN AND WOMEN OF THE HOME-O-NIZE CO.

John Van Lent, Editor

VOL. 2   MARCH

WHAT GOOD ARE PROFITS?

We read and hear a lot these days about profits--some of it favorable, some otherwise. There are those who say corporation profits are too high and want to skim off the top cream through heavy taxes. Industry, in the main, feels it needs these profits for further expansion and to build up a cushion against leaner days ahead.

There's not much point to arguing the question here. It might not be out of line, though, to analyze profits a minute and to realize what an important role they play if a company is to continue in business. There's one prime reason why a big majority of new enterprises fail--and that's lack of profits.

It takes profits to build up a surplus--surplus which may be used to help finance expansion of plant facilities, purchase of new equipment, and for research, experimentation and a lot of other expenditures a competitive industrial system demands.

A company has to make profits if it expects to obtain loans for necessary financing. It has to pay a reasonable dividend out of profits to stockholders for use of their money if it expects them to invest more money in additional stock.

And where it socks both you and me hardest is in the old wallet--because without profits there can be no such things as a steady job and an assured fair income.

※ ※ ※ ※ ※

WHAT'S YOUR NUMBER? . . . Safety experts say a worker violates a safe practive on the average of 300 times before he gets caught by an accident. Some guys will run over the 300 mark while others may get caught the first or second time. What number are you on?

SHOPTALK . . . Orchids to Manager Paul Slack's cage five which capped the runner-up trophy in the annual Y.M.C.A. tournament against tough competition . . . Home-O-Nize bowlers are away from the post with a burst of speed in the second half of play at Pla-Mor and at present are 'way out front... The Harmonizin' Home-O-Nizers, a bunch of smoothies from 'wayback, are hard at it, rehearsing for the annual Muscatine Club Barbershop Quartet contest. Let's be there to give them a hand.... Nygren, Boldt, Proffitt and the rest of our golfing brethren must really be sweating it out these first spring days ....But if it's exercise you're really wanting, "Wart" Thompson says to drop by his place and he'll let you sling some dirt out of the basement he's digging under his house. That's you he's looking at --not me!

FILE BOX SALES GAIN

Sales of index card file boxes for March had passed 10,000 by the 15th and appear on their way to a certain new monthly record. Some live new outlets have been opened up on the west coast, and efforts will be made soon to open up the eastern territory--giving us a nation-wide coverage on the item.

The latter part of March will see final assembly under way on the run of 2,000 88-inch belt pickups for Deere, and will also see the first completed units of the new run of steel cabinets come off the line.

※ ※ ※ ※ ※

"Next to a beautiful girl what do you consider the most interesting thing in the world?" "Listen, when I'm next to a beautiful girl I don't bother about statistics."

John Van Lent, who served as the company's first personnel director, edited Notes. *The newsletter explained what was happening in the plant and how the company was doing. The first one, shown here, was published in March 1947.*

Lessons learned in classes on methods, time, and motion, such as this early one held in the local high school basement, contributed to an improvement in quality and an increase in production.

Corporate Finance

The Prime-Mover Co. The finances of our wholly owned subsidiary, The Prime-Mover Co., were tight, but manageable, throughout the years of Operation Independence. Profits were not adequate to meet the scheduled maturities on notes payable to Bell, and we were seldom fully current on payments to creditors until near the end of the period. However, Bell wanted our acquisition of the Prime-Mover operation to succeed. Thus, they rearranged the maturities on the notes on several occasions to allow this to happen.

In January 1951, The Prime-Mover Co. negotiated with the Central State Bank a line of credit of $25,000, secured by engines, tires, and other purchased items placed in our bonded warehouse. Although helpful, this arrangement did not provide enough working capital to cover our expanding inventories and accounts receivable. To relieve this situation, the Prime-Mover board proposed, and Bell accepted, a deferral of payments on the inventory and working capital loans for 150 days. The extension was accomplished by issuing notes instead of cash as payments became due.

This carried us until late 1953, when the contract with Bell was amended again to reschedule the note payments and to credit Prime-Mover with a reduction of $27,000 on inventory notes for obsolete and unusable inventory for the Model 343. At the same time, Home-O-Nize accepted a note of $21,000 from Prime-Mover as partial payment on amounts due Home-O-Nize for fabrication of parts and assembly.

In December 1954, we were current on the Bell notes, and we expected profits for 1955 to liquidate the remaining payments due to Bell. During 1955, we arranged with Central State Bank for the discounting of notes, on a guaranteed basis, that we were accepting from dealers who stocked Prime-Movers for their floor plans.

As 1956 approached, we were encouraged by the stability of the Prime-Mover operation. Profitability had been achieved, new products were on the way, payments to Bell were current, and a new plant was being completed. Bell's satisfaction with Prime-Mover's progress was reflected in the attendance record of the directors representing Bell on the Prime-Mover board. Whereas their attendance had been regular during the early 1950s, Olmsted attended but two board meetings during 1954 and 1955, Gisel one, and Faneuf none. By the end of this period, Prime-Mover was established as a viable, self-sufficient operation, albeit a much smaller and less dynamic one than we had hoped.

The Home-O-Nize Co. The financial picture of Home-O-Nize, as distinct from that of Prime-Mover, moved gradually from extremely tight to tolerable. Cash flow was adequate, largely because of the mounting revenues from contract work and sales of office products. Gone were the days of fending off creditors.

The Prime-Mover operation had little effect on the finances of Home-O-Nize during this period, although the parent company increased its investment in Prime-Mover from $1,000 to $10,000 in 1952. The work that Home-O-Nize did for Prime-Mover, as a percentage of its total sales, declined from year to year during

Operation Independence, but it continued to provide a reasonable profit margin for Home-O-Nize.

Home-O-Nize's profits grew to $74,486 in 1955, compared with a loss of $5,032 in 1951 (after the corn picker write-off). This provided a substantial source of funds. In addition, common stock worth $1,900 was issued in 1951, and $66,900 in 1955.

In 1954, Home-O-Nize secured a term loan of $50,000 from the Central State Bank. The proceeds were used to retire the remaining $10,000 due on the earlier loan from the Smaller War Plants Corporation and to provide additional working capital. During these years, we continued with the Central State Bank our do-it-yourself factoring of accounts receivable on office products.

As our profits grew and our cash position became less stringent, we gave attention to rewarding our patient shareholders with a dividend. The board had declared the first dividend on our common stock in October 1951 but rescinded it as a result of the loss on the corn picker. Accumulated dividends on our limited amount of outstanding preferred stock were paid in January 1951 and September 1953.

Our profits for 1954 were such that we felt we should pay a dividend on the common. However, I was troubled by the effect on our cash position that payment of a fair portion of profits would entail. It was Stan Howe who suggested that we begin quarterly dividends, rather than annual, thus easing the impact on cash flow. The board then declared and paid the first dividends on common stock: $1 per share after each of the first two quarters of 1955 and $1.50 after each of the next two quarters. Dividends on common stock have been paid continuously since that time.

The financial position of Home-O-Nize was vastly improved at the end of Operation Independence in 1955. However, Home-O-Nize was still underfinanced, with expanding sales certain to require additional funding. Operations were approaching the physical limits of our facilities. Space would have to be constructed or leased, and equipment would have to be purchased. Working capital would have to be continuously infused to finance an expansion of inventory and accounts receivable. All of this would take money, but we were confident that financing could be arranged for the profitable company that Home-O-Nize had become.

PART THREE

OPERATION BOOTSTRAP, 1956-1965

As a result of the accomplishments of Operation Independence, Home-O-Nize had proved that it was more than just a survivor. The Home-O-Nize Co. had established itself as a small but growing enterprise among the more than 160 companies in the highly competitive office furniture industry. Through its Prime-Mover subsidiary, the company had carved out a small but profitable niche in the material-handling field.

In 1956, I prepared and implemented a plan that I called Operation Bootstrap. Largely by our own efforts, we were going to work toward greater market penetration in our businesses by expanding the sales of our office furniture and Prime-Movers, raising the productivity of our manufacturing, improving the quality of our products, and strengthening our financial position.

The result of Operation Bootstrap was a decade of explosive growth at Home-O-Nize. Annual sales (of both office products and Prime-Movers) passed the $5 million milestone in

Although the company was growing at an exciting rate, management never forgot its origins. The original group gathered for this reunion photo in 1981. From left to right: Bud Barton, Lyle McCullough, Wood Miller, Max Stanley, and Clem Hanson. Stanley hired McCullough to unlock the U.S. Button Co. building and clean it up.

61

1961 and moved beyond $10 million in 1965. During the years between 1956 and 1965, sales increased at a compounded annual rate of 28.6 percent—representing a 5.2-fold gain. Net income grew at a 22.2 percent compounded annual rate, to stand at nearly three-quarters of a million dollars by the end of Operation Bootstrap. Net profit as a percent of sales had increased to a comfortable 7 percent; return on beginning net equity had risen to a surprising 24.9 percent. The number of members who worked at Home-O-Nize and Prime-Mover more than tripled, from fewer than 200 at the beginning of 1956 to more than 500 at the end of 1965.

In 1964, Stan Howe was elected president, and I became chairman of the board. Because my primary occupation was chief executive of Stanley Engineering Co., I had been spending less and less time on Home-O-Nize business. Stan had been fulfilling most of the functions of president for a number of years.

Most of the company's spectacular growth stemmed from ever-increasing sales of office furniture, as the events during the decade of Operation Bootstrap prepared Home-O-Nize to move toward a position of leadership in the industry. Prime-Mover advanced more slowly. However, near the end of the period, the subsidiary was beginning to develop a line of material-handling equipment that would enable it to diversify successfully into industrial markets.

We had outgrown the need for contract work, which had contributed so importantly to the survival of Home-O-Nize in the company's early years. Our billings for contract work dropped from 28 percent of total sales in 1955 to just 4 percent in 1958, becoming negligible thereafter.

The unfolding of the remarkable progress made during the years of Operation Bootstrap is told in five chapters. Chapter 8 deals with product development and marketing of office furniture from 1956 to 1965. Chapter 9 discusses product development and marketing of Prime-Movers. Chapter 10 relates the work of the Production Division, which manufactured all of the office furniture and Prime-Movers sold by The Home-O-Nize Co. Chapter 11 addresses finance and related corporate policies. Finally, Chapter Twelve covers Home-O-Nize's policies regarding overall management and people.

CHAPTER EIGHT

Swift Progress in Office Furniture

Several developments combined to produce the considerable success that we achieved in the office furniture industry during Operation Bootstrap. We significantly broadened our product line, through acquisition as well as internal development. We made some important changes in the way that we marketed our office furniture, by developing sales through wholesalers and the organization of our own company sales force. In addition, lowered production costs and improved product quality contributed mightily to our success.

New Products as a Way of Life

As of 1956, we could examine a wide range of opportunities for enlarging our product line. We produced neither standard office desks nor chairs, and only an incomplete line of files. We had barely scratched the surface. We were convinced that introduction of new products should become our way of life, knowing that this would stimulate Home-O-Nize's growth and contribute to its economic health.

We followed three different paths in expanding our office product lines. We placed primary emphasis on internal product development, a process we could completely control. We also pursued aggressively, and with some success, a variety of acquisition opportunities whereby we could add product lines already on the market. A third approach was to import from Britain a unique product line for distribution to the American market—an adventure that turned out to be more interesting than profitable.

Internal Product Development. Phil Temple, with guidance from Howe and myself, directed our product engineering department, with numerous suggestions made by our sales people, product designers, and managers. However, a decision about the introduction of a new product was normally the result of a formal process that we developed during these years.

Before a new product was approved, it had to meet several criteria: favorable marketability, ease and economy of development, and suitability to our production processes. A product decision memorandum, requiring ultimate approval by the president, included a detailed analysis of design, tooling, and other preproduction costs, estimates of unit production costs, proposed selling price, expected margin, targeted market volume, and contribution to operating margin. Thus, budgets and costs were determined and agreed on before significant expenditures of time and money were made on production. This procedure minimized our chances of introducing a dud.

The HONOR line, specially designed for school use, included this desk for teachers. Shirley Garfoot, an office member, sits behind the desk.

Raleigh Rieke (left), an assembler, and Stub Fillingham, plant superintendent, examine a Million Line desk. Vinyl-clad drawer fronts and modesty panels made bright colors possible.

An Array of New Products for the Office. A year-by-year review of introductions shows the results of the efforts, made internally, to develop new products:

•1958   Ten models of steel drawer card cabinets and six models of steel cash and utility boxes were introduced. These well-styled items augmented our meager small goods line (the 3-by-5 and 4-by-6 card file boxes, soon to be fabricated of steel rather than aluminum). Suspension files in the 310 series were offered in two-, three-, four-, and five-drawer units, standard and legal sizes, with and without lock. These files were a shallower (26½ inches versus 28½ inches) version of our popular 210 series of files, incorporating nylon rollers.

•1959   The HONOR line of products for the schoolroom included files, teachers' desks, storage cabinets, bookcases, and room dividers. All were adaptations of office products then in production. The Million line of steel desks, with typists' returns and credenzas, incorporated square tubular legs and vinyl-clad steel drawer fronts. Although they represented a major step beyond the earlier hairpin-leg desks that they superseded, the Million Line itself would be replaced in 1965.

•1960   The suspension files in the 410 series were destined to become great promotional items. Offered in two-, three-, four-, and five-drawer models, standard and legal, with and without lock, these 24-inch-deep files were a streamlined, but popular, adaptation of the 310 series of files. The Convaire series was a conventional style of desks with typists' returns and credenzas. Styled similarly to those of many competitors, these desks are still offered to our customers.

•1962   We brought out VS, standing for Very Special, products—desks, credenzas, files, and bookcases. These higher priced items were intended for franchised dealers. The VS desks were similar to those offered by many Grade A manufacturers. The files were basically an improved version of our 210 series, given a face-lift with new drawer fronts and stylized hardware. The bookcases were an adaptation of the

Models 30 and 48 series with wood tops.

•1964 Tables styled to be compatible with Convaire desks were introduced.

•1965 The 50 series of desks with typists' returns and credenzas had contemporary styling, square tubular legs, and particle board tops with laminated surfacing.

Thus, a multitude of models of suspension files, desks, storage cabinets, bookcases, cash and utility boxes, and other items of office furniture emerged from the process of product development at Home-O-Nize. None of these products was particularly new to the trade. In fact, most of them were similar to those offered by competitors. However, in each case, H-O-N improved the quality of the product, lowered the cost of production by making changes in its design and manufacture, or both.

New Products by Acquisition

The experience we gained through the purchase of Bell's Prime-Mover in 1950 and Essington's costumers in 1954 helped us make acquisitions of existing companies or their assets as a way to expand Home-O-Nize's product line. During Operation Bootstrap, one minor and one fairly substantial acquisition augmented the aggressive internal expansion of our product line.

In September 1958, we purchased the designs, tooling, and inventory of a line of freestanding wood partitions from R.J.R. Industries, Incorporated. From this $10,000 investment, we reaped more experience than sales. Production of these partitions presented no serious difficulty, but marketing did. Our belief that such products could be sold through our open line H-O-N dealers and our manufacturers' representatives proved unfounded. The R.J.R. line had only limited sales and marginal profits, so within a few years, we dropped it.

Acquisition of Luxco. As H-O-N sales expanded, we became increasingly eager to produce and market chairs. In the summer of 1959, we seriously explored the possibility of purchasing the Rite-Form Chair Company, then operating in Quincy

The VS line, introduced in 1962, was designed to capture a portion of the higher end of the market. It was sold through special franchised dealers and had special treatment of details such as hardware and drawer design. Here, Ed Jones (right) confers with Harold Klein, a salesman, about the new literature for the program.

and Springfield, Illinois. However, we were not successful in negotiating an acceptable basis for purchase with Ray Voorheis, the major owner.

Thus, in late 1960, when Duval learned that the Luxco Company of La Crosse, Wisconsin, might be available for purchase, we actively pursued the possibility. Luxco, owned by Robert Luxford and his associates, manufactured and sold chairs, stools, and machine stands. It was earning a satisfactory profit on annual sales of about $540,000.

Howe, Duval, and I visited the plant at La Crosse, with lengthy negotiating sessions leading to a timely closing on March 2. Two days later, at the H-O-N Annual Sales Conference in Sarasota, Florida, Duval enthusiastically announced that we were in the chair business.

We purchased all outstanding shares of common stock of the Luxco Co. for a little more than $310,000—$200,000 of which was paid in the form of a promissory note and the balance in cash. Luxco continued to operate in La Crosse until October 1962, when it was moved—lock, stock,

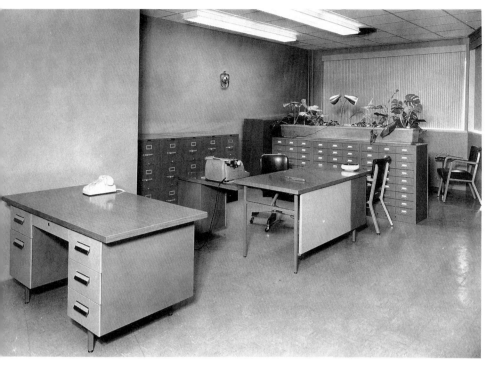

A modern office of the 1950s, equipped with bright HON Million Line desks and durable HON files.

Wooden partitions, acquired as a line from R.J.R. Industries, turned out to be more educational than profitable. They were easy to make but hard to sell.

and barrel—to a newly completed addition to our Geneva Plant in Muscatine.

Soon after acquisition, marketing of Luxco products was integrated into the H-O-N Division, and Luxco sales representatives were phased out. H-O-N territorial managers began selling Luxco products along with H-O-N files, desks, and other office furniture. Within a few months, some Luxco-designed items were being offered as H-O-N products.

We soon learned that Luxco chairs, although marketable, were not top quality and that Luxco's volume was inadequate to achieve low-cost production. It would take many years for us to learn the complexities of the seating business and to make significant penetration of the chair market. Nevertheless, the Luxco acquisition did expand H-O-N's product offerings to include chairs, stools, and machine stands.

Some Blind Alleys.   We made only two acquisitions during the decade, but we were constantly on the alert for other opportunities. We explored several that proved to be blind alleys.

Unfruitful discussions in 1957 with the Central Can Company regarding acquisition of their line of cash boxes was a factor that led to the introduction of our own line of cash boxes in 1958. Also in 1957, I went to Steubenville, Ohio, to discuss with Louis Berkman the purchase of the Steel Pride line of lockers and storage cabinets. On another occasion, I visited Hamilton, Ohio, to explore the possibility of acquiring a line of small rotary card index files. In none of these instances were we able to agree on purchase terms that I could recommend to our board of directors. Our tight cash position and the unproven value of our stock were still serious handicaps in negotiating an acquisition.

In 1964, we examined the feasibility of acquiring Peter Products, Incorporated, of Muscatine, whose principal product was a line of movable partitions manufactured for the Johns-Manville Company. Not only did the asking price seem high, but, based on our poor experience with the wood partitions acquired from R.J.R. Industries, we doubted our ability to market these products effectively.

Shannonvue: An Unsuccessful Import

The Shannonvue story began with Duval's chance meeting with Edgar Shannon of London at a National Stationers and Office Equipment Association (NSOEA) show in the fall of 1955. Shannon's company, located in Sussex, southwest of London, manufactured a line of shallow drawer index card files that visibly displayed key information, marketed under the trade name Shannonvue.

Shannon had a good business in Great Britain and was successfully exporting his product to many countries. However, he had been quite unsuccessful in penetrating the American market, so he was searching for an organization to import and distribute the product in this country.

The Shannonvue product appeared to be useful and well-made. At the same time, we wanted a broader range of products to channel through our expanding distribution system. After we indicated our interest, Shannon visited Muscatine to look us over and to let us examine the Shannonvue more carefully. A few months later when Betty and I were in Europe, I visited the Shannon plant, and we enjoyed a delightful English dinner in the Shannon home near Wimbledon, of tennis fame.

By mid-1956, we reached an agreement for Home-O-Nize to import the Shannonvue line of products. Andrew Woodward, a Shannonvue sales manager from London, came to Muscatine to discuss the product and its marketing. Sales literature was prepared, and our sales organization was briefed. We were enthused and ready to go.

Despite our determination and enthusiasm, however, the venture failed. Consumers were pleased with the product, but the sales takeoff normally experienced after the introduction and vigorous promotion of a new product was disappointing. The lesson learned was that our distribution system—manufacturers' representatives and dealers—was neither qualified nor eager to sell systems. Their forte was furniture, and sales of Shannonvue products required a systems approach.

Long before agreeing to sell Shannon

The acquisition of Luxco in 1960 launched Home-O-Nize into the seating industry. But it would take many years for the company to become a significant factor in the chair market. Shown in this photo are Emma Barko and Ray Tobias.

products, we should have realized the different sales approach needed to analyze a customer's systems needs. Moreover, the spread between imported costs and the net price to dealers was marginal. We searched diligently for a successful marketing program during a number of serious, but pleasant, meetings with Edgar Shannon and his son Lionel in the United States and England. Reluctantly, we finally dropped the line in 1961, but only after more than five years of fruitless endeavor.

Marketing

Our basic marketing approach remained unaltered. We continued to place primary emphasis on the middle market, between the Grade A manufacturers at the top of the office furniture market and the "price" product manufacturers in the bottom segment of the market. However, we did make major changes in our marketing methods, pioneering in the sale of office furniture through wholesalers and organizing our own force of territorial managers.

With the introduction of the VS line in 1962, we made an attempt to offer upgraded desks, files, and bookcases in competition with Grade A manufacturers. However, this venture was markedly unsuccessful. (More of this in a later chapter.)

Our offering of the Honor product line in 1959 was an effort to reach the then-expanding school market. Honor products were basically H-O-N desks, files, bookcases, and storage units with minor modifications and brighter colors. This venture was moderately successful for a few years. When the school market began to decline, Honor products were dropped.

A Change in Marketing Management.

As Home-O-Nize's second decade drew to a close, a change in marketing leadership occurred. In May 1963, Bill Duval left Home-O-Nize by mutual agreement, to be succeeded by Ed Jones as vice president of the H-O-N Division.

Bill Duval contributed greatly to H-O-N's progress. He stimulated considerable gains in office furniture sales—29 percent compounded annually from 1955 through 1962—and participated in many important decisions regarding selection of new products. His foresight and diligent effort launched H-O-N on the wholesale marketing route. He presided over a substantial upgrading of our sales literature and catalogs. (Because the reasons for Duval's termination were related to overall corporate management, they are discussed in Chapter 12.)

Duval was right for Home-O-Nize during the seven years he was with us. However, we found that Jones' more structured style of management, coupled with equal determination and enthusiasm, was better-suited for Home-O-Nize's transition from a relatively small regional company to our greater presence as a national entity in the years that followed.

A Company Sales Force.

Through the 1950s, increased sales volume normally resulted in the appointment of additional manufacturers' representatives. These

"reps," as is usually the case, sold H-O-N products along with those of other companies. Some of our representatives were very effective, but even the most capable held divided loyalties. With our own territorial managers, we believed that we could better introduce new products, promote special offerings, train dealer salespeople, and concentrate sales efforts on specific territories. The advantages of selling through company members appeared to be great.

Sometime around 1960, we began a transition to a sales force composed of company members. Minutes of the Operating Committee of top management show that salespeople were being employed regularly by the H-O-N Division at least as early as 1960. A one-week training session was held in Muscatine in early May of that year, with four members of the H-O-N sales staff in attendance.

Ed Jones completed the process. Soon after he assumed leadership of Home-O-Nize's sales efforts, he proposed that the company terminate its relationships with any manufacturers' representative who also handled competitors' products. By late 1965, the H-O-N Division's field sales force of 16 company-employed territorial managers had completely replaced the system of marketing through manufacturers' representatives. With the move to a company sales force, Jones instituted more intensive recruiting and training programs.

Among the earliest territorial managers were William Sasko (1963), who started in the Cleveland territory and later handled Miami for H-O-N; Edward Smarsh (1964), who started in the Rochester, New York, territory, and then handled the Atlanta area; and Clayton Gardner (1965), who started in the Minnesota territory and later became The HON Company's sales manager for the southeastern region.

Annual sales conferences, usually held in January, were instituted by Duval in 1959 at the Wagon Wheel Inn near Rockton, Illinois. Thereafter, they were held at more attractive, or at least warmer, locations, such as Biloxi, featuring a boat ride from New Orleans; Sarasota; and Fort Lauderdale. With annual sales conferences

During Bill Duval's tenure as sales manager, the company began to use the wholesale channel of distribution, a major factor in gaining leadership in the middle market for office furniture.

a company fixture, they later came to be held much closer to Muscatine. They proved to be most useful as a vehicle to launch the year's sales thrust, to introduce new products, and to train and stimulate members of the sales organization. Territorial managers could meet senior officers. Both Stan Howe and I have usually addressed the group.

Throughout the decade, the H-O-N Division's staff, assisted by the Clement T. Hanson Agency, substantially raised the quality of our catalogs and other sales literature. Clem Hanson continued to be active in the agency, although his son James was taking over day-to-day management.

For several years, we used loose-leaf catalog binders. At the shareholders' meeting in 1962, the 119-page edition of our catalog was described, perhaps somewhat extravagantly, as "the best in the business."

Under the guidance of Ed Jones, the four-color, slick-paper, bound-format catalog that became so familiar was adopted in 1965. Two versions of the 12-page catalog were printed, identical except for prices: one for the United States east of the Rockies and the other for the western states. Subsequently, catalogs have been revised and reprinted annually to accommodate the constant stream of new products and to reflect price changes. Separate brochures were prepared for the Honor line, the VS group, and for newly introduced products not yet included in the current catalog.

We maintained the programs of magazine advertising and trade association exhibits initiated earlier. Our advertising continued to be limited to *Office Appliances, Geyer's Dealer's Topics, Modern Office Procedures,* and other journals aimed at dealers. No consumer-oriented advertising was undertaken. Exhibits at the annual NSOEA show had become a regular event. In addition, we experimented with exhibits of products at such trade gatherings as the National Office Furniture Association (NOFA), the National Business Show (NBS), the National School Services Institute (NSSI), and the National School Supply and Equipment Association (NSSEA).

Special promotions were used from time to time. Sometimes, they helped to

Stan Howe kept in close contact with the sales force. Here, he is shown with John Doll (seated), a regional sales manager, at a sales meeting in Chicago.

introduce new products. They also were designed to stimulate orders when sales were slow because of a weak economy, such as occurred in 1957, 1960, and again in 1963.

The Wholesale Marketplace

Undoubtedly, the major marketing breakthrough of this period was our entry into the wholesale marketplace. Generally, office supply wholesalers did not then handle office furniture, although we had distributed some of our card files and combination cabinets through that channel. Usually, dealers placed quantity orders for factory shipments of office furniture directly from Muscatine through our territorial managers or manufacturers' representatives.

Duval proposed to wholesalers, including some who were already handling our small goods, that they take on the dis-

John Van Lent addresses the first Annual Sales Meeting in 1959 at the Wagon Wheel Inn in Rockton, Illinois.

tribution of our desks, files, and chairs. Of particular importance were his discussions with Ralph Moser, a leading figure in the wholesale business, then president of Carpenter Paper Company (later merged into Champion Office Products). By 1957 we began supplying office furniture, first to Carpenter Paper Co. and then to many other regional and national wholesalers.

These humble beginnings in using the wholesale channel gave H-O-N a significant marketing edge by providing a new approach to office furniture dealers. Now, smaller dealers—the so-called "mom and pop" stores as well as larger dealers needing fill-in's—could get products more expeditiously from the warehouse of a nearby wholesaler.

With our low production costs, we were able to develop a discount structure that we believed would provide wholesalers an adequate margin. Wholesalers, despite frequent arguments for the larger discounts that they traditionally had received on small-ticket office supplies, soon found that handling large-ticket office furniture expanded their total sales profitably.

Gradually, our business with wholesalers grew. By 1965, we were serving about 75 wholesalers' warehouses located throughout the United States. Significantly, by this time, some 35 percent of The Home-O-Nize Co.'s furniture business reached dealers through this channel.

This innovation gave H-O-N a lead over most of its competitors in the medium-priced office furniture market. Other companies tried to follow our lead, but they had only marginal success. Our low production costs provided the key to making wholesaling profitable for both the wholesaler and the manufacturer. Thus, by getting the jump on our competitors, we became well-entrenched in our market segment.

Selling to Sears

Selling sizable quantities of our products to Sears, Roebuck and Company was another important marketing innovation during this decade. Sears reached not only small offices and businesses but also the

H-O-N exhibits such as this one at Atlantic City showed the company's product offering to the trade.

home market. Our interest in these segments had been long-standing as some of our early products, particularly combination cabinets, were intended to serve them. We had had little success, however, with the Home Suite line, which we had introduced in 1954.

In 1963, Van Lent was calling regularly on Sears to sell them our card files and combination cabinets. He found that Sears' Middle West contract supplier of filing cabinets was unable to keep pace with the increasing sales of files in stores and through the catalog. Sears was looking for a supplier who was willing and able to expand facilities and output to fill the giant retailer's needs. Home-O-Nize met these specifications. A series of negotiating sessions involving Sears' buyers, Howe, and occasionally myself led to a tentative proposal to manufacture products for sale by Sears.

The cautious examination of this proposal by our board of directors reflected a concern about selling too high a proportion of our output to a single customer. Members of our board had also heard allegations that Sears treated suppliers unfairly—rumors we later found to be quite unwarranted. In any event, both the board and the management of the H-O-N Division were determined to avoid undue dependence on any one customer. The board thus stipulated that management must obtain approval should sales to Sears exceed 15 percent of the company's total volume. (It never has.) With this condition, our board approved the proposal.

So, in October 1964, we began to supply Sears with files and combination cabinets designed somewhat differently from our basic offerings. Products manufactured to Sears's advance schedules were warehoused on our premises and drop-shipped to Sears stores or customers. Thus began a long and favorable association, adding greater depth to our sales in the home and office markets. Our volume of sales to Sears increased over the years as Sears requested other products and used us to supply broader geographical areas. The designs of products supplied to Sears later provided the basis for H-O-N's Promotable

The first meeting of the western sales organization. Sibley Smith (left), owner of Wholesale Office Equipment in Los Angeles, was the distributor from the Rockies to the Pacific. Here, the group looks at the Shannonvue card filing system seen in the foreground.

line of products sold to high-volume, promotion-oriented office furniture dealers.

Sales and Marketing Staff

The staff of the H-O-N Division expanded along with the growing sales of office furniture. Among the first of Duval's recruits were Jerry Boulund and Lila Keller in 1956. Boulund, beginning as a salesman, carried out a variety of assignments, becoming sales manager, national accounts (West) of The HON Company. Keller, since the beginning of her employment, served as secretary to the head of the H-O-N Division (later The HON Company). With the employment of a new personnel director in 1952, Van Lent returned to sales; at the time of his retirement in 1974, he was advertising and sales promotion manager in The HON Company. John Hahn, who joined the company in 1956, was administrative assistant at the HON Division at the time of his untimely death in 1968. Irene Opitz supervised Home-O-Nize order processing from 1956 to 1963, when she left the company. She returned in 1964 and handled similar duties in our New Jersey warehouse until her retirement in 1973. As shipments grew, the need for a traffic manager was met by employing Ron Darnall in 1960. He continued as distribution manager of The HON Company until 1985, when he joined Hiebert, Inc.

By 1965, the regional structure of the sales force was well-advanced because of the substantial progress in the transition from manufacturers' representatives to territorial sales managers. Boulund and then James Coyle served as sales manager of the Central-South Division. Dar Swink, employed in 1965 after long service with other office product manufacturers, managed the Western Division. Art Arnold, who had started as a territorial manager, became manager of the Midwestern Division. Denison Waterman, long employed in the household furniture field by Chittenden and Eastman in Burlington, Iowa, became manager of VS sales in 1965 as a first step to broader responsibilities. Harry Klein, who joined us with the Luxco acquisition, managed Luxco sales while it operated separately and later undertook special sales assignments for the H-O-N Division until he resigned in 1966. He later promoted, through his own firm, HON sales to catalog houses. William French joined the organization as manager of customer services in mid-1965. He later transferred to the Production Division, where he has handled a number of assignments, and eventually became materials manager at the Geneva Plant.

CHAPTER NINE

Slow Growth at Prime-Mover

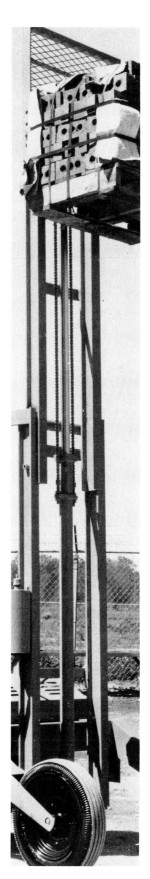

The growth of The Prime-Mover Co.'s sales did not keep pace with the staggering expansion of the H-O-N Division's office furniture during Operation Bootstrap. Nevertheless, the compounded rate of growth in Prime-Mover's annual sales was a healthy 10.3 percent from 1956 to 1965. Throughout the period, Prime-Mover consistently registered a comfortable profit margin. The division's progress was the result of new product introduction, stronger marketing, and constant efforts to reduce production costs.

Product Development

Prime-Mover was still a one-product company in 1956. The sole offering to distributors was the improved Model 15A, with bucket or platform and other accessories, which had been introduced in 1955. Accounting for 97 percent of Prime-Mover's revenue in that year, this dependable 1,500-pound walking-type concrete buggy continued to be an important revenue producer throughout the next decade.

The basic characteristics of the Model 15A were those of its predecessor—the original Model 15, which had been introduced in 1951. However, improvements made it easier to handle and more reliable and permitted important cost savings. Unfortunately, we had been forced to realize

that the market for such a concrete buggy was quite limited; sales would increase only modestly during the decade.

Prime-Mover's continued growth appeared to be dependent on two factors. First, we needed more products. Second, we wanted to lessen our dependence on the construction market by developing new products for the industrial market. The seasonal and cyclical nature of the construction industry would, we hoped, be offset somewhat by a steadier industrial market.

New products introduced during the decade were, with one exception, developed internally under Art Dahl's guidance. Our small design department was headed by Waldo Rodler until he resigned in June 1962, and later by David Horney, who joined Prime-Mover in January 1963. Robert Mangels served as a designer throughout the decade; before he retired, he transferred to The HON Company Robert Butler was employed as a draftsman in 1965; he later became a product engineer.

An Expanded Line for the Construction Market.
The introduction of the M-30 in June 1956 was the first of several new products for the construction equipment market. This 3,000-pound-capacity, riding-type concrete buggy was intended to compete with comparable units already offered

The M-30 was a 3,000-pound-capacity version of the original Prime-Mover. Because it was a completely new design, the company renegotiated the royalty agreement with Bell Aircraft.

by other manufacturers. The M-30 had few if any parts in common with the M-15. It used a purchased torque converter transmission and a heavy axle assembly, and it had a larger, square-shaped bucket.

Introduction of the M-30 led to discussions with Bell regarding the interpretation of our contract commitment to pay royalty on the first 25,000 Prime-Movers produced. We objected to paying royalty on the M-30 because it was a new product that we had designed rather than a version of the old Model 343. We reached a compromise: We agreed to pay royalty, but each M-30 was counted as the equivalent of 2.5 units against the 25,000 total.

Minor design changes during the production cycle added to the durability of the mason tender. These products continued working for years even under the most difficult conditions.

The L-10, introduced in 1957, was one of the first units designed in this country to handle small pallets or packages of brick or tile on construction projects. The L-10 was built on a Model 15A chassis, to which was added a forklift attachment. It could pick up 1,000-pound packages of masonry and place them on a scaffold. We called it a mason tender; it substituted mechanized for manual transfer of masonry products from stockpile to mason. Although the idea was a great one, few sales resulted. As a walking unit, the L-10 was cumbersome to operate.

The M-15B, introduced in 1959, involved only minor modifications of the M-15A, our reliable walking concrete buggy. The changes were intended to improve the handling and to reduce manufacturing cost. The M-30A, introduced in 1960, was a modification of our 3,000-pound riding concrete buggy. The changes, which improved its workability and reduced production costs, kept the product on the market until 1964 despite marginal sales.

Attention now turned to the M-20 concrete buggy. This unit was basically the M-15B, modified to provide a seat and steering mechanism that enabled the operator to ride. The M-20, introduced in September 1964, was still being marketed in the 1980s.

The L-812, a palletized masonry mover, replaced the L-10 in September 1960. Despite the high cost of the unit and its somewhat cumbersome operation, its successful marketing encouraged us to develop an apparatus specifically designed for the purpose. In May 1965, the L-36 and H-32 palletized masonry movers were introduced. The L-36 unit was power-operated; the H-32 unit was hand-operated. These units, supplemented by the L-812, won for Prime-Mover an important market with masonry contractors.

Aiming at the Industrial Market. After careful study of the potential market as well as the constructibility of the unit, we selected a flatbed, riding-type truck as our first product to be targeted specifically at the industrial market. The F-40, designed in 1958, was a two-ton truck with a 42-by-

122-inch bed and an 18-horsepower engine. The truck used the torque converter transmission and axle that we were already purchasing for the M-30. It was the highest priced item yet offered by Prime-Mover. Despite meager orders and difficulties with the supply of the torque converter transmission, the unit, later modified as the F-40A, remained in our product line until 1972. The Ford Motor Company, our best F-40A customer, placed units in many of its plants.

The M-15 continued to be a money-saving proposition for contractors because it increased the productivity of workers. Later, the introduction of concrete pumps and the use of cantilevered cranes cut out much of the market for these products.

The F-40 utility vehicle could be used for carrying materials or personnel. It was hoped this model would be popular for baggage handling in airports and other similar uses.

Late in 1958, pursuing a rumor, I traveled to the Milwaukee area to discuss with Allis-Chalmers officials the acquisition of their Chore-Boy truck. This unit, of lesser capacity than our F-40, would have doubled our flatbed truck offerings. When negotiations failed at an early stage, we went ahead with the design of our F-10, a half-ton industrial truck introduced in 1959. It used the transmission designed and produced by Prime-Mover for the Model 15. The F-10, modified later as the F-10A and then revamped as the F-20 with a one-ton capacity, was produced through 1968.

The F-10, with a capacity of 1,000 pounds, was intended for light duty such as baggage handling, maintenance supplies, and warehouse order picking. With seats added, it could be used as a personnel carrier. The F-40 (4,000-pound capacity) was intended for handling materials, supplies, maintenance equipment, and personnel in large industries. Although these units performed satisfactorily, they did not gain substantial volume. Hence, Prime-Mover's first entries into the industrial market were somewhat disappointing.

Looking for New Products in Europe.   In search of other products for either the construction or industrial market, I visited several European manufacturers who had indicated an interest in exporting products for us to distribute or in licensing us to manufacture their lines. One of these was the A.B.G. Company in Germany, manufacturers of vibrating drillers and soil compactors for the construction industry. Another was a Swedish company that produced the Tremix electrically activated concrete vibrator. Still another was the B/T Cooperative, also in Sweden, manufacturers of hand-operated pallet and skid trucks. The first of these European visits, made in 1959, produced nothing but the opportunity to enjoy a picturesque area of Germany that I had never seen before.

A second visit, made in 1960, led to the decision to import and market the Tremix line of vibrators. The unique design of these vibrators produced a high-frequency vibration in the head, although driven by a lower speed drive shaft and electric motor.

A vibrator, temporarily immersed in concrete that had been poured into a form, increased its density and eliminated air pockets before the concrete hardened. We introduced the vibrators in March 1961. With disappointing results, the line was discontinued in September 1965.

The earlier visit to B/T Cooperative turned out eventually to have more positive results. After extended negotiations, we were unable to determine a pricing structure that would provide adequate profit for us on products imported from B/T. Thus, we decided to design and introduce our own hand-operated pallet and skid trucks to offer in competition with the B/T line. The P-24 and P-45 pallet trucks, having capacities of 2,500 and 4,500 pounds, respectively, were put on the market in May 1961. Models S-25 and S-45 skid trucks followed in March 1964. The market's acceptance of these trucks was encouraging, but the total dollar volume of these low-priced items was not great.

Spare Parts.   Growth of spare part sales paralleled the increased volume of Prime-Mover products in service, giving Prime-Mover an advantage not enjoyed by the H-O-N Division. Dealers required constant replenishment of replacement parts to service the products they sold. Even in 1965 we were still supplying spare parts for the Model 343 Prime-Mover. Spare part sales represented about 8 percent of annual sales, producing a very good profit margin.

Marketing

The Domestic Market.   Prime-Mover's marketing during most of Operation Bootstrap was guided by Art Dahl, who served as sales manager as well as head of the Prime-Mover Division. With sales volume growing large enough to justify the separation of these responsibilities by late 1964, Gene Waddell was employed as sales manager, reporting to Dahl. Waddell graduated from the University of Illinois in 1957 with a major in journalism and a minor in advertising. He had acquired extensive sales experience with the Barber-Greene Company.

Prime-Mover's domestic sales organization throughout the decade consisted of company-employed district representatives supplemented by manufacturers' representatives in the far west.

Harwell Peterson covered the Midwestern Territory; he continued with the company until his retirement in 1974. Howard Worst served the Central Territory before he transferred to HON INDUSTRIES' advertising department. George Dunker was appointed customer service manager in 1967. Subsequently, he became product support manager, technical services manager, and sales manager of construction equipment.

Prime-Mover products reached customers through about 100 distributors located in major cities across the nation. Their functions included repair and servicing of equipment, as well as sales. Some distributors rented Prime-Mover equipment to contractors for a limited time, whereas others leased equipment to users for an extended period.

In 1956, the distributor organization still consisted almost entirely of firms that we had inherited from Bell, most of whom were in the construction equipment business. Many of these distributors, having been oversold by Bell, were disillusioned with the limited market for the concrete buggies. Primarily interested in larger and more expensive equipment, they tended to give little attention to our product. Their sales staff naturally preferred to sell a $20,000 piece of equipment rather than a $600 concrete buggy.

To stimulate our sales, therefore, we had to persuade distributors to push Prime-Movers aggressively, or we would have to replace them with dealers who would. But it was difficult, to find distributors with adequate sales and service capability who would handle Prime-Movers effectively. Introduction of products aimed at the industrial market further complicated the development of an adequate distribution network. Nevertheless, Prime-Mover strengthened its distributor organization appre-

ciably by the end of Operation Bootstrap. The number of distributors in the United States remained about the same, but they were selling more Prime-Movers.

Both the quality and quantity of sales literature—brochures, specification sheets, price lists, and promotional pieces—were improved from year to year. Clem Hanson and his son, Jim, worked with Art Dahl and his staff. Advertising programs were mounted with regular insertions in *Construction Methods and Equipment, Modern Materials Handling,* and *Contractors and Equipment*—journals that reached the kind of distributors we needed. Prime-Mover equipment was exhibited at the annual show of the Material Handling Institute. Art Dahl became active in relevant trade associations. He later served on the Industry Round Table of the Associated Equipment Distributors, which represented the construction equipment industry, and on the board of directors of the Material Handling Institute.

Arrangements were made with the Central State Bank to finance floor plans of Prime-Mover equipment in distributors' showrooms. But only a few distributors took advantage of this service, as its terms were not very attractive.

Seeking Export Markets. Frustration and discouragement were the hallmarks of Prime-Mover's foreign marketing efforts during Operation Bootstrap. Several European manufacturers were offering concrete buggies, mostly of the riding type, at prices that were extremely competitive when compared with the cost of production in the United States plus ocean shipping costs and import duties.

We also found the distributors that we had inherited from Bell to be uninterested in aggressively pushing the sale of Prime-Mover equipment. Bell had commissioned these distributors primarily because of their interest in Bell helicopters. In visiting our distributors during my frequent trips to Europe, I found that most were satisfied if they sold half a dozen units a year.

The one happy exception to the generally dismal European picture was in The Netherlands, where my continuing contacts with W. F. M. Muller of Stokvis & Zonen produced mildly encouraging results. The reduced prices that we had given Stokvis enabled the firm to increase its Dutch sales. Stokvis had associations with sales organizations in several other European countries, which seemed to hold promise of expanding Prime-Mover's marketing network.

In the late 1950s, Stokvis achieved a level of sales of Prime-Movers high enough to encourage us to consider a joint venture to manufacture Prime-Mover products in The Netherlands. Such consideration was stimulated by the progress of the European Economic Community in gradually lowering tariffs among member countries while maintaining high duties on imports from outside the Community. All of this greatly enhanced the benefits of manufacturing in one of the six countries that then formed the Common Market.

According to an agreement reached in July 1962, Stokvis would manufacture a pilot lot of 25 M-15B units. Transmissions and other complex parts would be shipped from Muscatine, while sheet metal parts would be manufactured in The Netherlands. Stokvis would sell these units not only in The Netherlands but also through established Prime-Mover dealers in Europe and through new distributors that he would commission and service. Our agreement also provided that after a suitable trial period, we would consider establishing a jointly owned company to manufacture and sell Prime-Mover equipment in Europe and, to the extent practicable, export products from there.

Soon thereafter, Stokvis established an assembly line and arranged for parts to be manufactured at its plant in Uden, which was then producing bicycles and related equipment. Some 125 M-15B units were manufactured in this plant through 1965.

However, the promising joint venture to manufacture Prime-Movers on a regular basis in The Netherlands never materialized. When Muller retired, new ownership and management took over Stokvis & Zonen. At the same time, it was clear that the concrete buggy would have difficulty in competing effectively with tower cranes and other advanced material-handling techniques widely used in the European construction industry.

Outside Europe, the export market for our products was practically zero. Developing countries needed labor-intensive, not labor-saving constructions methods. Few Bell-commissioned distributors outside of Europe displayed any continuing interest in our product.

Foreign interest in concrete buggies dwindled. Despite our desires and efforts, we were fading out of the export market.

By the end of 1965, it was evident that future growth of Prime-Mover depended primarily on successful marketing in the United States.

Prime-Mover's Dilemma

At the end of Operation Bootstrap, Prime-Mover was still too dependent on the construction industry. Concrete buggies—Models 15–B, M-30A, and M-20—along with palletized masonry movers, constituted the mainstay of our business. In America, as in Europe, the use of cranes for handling concrete in the construction of multistoried buildings was becoming increasingly common. In addition, more concrete was being centrally batched and truck-mixed and delivered. Thus, changing technology in the construction industry would discourage any tremendous expansion of the market for our concrete buggies.

Our position in the industrial field was still very weak.

Only a few F-10A and F-40A trucks were being sold. The quantities of pallet and skid trucks were encouraging, but their dollar volume was not great. Moreover, margins on the pallet trucks were severely limited by the vigorous competition of both domestic and foreign manufacturers.

Obviously, Prime-Mover product development was lagging.

Despite our efforts, we had not selected and introduced products capable of producing substantial gains in sales volume.

In the construction field, we had studied and developed models of a concrete conveyor, but we hesitated to put it into production. We had examined the possibility of designing or acquiring a line of concrete finishing equipment or other apparatus used by concrete and masonry contractors. Either of these products might have enhanced our participation in the market for construction equipment.

We developed and tested a small tow truck using the transmission system of our F-40A, but we backed away from introducing it. This truck, similar to those used extensively at airports, might have facilitated our entry into the sizable market for this type of material-handling equipment.

We also looked outside the construction and industrial markets. A three-wheeled golf cart was designed and tested. We backed away from introduction largely because of the seasonal nature of the market as well as the probable need to finance floor plans and to lease equipment. A determined effort was made to secure a contract from the U.S. Post Office Department for three-wheeled mail carrier trucks. We designed a good unit, featuring a two-cylinder engine with a torque converter drive, only to lose out in price competition to the one-cylinder clutch-type units that the department purchased.

In retrospect, we were undoubtedly too cautious in product development. At the same time, however, the rapid expansion of the office furniture business and its constant demands for plant expansion and working capital undoubtedly diverted the attention of top management and the board away from Prime-Mover.

Fortunately, the need for a new approach to the industrial market was fully realized, and ideas were incubating. Dahl, with his marketing and design staff, was close to recommending the production of a line of electrically powered industrial material-handling equipment.

Industrial materials handling proved the key to the future for The Prime-Mover Co. Here, Dick Duggan of the company's stores department maneuvers a pallet truck, which was the precursor of a complete line of electric material-handling products.

CHAPTER TEN

The Production Division at Work

Throughout the years of Operation Bootstrap, Home-O-Nize's Production Division manufactured the goods sold by both the H-O-N Division and The Prime-Mover Co. The Production Division embraced nearly 80 percent of the company's members, used nearly all of its physical facilities, and, through employment and purchase, accounted for most of the costs of operating The Home-O-Nize Co. The division had the complex task of transforming materials and labor into finished products of desired quality and cost, available as needed for shipment to customers.

The division's stellar performance during Operation Bootstrap established the foundation for H-O-N's continuing strength as a low-cost producer of office furniture. Production efficiency provided the solid foundation for the company's spectacular growth during the years of Operation Bootstrap and beyond. Low-cost production of quality products made possible the use of wholesalers and facilitated profitable penetration of highly competitive markets. Stan Howe, who headed the Production Division throughout the decade, deserves great credit.

In the early years of this decade, the Production Division's output included some contract work as well as office furniture and Prime-Movers. During 1958, military contract work ended, as did most other contract work, except that for Stampings,

Inc. In the next year, we ended our long-standing, mutually beneficial relationship with Stampings in an amicable way.

Plant Expansion

As advancing sales called for an increasing flow of goods over the shipping docks, new buildings and new production lines were needed. The several plant enlargements during the decade of Operation Bootstrap not only added to production capability but also led to significant economies in manufacturing through improved organization of production.

Oak Street Plant. The first of many expansions of the Oak Street Plant occurred in 1959. As the pressure for more space increased, we eyed with interest the three lots just across the alley north of the original Oak Street Plant. We acquired one of these in November 1955 after a fire destroyed the building on the site. The other two lots, the site of the William Glatstein junkyard, were then owned and operated by Abe Lieflander, who was planning to retire. After extended discussions, we reached a purchase agreement in July 1956 and soon took title to the property. Years later, Lieflander bewailed his reluctance to accept the Home-O-Nize stock that we initially offered in lieu of the cash he demanded.

Next, we approached the City of Muscatine about acquiring the alley between our original plant and the newly acquired property. This would allow us to build our new structure, Oak Street Building Number 2, as an extension of the original plant. The city, after due consideration, approved our request to purchase the alley, thus setting a precedent for abandonment of alleys and streets to permit future expansion.

The Stanley Engineering Co. was engaged to design a new 28,800-square-foot, high-ceiling structure to be used as a warehouse. Oak Street Building Number 2 was designed to receive packaged furniture from the assembly area of the original plant by means of a belt conveyor. The external style and materials of the building, as well as its internal treatment, set a pattern for subsequent expansions. This construction project was another contribution that HON made to urban renewal in Muscatine. An attractive new structure took the place of an unsightly junkyard and a burned-out building, thereby contributing to an improvement of the local environment.

Occupation of the new warehouse in 1959 nearly doubled the area of the Oak Street Plant. The enlarged storage space could accommodate the larger finished goods inventory needed to support the increasing furniture sales as well as making possible longer production runs.

A major advance in our manufacturing process triggered the next expansion, the construction of Oak Street Building Number 3 on a recently acquired lot across the street from the original plant. The steel cut-up facility housed in this 5,500-square-foot structure enabled us to use coiled steel instead of flat sheets. An overhead crane unloaded coils of steel from incoming trucks and placed them in storage or on the cradle at the head of the cut-up line. As the coiled steel was unrolled, it was fed to a straightener and then to a huge press where it was cut to size and shape. The investment in this equipment was quickly repaid, as it permitted the purchase of coiled steel rather than flat sheets at substantial savings. It also resulted in elimination of shearing and in lower handling and blanking costs. Oak Street Building Num-

Except for painting and repairing all the windows, the Oak Street Plant remained virtually unchanged from 1947 until the late 1950s when an expansion program began.

Digging the footings for expansion of the Oak Street Plant signified the dramatic growth of the company.

Stan Howe (right) and Harold Ogilvie, director of the Muscatine Industrial Development Commission, look at the new warehouse on Oak Street as it nears completion.

Working with flat stock required extra handling of raw materials. Here, Fritz Kramer (foreground) is cutting large sheets of steel. Otto Grothe and another member work at a shear in the background.

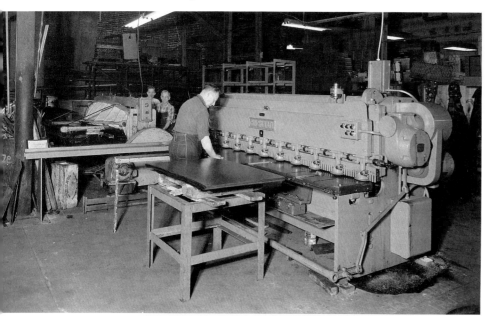

ber 3, although small, greatly increased our manufacturing capacity while lowering our production costs. Removal of steel storage and shearing operations from Oak Street Building Number 1 freed space there for production of more files and other furniture.

Space pressures at the Oak Street Plant were only temporarily relieved by the construction of Building Number 3 and the installation of the cut-up line. Increasing sales of files, plus the introduction of the Million line of desks and the contemplated introduction of the Convaire desks, called for additional production capacity. Having anticipated this need for several years, we had acquired property, lot by lot, in the block across Oak Street to the west of the original plant between Third and Fourth Streets. As temporary landlords, we rented, on short-term leases, the houses that were in reasonably good shape. Others were demolished, and the lots were graded and surfaced to provide parking areas for our expanding work force. By the fall of 1962, we owned all of the block to the west except the two lots parallel to Orange Street on the west end of the block. Hence, this area was selected for Oak Street Building Number 4.

Planning studies indicated that our primary needs were for more warehouse space for finished goods, space for a desk assembly and packing line, and better facilities for shipping products. These needs were met by constructing a 55,000-square-foot warehouse encompassing Building Number 3 and converting Building Number 2 from warehouse to desk manufacturing. An overhead conveyor across Oak Street would transfer packaged goods from both the file and desk production lines on the east side of Oak Street into the new warehouse on the west side. Railroad sidings were constructed to allow, for the first time, direct loading into cars from staging areas in the new warehouse. This eliminated time-consuming and costly trucking of products destined for rail shipment from the plant to remote sidings. With facilities for loading three boxcars, as well as four docks for loading trucks, the construction vastly improved the processes for transferring, storing, and shipping finished goods. The architectural style and materials of the new warehouse were the same as those used on Oak Street Buildings Number 2 and Number 3.

When the new warehouse was occupied in May 1963, an efficient desk production facility was organized in Oak Street Building Number 2. The installation of apparatus to produce desk tops using paper honeycomb core with laminated surfacing permitted substantial savings compared with the prior purchase of tops from outside sources. Dedicated press brakes, located near the assembly line, were used for forming the larger sheet steel pieces. Fork trucks transported blanks from the steel department across the street to the assembly area, thus simplifying material flow and reducing handling damage. A desk assembly line designed to produce one desk per minute not only speeded desk production but also resulted in substantial savings. The desk department continued to depend on the original fabrication department in Oak Street Building Number 1 for small parts. Transfer of desk assembly to Oak Street Building Number 2 released the full capacity of the assembly line in Oak Street Building Number 1 for the production of files, combination cabinets, and bookcases. The availability of this capacity made it possible for Howe to negotiate a contract with Sears to supply that company's needs for files. This new relationship grew substantially over the years, enabling us to gain access to a different segment of the market.

By the end of the decade, our production capacity was again becoming inadequate, particularly with respect to files. The time had come to build the most efficient file production facility that we could design. We selected an area just east of Oak Street Buildings Number 1 and Number 2. Negotiations with Huttig Manufacturing Company led to our purchase of adjacent property sufficiently large to accommodate the proposed facility and to provide a parking area. With the location determined, attention was given to the design of a single-product, highly efficient file production plant that was to produce one file every 40

Building Number 3, shown under construction here, was only 5,500 square feet; yet it enabled the Production Division to deal with coiled steel instead of flat stock.

Working with steel blanks and a roll form machine, Harold McKamey formed drawer sides at optimum efficiency.

Construction of a 55,000-square-foot warehouse encompassing Oak Street Building Number 3 provided badly needed space for storage of finished goods. A conveyor over the street, shown at right, moved product from the plant to the warehouse. Construction of railroad sidings allowed for the first time direct access to rail cars from the plant.

The first expansion of the Geneva Plant made it possible to make chairs, machine stands, stools, and Prime-Movers all inside one facility.

seconds. In August 1965, ground was broken for a $1.2 million construction project, another gigantic step forward. The dramatic effect of this plant, to be known as Oak Street Building Number 5, would not be realized until the next decade of Home-O-Nize's history. However, the announcement alone was a great morale booster.

Late in 1965, near the end of Operation Bootstrap, we negotiated the purchase of the 50,000-square-foot Hawkeye Button Company plant located across Third Street, south of the Oak Street Building Number 4 warehouse. This purchase, consummated in 1966, made us owners of a building in which we had been leasing 17,000 square feet. It would provide further warehouse space as well as opportunity for plant expansion.

Geneva Plant. In June 1956, Prime-Mover, B-47 fairings, and costumer production operations were moved to the 43,000-square-foot Geneva Plant, which had been completed and leased the prior year. The Sampson Street Plant was shut down, leases were allowed to expire, and the one Quonset hut owned by Prime-Mover was sold.

In 1957, production of small goods was transferred from Oak Street to the Geneva Plant. This allowed us to expand the product offering to include card cabinets and cash boxes, as well as card files and some small parts for other products. This facility contained sheet metal fabricating equipment, dip painting, and an infrared heat paint baking tunnel. Transfer of production of small goods from the Oak Street Plant, along with the use of new equipment, resulted in a badly needed gain of efficiency that improved profit margins on these products.

With the acquisition of Luxco in 1962, the Geneva Plant was expanded to provide space for that seating and machine stand operation. Planning studies had indicated that the Geneva Plant was the most desirable location for chair production. The owners of the building agreed to finance and construct an 18,000-square-foot addition, extend our lease to provide a 15-year base period plus two 10-year optional extensions, and, of course, increase the rental rate. Home-O-Nize outlined building requirements, Stanley Engineering designed the facility, and ground was broken in late spring 1962. When the Luxco Plant in La Crosse was shut down in October, selected equipment and personnel were transferred to Muscatine.

The extension of the Geneva Plant was designed and equipped to facilitate efficient production of chairs, stools, and machine stands. The parts fabrication and upholstery departments were largely equipped with machinery and apparatus from La Crosse. An overhead conveyor was installed to carry parts through a new painting facility and then to deliver them to a final assembly area where the products were assembled, inspected, and packed. By early 1963, the expanded plant was producing finished products.

Organization of the Production Division

Throughout the years of Operation Bootstrap, the functions of the Production Division remained the same—the fabrication of H-O-N and Prime-Mover products, planning, plant design and construction, industrial engineering, selection of equipment, production control, cost accounting, purchasing, design of H-O-N products, and, for part of the decade, personnel management. Design of Prime-Mover products and purchase of engines, tires, and other manufactured components were handled by The Prime-Mover Co.

However, as total employment at Home-O-Nize increased more than three-fold (from 167 to 521), changes had to be made in the organization of the Production Division. In 1956, managers exercised a broad span of control, typical of a growing, fledgling organization. Stan Howe, then vice president in charge of the division, had 10 people reporting to him (see chart at right). These included an assistant, the managers of the two plants, and those representing seven manufacturing functions.

We knew that the larger size of our operations required us to create another layer of management to relieve the burden

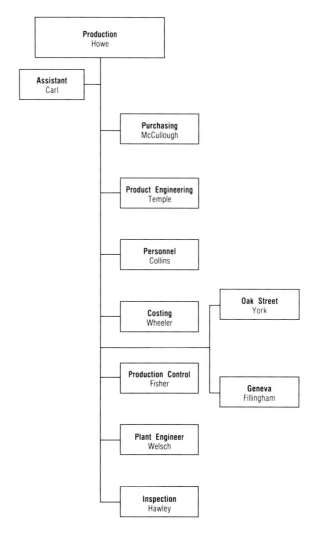

Production division organization in August 1956.

of supervisory responsibility that Stan Howe was carrying. We tried several arrangements. In 1958, we created a planning department that consisted of the purchasing, production control, cost accounting, and personnel sections. This new department was headed by Max Collins, who retained his personnel duties through later assignments.

In 1961, we assigned Rex Bennett to the newly established position of manufacturing manager. Heads of the functions of industrial engineering, tooling, maintenance, production control, purchasing, cost accounting, and quality now reported to Bennett, who, in turn, reported to Howe as vice president of the Production Division.

By April 1964, only four managers in the Production Division—the two plants and two functions—were reporting directly to Howe (see chart on page 87), who in 1961 had assumed the additional responsibilities of executive vice president, a newly created position. Personnel functions had been transferred out of the Production Division; Personnel Director Collins continued to report to Howe in Howe's role as executive vice president of The Home-O-Nize Co.

The frequent restructuring of the Production Division demonstrated our commitment to flexibility to meet changing conditions—expanding sales, changing products, and the growing talents of new and developing staff. In my experience, clinging to a rigid theoretical organizational structure usually paralyzes progress.

Yet, despite the many changes made in the structure, there was an amazing continuity of management personnel. Of the managers and supervisors in the Production Division of The Home-O-Nize Co. in 1964, 21, or 42 percent, were still employed by HON INDUSTRIES or one of its subsidiaries in 1986. Another 20 individuals, or 40 percent, continued with the organization until retirement or death. Thus, 82 percent of these members made, or are still making, HON their career. Such continuity of employment has been a major contributor to HON's efficient, low-cost, high-quality production.

Productivity

Expanding employment and enlarging space in a manner that reduces production costs is a great challenge—one that was fully met at Home-O-Nize during the years of Operation Bootstrap. Output per member—one rough measure of productivity—showed a significant improvement. A work force three times larger in 1965 than in 1956 produced goods worth 5.5 times more. (The general price level rose only gradually during this 10-year period.)

The remarkable emergence of Home-O-Nize as a low-cost producer of office furniture was not the result of any single or simple action. Our success resulted from a number of interlocking decisions, practices, and procedures. Most of these were initiated by the Production Division, but others involved the H-O-N Division and The Prime-Mover Co.

In the early years, our plant resembled a job shop, with few products and relatively short runs. From 1956 to 1965, we made the transition to the more efficient line-type operation with higher volume, so crucial to reducing production costs.

A constantly increasing level of sales, of course, made longer runs possible. But another significant factor was standardization of our products by limiting the range of models and colors normally offered. Salespeople frequently contended that just a little change in design, the use of a special color specified by the customer, or production of a few specialized items would let them close an important order. It took much self-discipline to resist these chants and to remember the attractive profit potential deriving from long runs of standardized products. The company grew and prospered by resisting most of the calls for special colors, designs, and the like.

Achievement of longer runs also depended on availability of sufficient warehouse space to accommodate the sizable runs of the more popular products. Maintaining reasonable shipping times required careful scheduling, taking into account the flow of orders as well as desired production scheduling.

The transition to line-type operations offered many opportunities for economies of manufacturing. Small parts could be produced in greater volume. Setup time on assembly lines was virtually eliminated. Material handling, particularly of sizable parts, could be reduced by arranging single-purpose equipment adjacent to assembly lines. This process reduced the need for handling of fabricated parts as well as investment in storage space and for work in process. It also greatly lessened the potential for damage inherent in moving large formed parts in and out of storage.

Unfortunately, the achievements of "just-in-time" production made at Home-O-Nize were not matched at Prime-Mover. Because of lower volume and the nature of

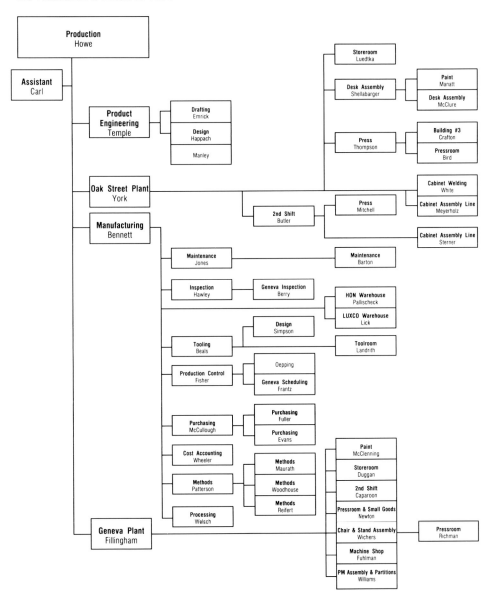

the products, the manufacture of Prime-Movers did not provide the same opportunities for highly efficient production methods. Although we did streamline, as much as possible, the final assembly of Prime-Movers, the manufacture of parts remained basically a batch-type operation. More efficient machining equipment, however, contributed to an overall reduction of production costs at The Prime-Mover Co.

A Philosophy of Manufacturing

The installation of increasingly sophisticated systems and clearly documented procedures during the period of Operation Bootstrap was no accident. It was an expression of our management philosophy. My natural emphasis on formalized standards, procedures, criteria, and records was reinforced by Howe's similar and more dis-

At The Prime-Mover Co., components still required individual stamping, forming, welding, grinding, and assembly. George Freeland is shown here working on the frame of a Model 15B. Low sales volumes prevented the introduction of a true assembly line production setup.

Jim Hawley, manager of quality control, shown testing a gear while a company-designed cycling machine tests a file drawer.

ciplined approach to production.

The development of systems and procedures within the Production Division was accelerated because Dahl and Winn shared our philosophy of management. This helped to simplify those matters involving interfaces between the Production Division, on the one hand, and The Prime-Mover Co., corporate finance, and office management on the other. Interfaces with the H-O-N Division were somewhat more complicated during Duval's regime, as he was less systems-oriented. Relations improved when Jones assumed responsibility for the management of the H-O-N Division.

Close linkages of production engineering and product design contributed significantly to the progress of Home-O-Nize toward low-cost production of high-quality products. Throughout Operation Bootstrap, Stan Howe saw to it that the two functions were not only coordinated but were also integrated at the appropriate times. While our production engineers performed their many normal functions—methods, rate setting, and the like—their talents were merged with those of our product designers before a product was released for production. The result was careful attention to manufacturability, use of common parts, and other factors that contributed to economical and efficient production while adding to the function, workability, style, and quality of the product. Through this integration, product designers became more aware of the impact of detailed design decisions on production costs and quality.

The paperwork systems that we established to manage production were not especially unique. By and large, they were adapted from systems in general use in progressive companies. They were, undoubtedly, more elaborate and extensive than those normally used in companies of our size. Blueprints, parts lists, and operation sheets were prepared for all parts and assemblies. Production control prepared weekly schedules using sales and inventory data and issued production orders for parts fabrication and assemblies, based on the explosion of the parts lists for each product. Time-keeping and accounting for time and materials were structured to provide accurate, ongoing information about costs. The cost accounting responsibility was located within the Production Division and was thus managed to provide the information most useful in the design and manufacture of products that provided the most function and quality for the money.

Well before the end of Operation Bootstrap, we were anticipating computerization of our systems. With this in mind, we employed specialists as consultants—Bill Cory and Al Hinkle. Each would later become a member of our board of directors. Under their guidance, our systems and manuals were structured for future adaptation to computers.

Another element of cost reduction was the introduction of group incentives in some of the production departments. This was initiated with the small goods line at the Geneva Plant in early 1958. Later, group incentives were applied to the cabinet, file, and desk lines at the Oak Street Plant. These group incentives were structured to allow members to earn about 20 percent beyond their base compensation. The system we adopted reflected our corporate judgment against the use of individual piece-rate work, a feeling that still prevails at HON.

The continuing emphasis on cost reduction had a positive rather than a negative effect on product quality. Cost-reduction measures were not approved unless they would improve, or at least maintain, quality. Better tooling, simplified methods, and reduced material handling are good

examples. Maintenance of quality was stimulated by intelligent use of inspection procedures on both parts and finished products. We emphasized building member awareness of their responsibility for ensuring fine and workable products.

Special machines were developed to cycle-test file drawers, chairs, and other pieces of office furniture. Concern for the quality of the product as delivered to the customer led to continued attention to packaging. Here again, special procedures were developed to test the packaged product at carton vendors' test facilities. Changes in packaging and often in product design were implemented as a result of such testing, supported by analysis of shipping damage.

Investment in Capital Equipment

Cost reduction became a way of life at Home-O-Nize during Operation Bootstrap. Beyond attention to manufacturability of new products, our production engineers were constantly seeking methods, equipment, and tooling capable of reducing production time. Equipment selection received careful attention. Many types of equipment—tape-controlled machines and cut-up lines for coiled stock, for example—could be purchased. But some equipment—such as the automatic welders for attaching tracks and stiffeners to the sides of file cabinets—had to be specially designed and manufactured, either in-house or through contract.

In 1961, we adopted criteria for making decisions about capital investments. A proposal prepared by Stan Howe called for a minimum of 25 percent annual return on assets employed. Careful analysis of costs and benefits would be made to determine whether such a return could be achieved. Only then would equipment purchases and plant modifications and additions be authorized. Following adoption of these criteria, Howe developed the procedures and documents necessary to analyze, review, and approve capital expenditures.

Implementation of this procedure greatly lessened the chance of an ill-conceived capital investment. It resulted in

close attention being paid to layout, design, and selection of equipment for new production lines. The criteria provided a basis for comparing proposed capital investments in order to select those with the greatest return first. Projects combining quality improvement and cost reduction could be readily justified in terms of return on investment.

Underpinning the significant achievements in product development and marketing made during Operation Bootstrap was the outstanding performance of the Production Division. Manufacturing costs were slowly, but surely, being lowered, while quality was being improved. As Operation Bootstrap ended, Home-O-Nize was firmly established as a low-cost producer in the office furniture field.

Don Flake (left) and Louis York at the packout station on the file line. Esther McCormick was the final inspector.

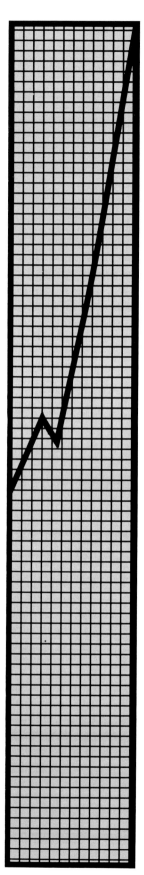

CHAPTER ELEVEN

Growing Financial Strength

Evidence of growing prosperity was visible around the office and factories of The Home-O-Nize Co.—new faces, new buildings and machinery, new products, and new marketing channels. However, the significant advances in marketing and production made during Operation Bootstrap could not have occurred without equally striking progress in the area of corporate finance. Key policies and practices developed during these years contributed to a significant strengthening of the company's finances. A strong financial position was an important heritage of Operation Bootstrap.

Financial Administration

We did not overlook the fact that efficient use of assets improved the profit performance of a company. Optimization of inventory, we knew, required a delicate balance among such factors as size of production runs, delivery schedules to customers, and costs of maintaining inventory. Too little inventory and delayed shipments could reduce sales volume, whereas too much inventory needlessly consumed capital. Optimization of accounts receivable depended on terms offered, credit policies, and collection aggressiveness. Increasing experience and better systems improved the ability of Home-O-Nize to manage these components of working capital.

Administration of our financial affairs was the responsibility of Fred Winn, our secretary-treasurer, and his staff. Their responsibilities included billing, accounts receivable, accounts payable, payroll, general accounting, banking, and related financial transactions. Great credit should go to Winn for the efficient manner in which he handled these functions for the company.

Ladd Steinmetz, a native of Muscatine, a graduate of the University of Iowa, and a veteran of World War II, was employed in 1955—one of the first professionals to be added to Winn's staff. (Ladd had been a member of a church school class I taught during the 1930s.) A year later, Kermit Cook, who grew up in Winterset and Earlham, Iowa, and graduated from Simpson College with a degree in business administration, joined the organization. John Axel, another native of Muscatine and a graduate of Iowa State University and the University of Pennsylvania's Wharton School of Finance and Commerce, was employed as an internal auditor in December 1965. Two of these men are still with the organization: Cook as controller of The HON Company, and Axel as vice president of finance of HON INDUSTRIES. Steinmetz was assistant credit manager when he retired in 1983.

Winn's other staff members during the decade were clerks, stenographers, and bookkeepers. Among those who had extended service with the company were Betty Brown, assistant credit manager (22 years); Ruth Naber, truck fleet dispatcher (26 years); Genevieve Allbee, accountant (23 years); Jack Plogh, tab department supervisor (11 years); and Carole Holcomb, senior data entry operator (27 years).

An End to Crisis Money Management

At the beginning of Operation Bootstrap, Home-O-Nize was in an extremely tight cash position. The company's debts included $44,000 borrowed on factored accounts, $46,250 secured by a mortgage to the Central State Bank, and $61,000 secured by short-term notes. In addition, Prime-Mover had notes outstanding to Bell of $103,363. Of the combined debt owed by Home-O-Nize and Prime-Mover, $297,290 was a current liability due within 12 months. Only $199,495 had maturities beyond one year. Of the combined current assets, only $23,990 was in cash; the balance was in accounts receivable and inventories.

Operation Bootstrap did not move Home-O-Nize from rags to riches. However, during these years, we did make the transition from crisis management to a more normal style of fiscal operation. Well before the end of the period, Treasurer Winn was able to meet payrolls on time and to take cash discounts on payables. This was done by forward planning and use of credit, rather than by chaotic maneuvering. Moreover, our production facilities were substantially enlarged without undue financial strain on the company.

Demonstrated profitability was, of course, the foundation for our improved financial condition. Profits provided a source of capital in the form of retained earnings, which increased shareholders' equity. Between 1957 (the first year of consolidated statements for Home-O-Nize and Prime-Mover) and 1965, the accumulated amount of earnings retained for use as capital rose from $199,800 to $1.76 million—nearly a ninefold gain. This rise in retained earnings was accomplished even while we were gradually increasing cash dividends.

Our retained earnings were substantial, but we found it necessary to look beyond them for working capital and the funds for plant expansion. Accounts receivable and inventory, the major elements of working capital, increased from month to month almost in direct proportion to sales. Larger blocks of funding for plant expansions were necessary. Continuing profits encouraged lenders and suppliers to extend long-term and short-term credit to Home-O-Nize.

Factoring

At the beginning of Operation Bootstrap, we were using a kind of do-it-yourself program of factoring office furniture accounts receivable. The Central State Bank made short-term loans, with recourse, secured by our pledge of accounts receivable. Although the program was helpful, it only partially converted our receivables into quick cash. At the end of 1955, borrowings on factored accounts were about $44,000, compared with total receivables of $204,000. Neither was this arrangement easily managed. Because the bank was not in the factoring business, the systems we had devised to provide security, handle collections, and make repayments were awkward.

Home-O-Nize net income during the Operation Bootstrap years.

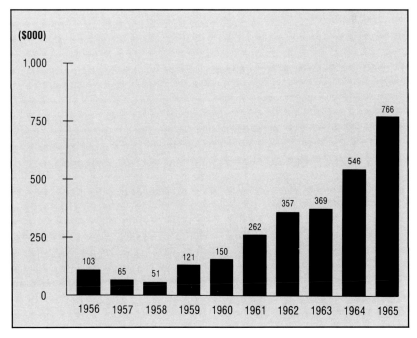

($000)

1956	1957	1958	1959	1960	1961	1962	1963	1964	1965
103	65	51	121	150	262	357	369	546	766

We recognized that factoring was an acceptable route to short-term credit, quickly converting receivables into cash, although it was not without its limitations. However, the problems we encountered in working with the Central State Bank encouraged us to seek to make factoring arrangements with an institution that specialized in that form of financing.

As a result, in 1957 we concluded a factoring agreement with the William Iselin Company of New York City. This firm made loans to us against our accounts receivable in office products and collected these accounts, charging a percentage as a fee.

Our negotiations with the William Iselin Co. included another very important item—a term loan of $200,000 maturing over five years with interest of 5 percent. This loan was secured by a mortgage on specified plant and equipment not otherwise pledged on the mortgage held by the Central State Bank. Our cash position changed dramatically for the better as we phased out the factoring arrangement with Central State and paid off many of our notes. Our relationships with the Iselin firm and with Leonard Kinsman, who serviced our account, were both helpful and pleasant.

The combination of financing from Iselin and retained earnings greatly improved our cash position. When we gathered at the annual meeting of shareholders in March 1958, we could report that we were on a current basis with all of our creditors. In addition, we were prepared to pay off the remainder of the indebtedness to Bell Aircraft during the year. Relief and congratulations were the order of the day.

Some Ad Hoc Financing

But there was no time to relax. Financing had to keep pace with the sales growth. In 1959, the Iselin term loan, which had been partially repaid, was restored to its original amount of $200,000.

During the same year, we benefited from the sale of convertible subordinated debentures, in the amount of $125,000, at 6.5 percent. Director George Olmsted, who had proposed this action, arranged to place these debentures with the Hawkeye Security Insurance Company and the United Security Insurance Company of Des Moines. Proceeds from the sale of these debentures financed the construction and equipping of Oak Street Building Number 3—the steel receiving center and cut-up line. By 1964, when our financial situation had improved, we were able to convert these debentures into 19,087 shares of common stock.

In 1960, we again went to the Central State Bank for a loan of $85,000 to finance the construction of the new warehouse, Oak Street Building Number 4. This was a 10-year loan at 5.5 percent, secured by a first mortgage. In 1961, we paid off the $200,000 term loan with the Iselin firm and negotiated a new first mortgage loan of $400,000 at 7 percent. The new loan called for annual payments of $50,000 over five years, with a balloon payment at the end.

New Efforts at Equity Financing

Although these ad hoc arrangements kept our head above water, it was increasingly evident that we were outgrowing the sources of finance to which we then had access. It seemed that we were scurrying

Home-O-Nize net sales during the Operation Bootstrap years.

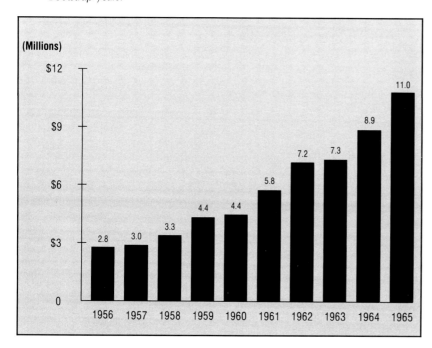

around much of the time trying to arrange debt financing on rather short maturities.

Our common stock was still regarded as very speculative, with sales negligible during the first few years of Operation Bootstrap. In 1959, common stock in the amount of $21,300 was sold, together with $4,400 of preferred stock. We sold common stock worth $50,000 in 1960, and the same amount the following year. Annual stock sales of this magnitude required only relatively simple filings with the Securities and Exchange Commission. Most of these sales were made to existing shareholders, including many of our members. Obviously, the time had arrived to consider new approaches to equity financing.

After considering various regional investment bankers, we enlisted the services of John Quail, owner of Quail and Company of Davenport, Iowa, whose firm later merged into Dain, Kalman & Quail. After due deliberation, we rejected his proposal to market an issue of Home-O-Nize common stock. We thought his proposed sale price to be too low—in terms of the price-earnings ratio—and his commission for underwriting to be too high. Instead, in 1962, we raised $300,000 with the sale of an issue of preferred stock carrying a dividend of 6.5 percent. No further equity financing occurred within the Bootstrap years, except for a precedent-setting common stock offering of $41,300 made to our members in 1964.

Obviously, our efforts at equity financing were not providing the capital needed to finance our growth. Our major source of debt financing—the Iselin term loan—was tied to factoring, a process we increasingly wished to discontinue. The factoring process, although it provided us with funds, was time-consuming and complicated. From our contacts with dealers, we had learned the conventional wisdom of the day, which held that factoring implied financial weakness and thus carried a degree of stigma.

Long-Term Debt: "A Piece of the Rock"

We therefore initiated a search for a long-term loan, focusing our attention on insurance companies. I particularly remember one futile trip to Des Moines. Neither our Iowa location nor my presentation of Home-O-Nize's progress and outlook impressed the loan officers whom I visited. Perhaps their attitude reflected the prevailing view from the capital city, which cast doubt on the viability of any venture beyond its environs.

We fared better with the Prudential Insurance Company, one of several non-Iowa organizations that we investigated. Following the suggestion of John Quail, to whom we paid a finder's fee, we made initial contact with William Grant, regional manager of Prudential's Small Loan Department in Minneapolis. A Prudential team, after reviewing the financial documents we submitted, came to Muscatine to look us over. Within a few weeks, we had reached an agreement in principle. The commitments in the agreement were reasonable ones with which we could live.

The unsecured loan from Prudential, made in 1962, was for $1 million at 6.25 percent for 15 years. This represented a major breakthrough in our battle for more adequate financing. In December, we drew down $400,000 to pay off the Iselin and Central State Bank loans, thereby discontinuing factoring. The remaining $600,000, drawn down in early 1963, enlarged our working capital and provided funds for plant expansion.

This was just the beginning of a long association. In October 1965, just before the end of Operation Bootstrap, we negotiated an increase in the loan amount to $2 million including $800,000 remaining on the original note, with a closing date scheduled for April 15, 1966. The aggregate was rescheduled with maturities over a 15-year period, carrying a composite interest rate of 5.94 percent. Our arrangements with Prudential brought to Home-O-Nize the kind of financial security implied in that company's "Rock of Gibraltar" advertisements.

As we reached the end of Operation Bootstrap, we thought, quite correctly, that we had cause for celebration. We had distanced ourselves from the cash stringencies of the 1950s. The Prudential loan helped to ease cash flow. What was even more important, from a larger perspective, it allowed managers to reallocate the time and attention they had been giving for so long to the often frantic search for funds.

Relations with Shareholders

Despite our unsuccessful efforts to market common stock during from 1956 to 1965, we expected that Home-O-Nize's continuing profitability would facilitate such financing before long. Therefore, we took several actions that we thought would improve the marketability of our stock and enhance the image of Home-O-Nize in the eyes of our shareholders.

Several stock splits were made for the purpose of increasing the float and broadening the market for Home-O-Nize shares. A 10-for-1 split occurred at the end of 1957, a 5-for-1 split in November 1962, and a stock dividend of 5 percent at the end of 1964. These actions were intended to keep the price of the stock below $20 per share and also to encourage existing shareholders to sell some of the additional stock that they received. Little of the additional stock, however, found its way into the market. The earlier purchasers of Home-O-Nize stock, having ridden out our depressed years, simply added the new shares to their portfolios.

The 1959 annual report included, for the first time, photographs of the company's facilities and products. Previous annual reports were typed on stencils and printed on office duplicating machines.

Information for shareholders was also important. Through 1958, our annual report had been a copy of a typewritten communication issued over my signature, using the data developed by our auditors but omitting their accountants' opinion. The annual report for 1959 included, for the first time, photographs of our facilities (Oak Street Building Numbers 1, 2, and 3, and the Geneva Plant); photographs of H-O-N products and Prime-Movers; a map showing H-O-N warehouses and Prime-Mover distributors; a president's letter to the members, stockholders, and friends of The Home-O-Nize Co.; condensed comparative balance sheets; an income statement; a 10-year summary of financial data; a consolidated balance sheet; a consolidated income statement; a consolidated statement of surplus; and an "Accountants' Opinion" as prepared by McGladrey, Hansen, Dunn & Company. Finally, the report listed the directors and officers of Home-O-Nize and Prime-Mover, together with our legal counsel and auditors. Although the design varied from year to year, subsequent reports contained similar information in sufficient detail to inform shareholders of the company's progress.

We first employed McGladrey, Hansen, Dunn & Co. as corporate auditors for 1956. Their audit reports were used internally by the board of directors and officers. As they related to The Prime-Mover Co., they had been submitted to Bell.

Dividend Policy. Since the payment of quarterly dividends on Home-O-Nize common stock was initiated in 1955, not a quarter has been missed. In 1963, a year-end extra dividend was added, a practice that continued for several years. Cash dividends on common stock increased each year from the 1956 to 1965 with only one exception, the result of a drop in earnings associated with the recession of 1958–1959. In the aggregate, the purchaser of one share for $100 in 1955 received $170.99 in dividends during the ensuing 10 years. Not a bad return!

Throughout the years from 1956 to 1965, 25.1 percent of net earnings was paid out in common stock dividends, and

ANNUAL REPORT
1959
THE HOME-O-NIZE CO.
MUSCATINE, IOWA

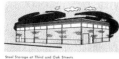

3.9 percent in preferred dividends, making a total payout of $809,313. By the end of this period, the board had formally adopted a policy of limiting the payment of annual dividends to between one-fourth and one-third of the net earnings of the previous year. This guideline emerged out of the experience of the Bootstrap years, when retained earnings provided much of the badly needed cash flow to support our expanding operations. The policy resulted in a continuing enlargement of equity in addition to providing funds for greater working capital and fixed assets.

In addition to receiving an increasing amount of dividends, Home-O-Nize shareholders had other reasons for rejoicing. A high return on equity, which stood at nearly 25 percent in 1965, coupled with the company's record of growth, resulted in substantial gains in the market value of our stock. With the market price adjusted for splits and stock dividends, the increase was about sixfold over the 10 years following 1956.

Sources of Capital

Throughout the years of Operation Bootstrap, we remained optimistic that the price-earnings ratio at which our stock sold would increase enough to justify appreciable equity financing. The ratio gradually improved to just less than 10 times earnings by 1965.

We also began to appreciate the leverage offered by long-term debt of the type represented by the term loan from Prudential. By maintaining a ratio of debt to permanent capital (equity plus debt) of between 20 and 40 percent, we increased our ability to show a high return on our equity. Consolidated net income as a percentage of equity advanced from just more than 10 percent in 1957 to nearly 25 percent in 1965.

Without quite realizing it, we were putting into place the elements of a program for self-financing our continued expansion. Retained earnings, resulting from our policy of limited dividend payout, plus the leverage obtained by substantial use of long-term debt, would combine to fund future expansion at an annual rate of 15 to 20 percent.

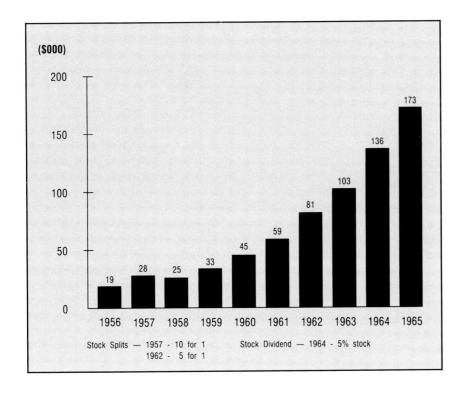

Common stock dividends during the Operation Bootstrap years.

CHAPTER TWELVE

People and Policies

Expanding product lines and production facilities were essential to the success of Home-O-Nize. Without effective marketing and distribution, our growth would have faltered. Without sound business practices and adequate financing, the fledgling Home-O-Nize could not have prospered. The company's progress in each of these areas was the result of the competence, loyalty, dedication, imagination, and hard work of our members, guided by the policies and programs developed by management, authorized by the board of directors, and implemented by management.

Board of Directors

At the beginning of Operation Bootstrap in 1956, our five-man board consisted of Clement T. Hanson, H. Wood Miller, Carl Umlandt, Kenneth Fairall, and myself. I was the only person on the board having management responsibility. Although founders of the company, neither Hanson nor Miller was then active in the business. Umlandt, who had joined the board in 1949, was in the button business in Muscatine, and Fairall, on the board since 1950, operated a paint store and then served as postmaster.

A number of new faces would appear on the board during the ensuing 10 years. Two of these new faces were members of

Home-O-Nize management. But more of them were outsiders, continuing our policy of having a largely outside board of directors.

Changes in Personnel. The annual meeting of shareholders in March 1958 was a time of major change. The size of the board was increased from five to seven. Hanson, Umlandt, Fairall, and I continued to serve; but Miller, whose interests were not strongly oriented toward board deliberations, retired.

Three new directors were elected—Stanley M. Howe, William Duval, and George H. Olmsted. Because Howe and Duval held important management positions, their board participation was considered desirable. Olmsted, with whom we had become well-acquainted during his service for Bell on the Prime-Mover board, brought to the Home-O-Nize Board a broad background of managerial and financial experience.

With these changes, we had three insiders—Stanley, Howe, and Duval—and four outsiders—Hanson, Umlandt, Fairall, and Olmsted. This division was consistent with our belief that the diverse experiences and talents of outside directors would broaden the composite viewpoint of the board. It would also distinguish the role of the board—approving the strategy of the corporation and appraising performance—

from that of management—developing the strategy and the tactics to carry out that strategy.

Miller's departure from the board of directors in 1958 marked the end of his active participation in the affairs of Home-O-Nize, although he continued as a shareholder and, on occasion, undertook industrial design assignments for our product engineers. Hanson and I were distressed at the loss of an original partner, but we recognized that Miller would be happier doing industrial design work in his own company. Later, Miller joined Sears Manufacturing Company of Davenport, manufacturers of tractor accessories and components, where he was employed in the industrial design area until his retirement. When Miller left the board, we paid tribute to the role that he had played in the early days of Home-O-Nize. Without his interest and imagination, we might never have been enthused about the manufacture of kitchen cabinets and appliances, and Home-O-Nize might never have been born.

In March 1959, we elected to the board John S. Latta, president of Latta's, Incorporated, a wholesaler and retailer of office furniture and supplies in Cedar Falls, Iowa. He replaced Fairall, who had left Muscatine to accept a government appointment in Des Moines. Latta was selected on the basis of Duval's recommendation, following a careful review of Home-O-Nize's most effective customers. He provided the viewpoint of the wholesaler, the retailer, and the purchaser of office products—a most valuable insight for the board. John was a fine addition—an experienced, pleasant, outgoing, and capable executive.

No further changes occurred in the board until August 1961, when Olmsted resigned because of the growing pressures of his work for the International Bank in Washington, D.C. We were reluctant to lose the sound judgment that Olmsted had brought to our deliberations. In November 1961, the board elected James H. Delaney, a partner of Delaney & Woods, a certified public accounting firm in Chicago. Northern Trust of Chicago recommended Delaney, one of whose clients was a local

manufacturer. Delaney brought broad experience in corporate finance, including active participation in a number of turn-around situations of faltering companies.

The next change in the composition of the board occurred on the eve of the annual meeting in April 1963, when directors were informed about Duval's termination. To avoid a reduction in the size of the board at the last minute, David H. Stanley, my eldest son and attorney for the company, was elected to the seat vacated by Duval. Dave resigned within a few months, however, because of the heavy demands of his legal work and his obligations as a member of the Iowa House of Representatives. We operated as a board of six until the annual meeting in April 1964. At that time, my younger son, Richard H. Stanley, was elected to the board. Dick was then a vice president and secretary of Stanley Engineering Co.

In the latter part of 1965, further changes were necessitated by a resignation and a death. Delaney's resignation in August was mutually agreeable. Jim, an extremely conservative individual, was uncomfortable with our growth process, which he felt was unnecessarily risky. He advocated slower growth and tighter financial practices, but the board and management could not accept such a conservative approach to business policy-making. Then Carl Umlandt's unfortunate death in December 1965 deprived us of an experienced director who had made important contributions during our formative years.

To replace these two directors, we elected Albert H. Hinkle of Cedar Rapids and Clarence D. Ager of Muscatine. Hinkle, a certified public accountant with an engineering background, had formerly been a partner of Ernst & Ernst. He was then operating a retail business in Cedar Rapids, but he had undertaken several consulting assignments for Home-O-Nize. We valued his experience and point of view. Ager, then manager of the F. W. Woolworth store in Muscatine, was selected to succeed Umlandt to reflect the point of view of local investors.

With these changes, the directors at the end of 1965 were, in order of seniority,

Howe Given Home-O-Nize Promotion

STANLEY M. HOWE

The Home-O-Nize Co. announced today that Stanley M. Howe has been elected Executive Vice-President by the board of directors.

As executive vice-president, Howe will be responsible for all operations of The Home-O-Nize Co., including Luxco Co. in La Crosse, Wisc. He will continue as vice-president of the production division.

Howe has been an employee of The Home-O-Nize Co. for over 13 years. He is chairman of the Commission on Education of the First Methodist church, president of the Rotary club and is serving on the Library board of trustees.

Howe and his wife, Helen, live at 715 West Fourth. They are the parents of two sons and one daughter.

Stanley Howe becomes executive vice president, April 1961 (from the Muscatine Journal).

C. M. Stanley, Hanson, Howe, Latta, R. H. Stanley, Ager, and Hinkle—two insiders and five outsiders.

Changes in Procedures.   Board changes were not limited to membership. The style of operation was changing as well. Advance scheduling of quarterly meetings replaced the haphazard practice of meeting on short notice at the call of the president. This change was made primarily to accommodate directors residing away from Muscatine, but it also proved generally beneficial to the decision-making process. Scheduled quarterly meetings encouraged more adequate preparation of agenda, reports, and other materials for advance circulation among directors. The result was more thorough discussion of matters requiring board action.

Another change involved the role of the Prime-Mover board, made in 1961. This became possible with Prime-Mover's payment of the last of the Bell notes in 1958. At that time, Olmsted and Gisel, the Bell representatives, had withdrawn from the Prime-Mover board, and were replaced by Howe and Dahl. As the result of a policy decision made in 1961, Prime-Mover would be considered a Home-O-Nize operating division even though it continued legally as a separate corporation. Policy matters requiring board consideration were, henceforth, dealt with by the Home-O-Nize board. Subsequently, the Prime-Mover board acted primarily to legitimize the policy decisions taken by the parent company's board and to function as legally required. This decision permitted the Prime-Mover board to be reduced to three members—Stanley, Howe, and Dahl. This action was significant for the subsequent history of HON INDUSTRIES because it established a pattern regarding the size, membership, and function of boards of directors of subsidiary companies that would be acquired.

An Outside Board

From an early date, we had seen the advantages of a board of directors made up predominantly of outsiders to Home-O-Nize. Independent outside directors, properly selected, owed no allegiance to managers. Bringing many different perspectives to bear on the issues under discussion, they could represent the interests of the shareholders, challenge management, and view the overall picture.

Gradually, with the shift to more outside directors, the board would focus to a greater extent on establishment of broad corporate policies and long-range objectives. Step by step, greater separation of the responsibilities of the board and of management resulted, with the proper roles of each becoming better understood and respected. The growing strength of outside membership aided this process.

Management

A gradual shifting of greater responsibility to Stan Howe was, undoubtedly, the major change in the organization of corporate decision making during this period. With his elevation to executive vice president in April 1961, he became our chief operating officer. This move relieved me of part of my executive responsibility and allowed me to direct my attention more to policy and planning. The change also provided greater coordination of the various divisions. With the implementation of this arrangement, Stan and I strengthened our personal relationship, developing a special pattern of operation with respect to making and carrying out important decisions.

I made the decision to advance Howe to the position of executive vice president despite my recognition that such action would likely result in Duval's resignation. Duval had appeared to be restless or uneasy about something almost from the beginning of his employment in 1955. However, whatever problem existed only simmered for the next six years. After the appointment of Howe as executive vice president, it became increasingly clear to me that Duval would never be happy except as heir apparent to the president. As this was not possible, the only course of action was to encourage his resignation. Our parting in May 1963 was amicable. Duval went on to organize and subsequently liquidate a company of his own and then served as sales manager for a competitor. In 1972, we called him back to serve as sales manager of what turned out to be a short-lived new product program.

The Howe-Stanley relationship functioned well in the years after Stan's appointment as executive vice president. At the annual meeting in April 1964, Howe was elected president. I became chairman of the board, retaining my position as chief executive officer.

The organizational structure gradually became more formal as functions within divisions were more precisely delineated. With growth, each division appointed executives and supervisors to handle specific responsibilities. There came to be more specialists and fewer jacks-of-all-trades.

Changes in the titles of our key executives reflected this growing tendency toward more sharply defined areas of responsibility and lines of authority. In 1964, Rex Bennett was elected vice president of manufacturing services. A year later, Phil Temple became vice president of product engineering. In the same year, Max Collins was elected vice president of personnel. Bennett and Temple reported to Howe in the latter's capacity as head of the Production Division, and Collins reported to Howe in his other role as president of The Home-O-Nize Co.

By 1955, we concluded that our profit-sharing program did not provide sufficient incentives to management. Therefore, we established a bonus program for officers based on the previous year's performance. In the ensuing years, we developed formulas and guidelines to determine the amount of each individual's bonus.

Personnel Policies

From the beginning, we regarded people as Home-O-Nize's greatest strength and resource. Home-O-Nize could never have survived and prospered in highly competitive markets without able people. We had no lead in technology and no entrenched market position. Thus, we believed it was essential to develop personnel policies that strengthened Home-O-Nize's ability to re-

Stan Howe and Max Stanley formed a dynamic team. Howe, with manufacturing genius and administrative acumen, shared Stanley's vision and desire for growth. Howe became vice president, production in 1954, executive vice president in 1961, president in 1964, and chairman after Stanley's death in 1984.

Organization of the Home-O-Nize Co. in April 1964.

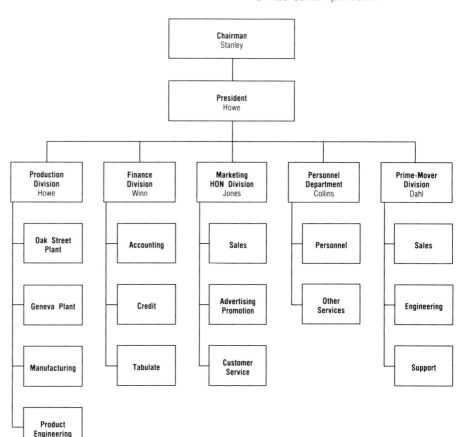

cruit and hold loyal, dependable, competent, and cooperative people at all levels. The principles of human relations that we set forth in the early days of the company were reflected in the programs and practices established during Operation Bootstrap.

Compensation.   Adequate wages and salaries continued to be the cornerstone of our approach to member relationships. We sought to pay our members more than the prevailing medians in the various markets from which we recruited. Plant and office workers were recruited primarily from Muscatine and the surrounding area. But for toolmakers and certain other skills, we had to look toward the Quad Cities of Iowa and Illinois. For experienced managers and technicians, we were competing nationally. Surveys furnished us with information about prevailing wages and salaries for each classification of plant and office workers in the relevant market area.

For each classification of plant workers, officeworkers, supervisors, and professionals, minimum and maximum rates were calculated, along with rates at the quarter-point, midpoint, and three-quarter–point between the minimum and maximum. Newly employed workers were normally paid at the minimum, or entry, rate for the classification. If their work proved to be satisfactory, they were advanced automatically to the quarter-point and midpoint rates. Advance beyond the midpoint depended on merit.

A cost-of-living adjustment, established in 1947, was continued through the years of Operation Bootstrap. As the cost-of-living index rose, upward adjustments were made in payrolls. Accumulated cost-of-living adjustments were wrapped into an annual across-the-board wage or salary adjustment, normally made at the end of the calendar year.

Group incentives for production workers, as described earlier, were implemented initially in 1958 for the purpose of encouraging teamwork and cooperation, thereby improving productivity. Group incentives were structured to allow an average bonus of about 20 percent above

hourly rates. We gradually expanded the use of group incentives.

The performance of each member was reviewed at least annually. New and lower echelon members were reviewed more frequently. Evaluation of performance provided the basis for merit adjustments above the midpoint of each classification as well as for advancement into positions of higher classification. The performance of executives was reviewed annually, at which time salary increases were considered.

Fringe Benefits.   Fringe benefits were constantly improving, generally keeping a few steps ahead of local practice. By 1965, we were granting seven-and-one-half days of paid holidays, as compared with six in 1955. Our health and life insurance programs improved. Our vacation policy, calling initially for two weeks of paid vacation after one year of employment, added another half day for each year of service up to a total of three weeks. This permitted members to take a day off now and then without cutting into the traditional two-week summer vacation, usually scheduled at the time of the annual plant shutdown. A formal sick leave program allowed up to five days per year, noncumulative, to members who had been employed at least one year. Members with longer service could accumulate up to two weeks of sick leave.

Although no formal educational assistance program had been established by 1965, we had started to grant tuition refunds to individuals who took night or Saturday courses deemed by management to be relevant to their jobs. Starting in 1958, continuing education programs from Iowa State University, the University of Iowa, and other institutions were available to members at various levels. Beyond this, on-the-job training was a continuing responsibility of all supervisors, whether in the plant or in the office.

Financial Participation by Members

Our previously established profit-sharing program continued to be the cornerstone of financial participation by our members. The formula for computing profit sharing, adopted earlier by the board, provided one pre-tax dollar for profit sharing for each three dollars of after-tax net income. Although the details of distribution varied somewhat from year to year, cash profit-sharing payments in 1965 consisted of 1) the equivalent of 1.25 weeks' pay, disbursed in June before the shutdown of the plant for vacation; 2) the equivalent of 2 weeks' pay disbursed in December before the holiday season; and 3) the equivalent of 3 weeks' pay paid into the retirement fund. All of this amounted to an equivalent of 6.25 weeks' pay for each eligible member.

The opportunity for further financial participation by members through stock ownership continued. Members had an opportunity to purchase common stock at below market price during special offerings made in 1960, 1961, and 1964.

Our retirement program, established in 1960, became an important element of financial participation by members. A trust agreement set up a profit-sharing trust fund to which contributions were made annually. Initially, eligible members contributed 2 percent of their base pay through payroll deduction, with the company matching this amount. In addition, about one-half of the annual profit-sharing fund was paid into this retirement trust fund, the other half being disbursed in cash payments to members as mentioned above.

All members who were at least 25 years old and who had been employed for one year participated in the profit-sharing retirement program. Their interests were vested over a 10-year period. If the members were terminated before full vesting, the unvested portion was forfeited to the benefit of the other participants. Members could voluntarily contribute up to 10 percent of their base compensation through payroll deductions. Such personal contributions were fully vested, but they were not matched by the company, and they were not considered in the pro rata distribution of forfeitures or of company contributions.

Hanson, Duval, and I were the initial trustees of the fund, with Howe replacing Duval in 1963. Stein Roe and Farnham of Chicago, our investment counselors, managed the account as a balanced fund. The magnitude of the fund increased not only with contributions but also with the appreciation of the investment portfolio, plus interest and dividends earned, plus forfeitures of nonvested portions of the accounts of terminating members.

Information Participation by Members

As is so often the case when a company grows, the early informal policies and procedures must give way to more formal programs. From the inception of Home-O-Nize until about 1960, I had a personal acquaintance with nearly every member. Until near the mid-1960s, Stan Howe had similar personal relationships. Nevertheless, as the number of members increased, member-management relations needed to be systematized to preserve and, in fact, to strengthen our objectives of fair treatment, openness, and member involvement.

The vital communication process was improved in several ways. Instead of one large meeting of members, we scheduled several back-to-back sessions with smaller numbers of members in order to encourage questions and comments from those in attendance. Through most of the years of Operation Bootstrap, Howe and I shared the presentation at these meetings. We endeavored to keep our members informed about the financial progress of the company, expansion plans, new product introductions, member benefit programs, corporate problems, and the like.

Howe and Collins developed a new pattern for the two-way communication meetings that we had started earlier. About a dozen members, selected at random from office and plant, attended each session. We took care that a wide range of skills and positions was represented at each meeting and that no individual met with his or her immediate supervisor or subordinate. The chairman of the meeting, usually Stan Howe, devoted only a few minutes to a formal presentation; he then solicited questions and comments. The result was genuine two-way communication between management and members. A further step in the communication process was the continuation and improvement of the house organ, now called *ON TARGET,* edited by the personnel director and his staff.

These group meetings supplemented the normal personal communication through line organization. Supervisors, maintaining day-to-day contact with their subordinates, were responsible for answering questions and providing information as well as directing the work of members and helping them to improve their skills. Supervisors counseled with each member under his or her supervision at the time of performance reviews, made annually or more frequently in connection with merit adjustments. We expected in these ways to provide an opportunity for one-on-one discussions of performance, opportunities, and problems between a member and his or her supervisor. To improve their counseling skills, supervisors were brought together from time to time for discussion of counseling techniques.

We continued the practice of holding annual dinners for members and their spouses to recognize length of service. Very soon, we had our first 15-year veterans of Home-O-Nize. In the mid-1960s, we established "one year" dinners, inviting members, with their spouses, who had completed one year of service. This was intended to mark graduation from probationary status into full membership in the company.

During Operation Bootstrap we prepared our first comprehensive member manual, which contained complete information about our compensation policies and benefit programs. It also outlined the company's expectations regarding performance and relationships among members.

Committees that had been established earlier continued their important work. For most of the decade I chaired the General Policy Committee, but Stan took over when he was elected president. The committee met regularly to discuss member-related programs and problems.

The first annual recognition dinner was held in 1956 on the anniversary of ten years of operation. The total number of members with five years of service or more was 47.

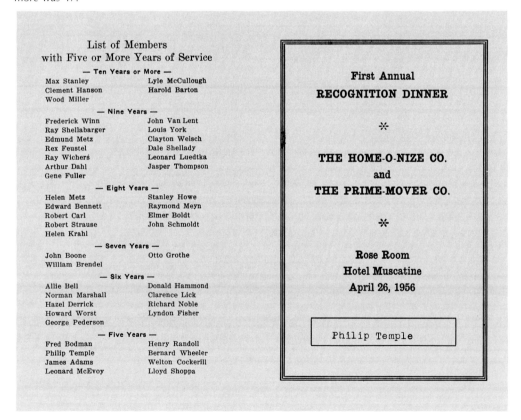

List of Members
with Five or More Years of Service

— Ten Years or More —

Max Stanley	Lyle McCullough
Clement Hanson	Harold Barton
Wood Miller	

— Nine Years —

Frederick Winn	John Van Lent
Ray Shellabarger	Louis York
Edmund Metz	Clayton Welsch
Rex Feustel	Dale Shellady
Ray Wichers	Leonard Luedtka
Arthur Dahl	Jasper Thompson
Gene Fuller	

— Eight Years —

Helen Metz	Stanley Howe
Edward Bennett	Raymond Meyn
Robert Carl	Elmer Boldt
Robert Strause	John Schmoldt
Helen Krahl	

— Seven Years —

John Boone	Otto Grothe
William Brendel	

— Six Years —

Allie Bell	Donald Hammond
Norman Marshall	Clarence Lick
Hazel Derrick	Richard Noble
Howard Worst	Lyndon Fisher
George Pederson	

— Five Years —

Fred Bodman	Henry Randoll
Philip Temple	Bernard Wheeler
James Adams	Welton Cockerill
Leonard McEvoy	Lloyd Shoppa

First Annual

RECOGNITION DINNER

✳

THE HOME-O-NIZE CO.
and
THE PRIME-MOVER CO.

✳

Rose Room
Hotel Muscatine
April 26, 1956

Philip Temple

The Activities Committee planned a number of recreational occasions, partially financed by the net proceeds from the vending machines in the office and plant. Organizing the company picnic in September was the committee's major function. As the number of members increased, these picnics became more complex and elaborate. The location of the picnic was moved from the Box Car Ranch to Erikson's Grove and then to the Kent-Stein Recreational Area to accommodate the ever-increasing attendance. By 1965, some 1,200 people—members and their families—gathered at a nearby park on a Sunday. The menu was charcoal-broiled chicken, coleslaw, beans, and rolls, with ice cream and soda pop at a nearby stand. Entertainment included rides for the kids, horseshoe pitching, music, bingo, and drawing for door prizes. On more than one occasion, the committee sweated out unpredictable weather, making a decision at about 2 A.M., which allowed for the lead time needed to prepare broiled chicken. Other festivities organized by the Activities Committee included separate Christmas parties for members and their teenaged children, a Christmas gathering for youngsters, dances, baseball and basketball teams, bowling and golf leagues, and trap shooting groups.

The Safety Committee, including members from both management and the shop floor, continued to work toward upgrading safety precautions and strengthening safety attitudes. They sought to remind both supervisors and members about the need for more careful attention to safety precautions. As a result, Home-O-Nize's safety record was well above average.

A Test of Our Human Relations Concept

During this period, we witnessed a test of the human relations concept that had originally inspired Hanson and me to found Home-O-Nize. We believed Home-O-Nize to be a good place to work. Physical facilities that were already generally satisfactory were being improved. Generous benefits were being enlarged. Continued growth of our business protected

A chorus made up of Home-O-Nize members and their spouses was featured at the third annual company family Christmas party. The chorus was directed by Max Collins and accompanied by Bill Duval.

against layoffs and provided opportunities for advancement at all levels. Above all, managers and supervisors dealt fairly with members, who were treated as human beings rather than as a commodity to be hired, used, and fired.

The test occurred in 1963, when the Teamsters Union tried to organize the plant workers at Home-O-Nize. Rumors had circulated for several years that various unions were about to launch organizing drives. Home-O-Nize was certainly an attractive target. Our employment was then close to 500, with about half of our members eligible for inclusion in a plant bargaining unit. Accordingly, it was not a surprise when we learned that the Teamsters had initiated sign-up activities. In response to a petition by the Teamsters, the National Labor Relations Board (NLRB) ordered that an election be held.

As activities by the Teamsters accelerated, we engaged legal counsel experienced in plant election procedures, established company policies to deal with the organizing effort, and began briefing our supervisors as to the do's and don'ts of

*Occasional open houses
enabled members to show
their friends and family the
products they made and
the work they performed.
Open houses also helped
recruit new members.*

handling the situation. In a way, we welcomed the test and prepared to use it as a means to present our philosophies clearly and vigorously.

We were not antiunion in principle. We fully agreed with the right of our members to designate a bargaining agent if they desired to do so. My personal beliefs then and later give great credit to the role that unions have played on behalf of workers. They have helped to counter the effects of management's lack of responsiveness to the need for fair play and equity in labor relations. Union activity in the United States before World War II greatly improved wages, benefits, and working conditions. It gave many workers a means of bargaining with management, thus bringing about a sorely needed balance to labor-management relations. As long as the increased wages and benefits obtained through collective bargaining are accompanied by growing productivity, all parties benefit—workers, industry, and the economy.

Our posture was not antiunion, but

promember. We maintained that our members did not need a union to get a fair deal at Home-O-Nize. We contended that our personnel practices, including our generous profit-sharing and retirement programs, were more beneficial than members could gain through collective bargaining. Thus, we wanted to counter the union's organizing efforts by presenting a positive, dynamic posture. We refused to be backed into a defensive position. Armed with legal advice regarding management's rights, we launched a vigorous, but factual, counter campaign presenting the company's case to the members.

The Teamster's organizers used handouts, called meetings of our members at their headquarters, and encouraged members favoring unionization to speak with their fellow workers. We responded by using handouts, calling meetings of members to present our case, and prepared our supervisors to answer questions. Of course, we hoped that those of our members who did not favor unionization would be persuasive with their uncommitted fellow employees.

After a long four weeks, September 13—the day of decision—arrived. Eligible members at the Oak Street and Geneva Plants voted under the watchful eyes of the NLRB. The polls closed, and the 243 votes were counted. About 6 P.M. we had the news: 62 votes for the Teamsters Union, 173 votes against. We were elated. We saw the margin of nearly three to one as an endorsement of the member relations programs that we had developed and cultivated since 1947.

However, the unsuccessful effort of the Teamsters did not discourage the International Association of Machinists from trying to organize the workers at Home-O-Nize. In 1965, confronted with claims that a majority of the workers in the bargaining unit had signed cards designating the Machinists as their bargaining agent, we took the lead by petitioning the NLRB for an election. Again, a clear majority of the members working in our Muscatine plants showed that they did not favor unionization. Of the 298 votes cast, 110 were for the union, and 188 against.

Corporate Citizenship

As Home-O-Nize began to prosper, we believed that much of our success was due to our willingness and ability to respond fairly to the expectations of each of several groups—shareholders, members, customers, and the general public. However, we were aware of the rising level of expectations about the performance of business in the 1950s and 1960s. Thus, we realized the importance of directing even greater attention to the area of corporate citizenship.

The increased profitability of the company during the period of Operation Bootstrap served our shareholders well, with growing dividends and higher stock prices. That members chose to turn back a strong union organizing effort appeared to demonstrate their satisfaction with corporate policies and practices. Mounting sales indicated that customers were satisfied with the way in which we were meeting their needs for products that combined high quality and moderate price.

The fourth constituency consisted of the institutions through which the expectations of the general public were expressed—federal, state, and local governments. The board of directors and management shared a conviction that the company should adhere to the spirit as well as to the letter of the law.

From the beginning we had engaged continuing legal counsel to monitor our corporate decisions. During the period of Operation Bootstrap, we initiated a practice of asking our legal counsel to make a regular and continuing review, conducted on an informal basis, of corporate compliance with the many federal and state laws and regulations that applied to our operations.

The law firm later known as Stanley, Lande, Coulter & Pearce was our legal counsel through this period and beyond. David Stanley personally handled the business of Home-O-Nize until about 1963, when Terrence Mealy took this responsibility for several years. Roger Lande assumed the role of corporation counsel in 1966.

During this period, several Standard Practice Instructions (SPIs) were written to guide officers and supervisors in matters having legal and ethical implications. A crucial matter was the structure of discounts allowed on sales of office furniture to wholesalers and dealers. SPIs were issued to make sure that our discount structures complied fully with the letter and intent of regulations promulgated by the Federal Trade Commission and other government agencies.

As Home-O-Nize and Prime-Mover became more visible in the Muscatine community, and as we employed more and more people, our efforts at responsible corporate citizenship expanded. We had always supported the United Way and other local drives. Because we wanted to do our share, we were beginning to develop a planned corporate program of philanthropy. Initially, the amounts of our gifts were determined on the basis of our best ad hoc judgment. Later, we developed a formula based on pre-tax profits.

Home-O-Nize became a member of the Chamber of Commerce, and we supported a number of individual memberships in the Junior Chamber of Commerce. We also encouraged our members to become involved in community activities.

PART FOUR

A Surge of Growth, 1966-1972

As a result of the rapid growth experienced from 1966 to 1972, the company—its name changed from The Home-O-Nize Co. to HON INDUSTRIES Inc.—became a more important factor in the national office furniture market and a more complex organization. Internal expansion of the company's office furniture business was supplemented by two substantial acquisitions: Holga Metal Products Corporation of Van Nuys, California, and Corry Jamestown Corporation of Corry, Pennsylvania. These acquisitions helped to maintain the momentum of corporate growth, more than offsetting the adverse effects of the recession of 1970–1971.

Although Prime-Mover did not enjoy as much growth during this period as did the company's office furniture business, some increase in its sales of material-handling equipment occurred. During these years Prime-Mover gradually enlarged its product offerings to the industrial market, thereby positioning itself for later growth.

This seven-year surge of growth is discussed in four chapters: Chapter 13 provides an overview, with discussions of policy, finance, and management. Chapters 14 and 15 trace the progress of The HON Company and Prime-Mover, respectively. The two acquisitions are discussed in Chapter 16.

CHAPTER THIRTEEN

From Home-O-Nize to HON INDUSTRIES

AN OVERVIEW

From 1966 to 1972, sales increased 4.5-fold, equivalent to 24 percent compounded annually. Net income grew four-fold, or at a rate of 21.7 percent compounded annually, and averaged 6.73 percent of sales. The total number of members recorded a 3.6-fold gain. Return on equity ranged between 15.8 and 24 percent for an average of 20 percent. The data shown in the bar graphs on these pages reflect two full years of operations at Holga Metal Products (acquired in 1971), but only eight months of operations at Corry Jamestown (acquired in 1972).

The basic objectives formulated during Operation Bootstrap continued to guide HON INDUSTRIES during the 1966–1972 period. Certainly we grew. We increased our total profits; we improved our economic soundness; and we became more competitive. Service to customers improved. HON INDUSTRIES became a better place in which to work as well as a better corporate citizen. The increased size and complexity of HON INDUSTRIES, however, required that we implement a basic change in our management structure, which occurred near the end of this period.

Personnel Policies

Expansion required greater attention to personnel practices. The 3.6-fold increase in members, which was only partially due to the Holga and Corry Jamestown acquisitions, required not just more people, but talented and motivated people at all levels. This necessitated an intensification of recruiting efforts. It also provided numerous opportunities for promotion from within.

Some established personnel policies were sharpened and fine-tuned, but relatively little basic change occurred. Fringe benefits were upgraded during this period. By 1972, nine-and-one-half holidays were granted annually, as compared with seven-and-one-half in 1965. The Friday after Thanksgiving and a floating holiday were added. Sick leave was raised to six days per year, with 30 days of allowable carryover from one year to the next. Benefits from our medical and hospital group insurance policies for members and their families were raised from time to time. In 1972, the company's contribution to these policies was increased from 50 to 75 percent of the premiums.

The growth of our Profit-Sharing Re-

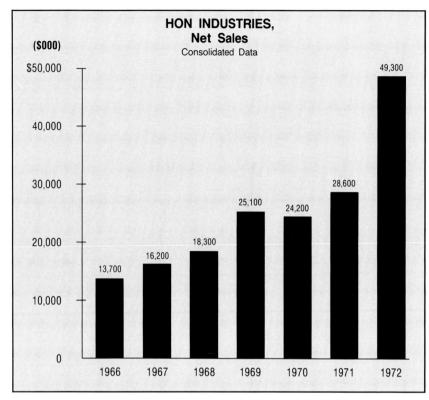

HON INDUSTRIES, consolidated data on net sales (above), net income (below), income as a percent of sales (opposite, above), and number of members (opposite, below) from 1966 to 1972.

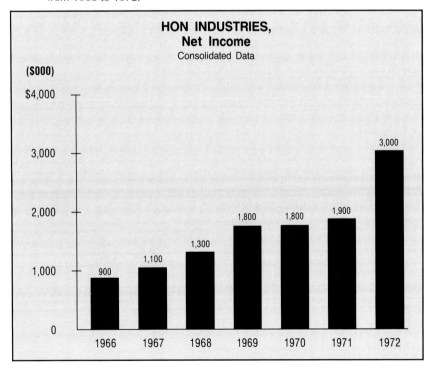

tirement Plan was most encouraging. The fund amounted to just over $6 million at the end of 1972, despite the fact that cash payments out of profit sharing averaged 2.7 weeks of pay during the period. Mandatory member contributions to the retirement fund were discontinued in 1967 when the company increased its contribution from 2 percent to 4 percent of eligible member compensation.

The success of the profit-sharing retirement program came none too soon, for 16 of our earliest members retired during the years between 1967 and 1972, including cofounder and director Clement T. Hanson. Their departures, recognized by appropriate ceremonies, plaques, and gifts at the next annual recognition dinner, provided the opportunity for them to be thanked for their contributions to HON INDUSTRIES in our troubled early days. These occasions forced us to recognize that we were no longer a fledgling company; we were moving toward maturity.

Retirement has not meant the end of our contact with the retirees, as they have been regularly invited to attend annual recognition dinners. Many of them, from time to time, have dropped by the office or the plant to visit their friends. Because the profit-sharing retirement program was relatively new, the benefits to the early retirees were less than we desired. This indicated the need for supplements, which were later provided.

All types of member participation, including profit sharing, stock offerings, and information sharing, continued. As the company grew, several executives in addition to Stan Howe became involved in the periodic member meetings. Activities such as the annual recognition dinner in the spring and the picnic in early fall continued.

The validity of our personnel policies was tested in Muscatine from time to time during this period. Union activity by the International Association of Machinists occurred again in 1967 and 1969, but no election was ordered. When the union mounted another drive in 1970, we asked the NLRB for a hearing, held in February 1971, at which the Machinists temporarily withdrew their petition for an election. Later that year, however, the Machinists petitioned again for an election, held in August. The vote, 24 percent favoring the union and 76 percent against, was even more decisive than it had been in November 1965.

Finance

The program for financing expansion, including the Prudential connection developed near the end of Operation Bootstrap, proved adequate from 1966 to 1972. Retained earnings supplemented by a moderate amount of equity financing enlarged the shareholders' equity, thereby providing the foundation for increasing the company's long-term debt held by Prudential.

During this period, retained earnings rose from $1.8 to $10.6 million. This six-fold increase was accomplished even though quarterly dividends on common stock were frequently raised.

Equity financing included a 15,000-share offering to existing shareholders in 1966; a public offering of 100,000 shares in 1970; and offerings to members of 4,829 shares in 1967, 11,450 shares in 1970, and 10,780 shares in 1971. Not all of these shares were new issues, as some shares that were sold to members during these years had been purchased earlier from shareholders to be held as treasury stock.

In response to queries from individuals, estates, and others who wished to divest themselves of the preferred stock issued earlier, we initiated a program to make an annual purchase of 100 of these shares. Each year, owners of preferred stock were invited to propose a price at which they would sell their shares to HON INDUSTRIES. One hundred shares were then purchased from the lowest bidders.

On balance, these equity transactions increased the book value of capital stock, including paid-in capital, from $1.32 million at the beginning of the period to $4.5 million at the end, a net gain of $3.26 million.

The size of the Prudential loan changed several times during these years. From a level of $1 million, we negotiated

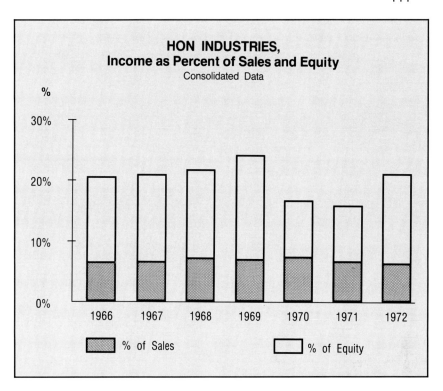

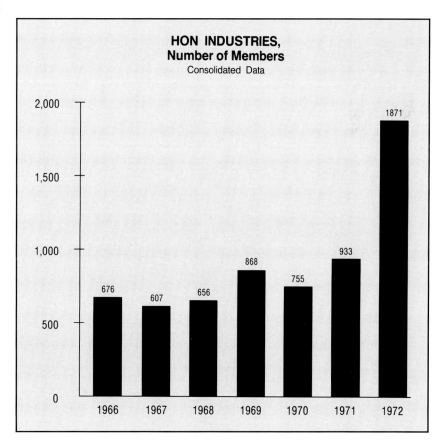

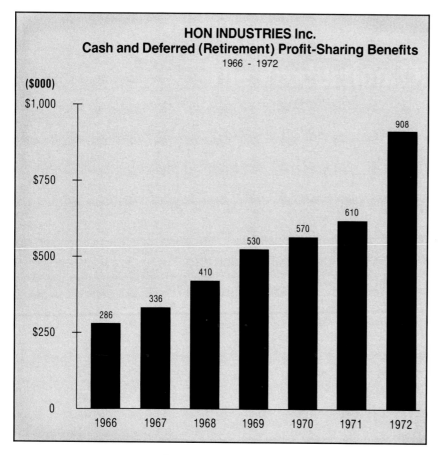

HON INDUSTRIES Inc.
Cash and Deferred (Retirement) Profit-Sharing Benefits
1966 - 1972

($000)

$1,000

$750

$500

$250

0

908
610
570
530
410
336
286

1966 1967 1968 1969 1970 1971 1972

*HON INDUSTRIES, cash
and deferred (retirement)
profit-sharing benefits, from
1966 to 1972.*

*When Esther McCormick
retired in 1974 after more
than 20 years of service,
she took more than this
rocking chair with her. The
Member Profit-Sharing
Retirement Trust, which
was started in 1960,
helped add prosperity to
years that had traditionally
been bleak for many
Americans.*

an increase to $2 million in 1966, to $3 million in 1967, and to $5 million in 1969. Each time, the composite interest rate on the loan rose—from 5.94 to 6.5 percent and then to 7.85 percent. The rising interest rates were a sad omen of what was yet to come.

At the time that we negotiated the 1969 increase, we expected to draw down the funds in 1970 to finance plant expansion and to increase working capital. When the immediate need vanished because of the recession of 1970–1971, the increase was canceled, with the amount of the Prudential loan reverting to $3 million.

We financed the Holga acquisition in 1971 without additional equity or long-term financing. However, the purchase of Corry Jamestown in 1972 called for sizable financing. The Prudential loan was increased to $8 million at an 8 percent composite interest rate, with semiannual installments to run from 1977 to 1987. This financing was supplemented by a $3 million term loan from Northern Trust Company, with interest at 115 percent of prime rate. Principal payments on the Northern Trust loan ran to 1976 with payments made semiannually.

Investor Return

The financial situation from 1966 to 1972 improved for our investors as well as for the company. Stock splits and stock dividends, as well as larger cash dividends, sweetened the return to those shareholders who held their stock. A 3-for-1 split in 1968 and a 2-for-1 split in 1969 were supplemented by a 5 percent stock dividend in 1966. As a result, at the close of 1972 each shareholder had 630 shares for every 100 shares he or she had held at the beginning of 1966.

Payment of quarterly cash dividends continued. By the end of the period, the 71st consecutive dividend had been paid. The amount of dividends paid increased every year except for the recession year of 1971, when they were held at the same level as 1970. The magnitude of cash dividends per share, after adjustment for stock splits and stock dividends, was 2.67 times that received in 1965. Shareholders who retained the additional shares resulting from stock dividends and stock splits would have received $17.39 in cash dividends in 1972 for each dollar received in 1965. Both managers and shareholders were gratified by these results.

The market value of shares of HON INDUSTRIES increased significantly from 1966 to 1972. The stock's price-earnings ratio advanced from 9.7 to 18.7, with an interim high of 25.7 at the end of 1969. These were bonanza days when many growth stocks were enjoying very high price-earnings ratios. We were not to see such high ratios again for another decade.

We were more than gratified that our early investors were being rewarded for their patience in holding on to their stock. The company's increased prosperity made possible these improved returns to shareholders. At the same time, this economic well-being allowed a substantial increase in retained earnings, which, along with long-term debt, financed plant expansion and enlarged working capital. During this seven-year period, aggregate dividend payments represented only 26.3 percent of earnings, consistent with our guidelines relating to payout.

Introduction of the Computer

In July 1968, HON INDUSTRIES took a mighty step forward when our first computer, a Honeywell Model 120, came on-line after several years of preparation for computerization. The growing magnitude and complexity of our operations necessitated mastery of the intricacies of electronic information processing. Never again could we be solely dependent on manually processed data. We would be constantly challenged by the rapid development of computer technology as well as by the expanding needs of our own data processing. I'm sure that in 1968 we failed to realize how difficult it would be to keep up and what a minor step we had taken with the Honeywell 120.

Contrary to the experience of so many companies, installation of computer hardware and software at HON INDUS-

Volleyball, picnics, and open houses remained an important part of member relations. Such activities were organized through the efforts of the personnel department.

The introduction of computers was smooth and complete, largely because of the commitment of Stan Howe and Max Stanley and the work of William F. Cory, a consultant who later became a board member.

TRIES created relatively few headaches. The early success of our computer program was due to several years of advance preparation, outstanding performance by those responsible for installing the system, and, of major importance, the support, guidance, and leadership of top executives.

Preparation for computerized data processing had been under way at HON INDUSTRIES for several years. William F. Cory, later to become a member of our board of directors, had been employed as a consultant to work with the company's staff and develop manual systems that could be readily adapted to electronic operation. These systems included production and material control, payroll, accounting, and management information.

The Honeywell 120 was installed on the second floor of Oak Street Building Number 1, the old brick button plant in which Home-O-Nize had started many years before. Air conditioning and climate-control devices were installed to maintain appropriate temperature and humidity. A staff of 13, supervised by Robert Putnam as data processing manager, took over the programing, keypunching, and other operations.

We had hardly congratulated ourselves for our new computer when we were face-to-face with the ever-continuing necessity of upgrading both hardware and software. Only 15 months later, the Honeywell 120 was upgraded to a 125 by adding

memory capacity. Two years later, in 1971, a Honeywell 115/2 mainframe was installed. Then in 1972, a major upgrading to a Honeywell 2200 occurred. The Model 120 had been only a beginning. In just over four years, three new configurations of hardware and constant upgrading of software were needed to carry on data processing operations at HON INDUSTRIES.

Our electronic progress in this period can be measured by comparing the capabilities of the Model 2200 and the initial Model 120: The Model 2200 had between four and five times the speed of the Model 120 and at least three times the memory. Significantly, it allowed a change from tapes to disks.

Keypunch operations were initially performed by the computer staff, but they were later transferred to other departments. At the end of 1972 the computer staff, headed by Gail Kauffman, included six people.

A Change of Name

Despite the cheerful appeal of the two quarter notes in the O of Home-O-Nize, the corporate name became increasingly out of tune with the thrust of our office furniture and material-handling businesses. As mentioned earlier, we had begun in the early 1950s to use H-O-N to identify our office products division, but our dealers and customers had disregarded the hyphens and substituted one syllable, HON, for the three syllables, H-O-N. Heeding the adage that the customer is always right, we dropped the hyphens and began using HON on our office product catalogs and literature. By the end of 1966, we were using The HON Company to identify the office furniture division of the corporation.

These changes met an immediate need, but Home-O-Nize as a corporate identity became less and less appropriate for our business. Although well aware that we needed a change, we agonized for several years over what the new name should be. A name change contest among our members produced 190 different suggestions, with prizes in the form of a share of company stock awarded to each of 10 members. Some proposals incorporated a geographic name, such as Iowa, Muscatine, or Middle West. Others included a product name. Such suggestions seemed inappropriate as we were already a multi-product company, and we anticipated expansion beyond the Middle West. Several members urged that the name include Stanley, an idea I quickly vetoed. Two of the winning contest suggestions included HON. Finally, after months of serious consideration by management, we recommended to the board of directors that our corporate name be changed to HON INDUSTRIES Inc. Acting on the board's recommendation, shareholders at the 1969 annual meeting amended our charter accordingly.

HON INDUSTRIES Inc. continues to serve as our corporate identity, even though we have frequently been asked to explain its origin. The use of three letters—HON—is in keeping with the tendency of many corporations to shorten their names. The inclusion of the word "industries" avoids any problem resulting from changing product lines. HON INDUSTRIES has been a comfortable name to live with; after all, a rose is a rose by any name.

Management

From its early days, The Home-O-Nize Co. and then HON INDUSTRIES functioned as one big family. Manufacture of office furniture and material-handling equipment was integrated into a single product division. The HON and Prime-Mover Divisions were concerned primarily with sales, although Prime-Mover later handled design of products and purchase of outside parts. Such functions as personnel, accounting, and finance were totally integrated. Although revenues, costs, and operating margins were calculated separately for the office furniture and material-handling equipment businesses, the company functioned as a single profit center.

The acquisition of Holga in 1971 and Corry Jamestown a year later signaled the need to modify our organizational structure and management pattern. These acquired companies could not readily be in-

tegrated into our existing organizational pattern. It was time to create a corporate staff and to treat HON, Prime-Mover, Holga, and Corry Jamestown as separate profit centers.

Stan Howe, as president of HON INDUSTRIES, headed the newly organized corporate staff, which initially included functions related to finance, accounting, personnel, data processing, and planning. To assist Howe, Art Dahl began in March 1969 to divide his time between Prime-Mover and HON INDUSTRIES; in December 1970, he became full-time senior vice president of HON INDUSTRIES. Other officers assigned to the corporate level included Max A. Collins, vice president of personnel; Robert Putnam, vice president of systems and data processing (who resigned within a year); and Fred S. Winn, secretary-treasurer.

Functions transferred to the corporate

THE H-O-N CO., MUSCATINE, IOWA

HON INDUSTRIES

(top) The original Home-O-Nize logo designed by founders Hanson and Miller in 1945.
(center) In the 1950s, H-O-N identified by the company's office products division.
(bottom) The final corporate name was determined after a contest among members and months of consideration by management.

staff included plant engineering headed by Maurice Jones, and manufacturing research headed by Clare Patterson. Among the individuals assigned to the corporate staff were Robert Carl, assistant to the president; Kermit Cook, assistant secretary and assistant treasurer; and Mary Ann Stange, an assistant to Collins.

Stan Howe wore two hats—president of HON INDUSTRIES and operating head of The HON Company. Because of managerial problems that emerged at Corry Jamestown, Howe assumed a third role as president of that subsidiary. Gene Waddell, promoted to the position of vice president and general manager of The Prime-Mover Co., reported to Stan Howe, as did Jim Arthur, whom we retained as president of Holga.

By the end of 1972, a good start had been made toward an organizational structure better-suited to expansion. Functions of the corporate staff were limited to those operations related to overall corporate matters and to those operations that could be handled more effectively at the corporate level. The restructuring called for substantial changes in the accounting system to accommodate four profit centers plus a corporate staff. Performance of each of the operating divisions was closely monitored. The primary measure of profitability was the ratio of operating income to total assets employed in the division. A secondary measure was operating income as a percentage of sales of the division.

As the shape of the revised structure became clear to management and the board of directors, we became increasingly aware of the need to assure the availability of an adequate number of capable executives to manage the operating units and to staff the corporate organization. This led to greater emphasis on internal executive development and recruitment.

Board of Directors

Several changes made during this seven-year period strengthened our board of directors. We established even more firmly the principle of an outside board. This, in turn, led to the creation of several committees of the board to facilitate its functioning.

In 1966, I invited Thomas G. MacGowan, a retired Firestone executive, to join our board. I had known Tom for several years through our mutual activities in the World Federalist movement. Tom brought to the board experience in marketing and planning. Unfortunately, he resigned the following year after he had made new business connections deemed to be incompatible with continued service on our board.

To replace MacGowan, we selected Dr. Dan Throop Smith, a professor at the Harvard Graduate School of Business Administration. I had become acquainted with Dan while we both were members of the board of trustees of Iowa Wesleyan College located in Mt. Pleasant, Iowa, Dan's hometown. An expert in the field of taxes and finance, Dan had served as an assistant secretary of the treasury during the Eisenhower administration. He possessed a keen mind and had the ability to ask perceptive questions at the right time, so he proved very quickly to be a most effective addition to the board. Soon after he came on our board, he gave up active teaching at Harvard to become a Fellow at the Hoover Institute of Stanford University in Palo Alto, California. Serving on other boards of directors, writing, lecturing, traveling, and bird watching with his wife, Dan was a busy person. He and his wife, Martha, immediately became respected and cherished members of the HON family.

No other changes were made until 1970 when William F. Cory and Austin T. Hunt, Jr., joined the board. Cory, an independent consultant who was serving several industries in Iowa and nearby states, had done a good deal of work for Home-O-Nize in preparation for the installation of our computers. Cory's education in general engineering plus experience with Ernst & Ernst, the accountants, gave him a sound knowledge of business problems, particularly those related to accounting and information systems. Cory's down-to-earth, cautious, and somewhat conservative approach was to contribute much to board deliberations in the years ahead.

Austin Hunt, educated as a mechanical engineer at Massachusetts Institute of Technology, was then corporate director of manufacturing at the J. E. Baker Company in York, Pennsylvania. He was attractive to us because he had previously worked for the Cole Steel Equipment Company, then a strong competitor of The HON Company in the office furniture field. At Cole, Austin had served in both production and general management, including a time as head of the company's Canadian operation. His knowledge of manufacturing in general and of office furniture in particular was useful to the board.

In 1971, Clarence D. Ager and John S. Latta resigned from the board after long and useful periods of service. Both were retiring from their regular occupations and wished to lighten their responsibilities. To replace them, we engaged Hal Batten of Batten, Batten, Hudson & Swab to search for desirable candidates. From his several recommendations, we selected J. Harold Bragg and Ralph Hofstad.

Bragg was then vice president and general manager of the Marshalltown Division of Lennox Industries, Inc. Educated as an engineer, he brought a background of manufacturing, product development, and marketing, together with experience in a company substantially larger than HON INDUSTRIES. He had many contacts in the Iowa and national manufacturing circles, which stood us in good stead. In our board deliberations, Bragg frequently displayed the "show me" attitude of his native Missouri as he raised pertinent questions.

Ralph Hofstad's background was considerably different from that of the other directors. Hofstad, with a business management degree from Northwestern University, had been president and general manager of the Farmers Regional Cooperative in Fort Dodge, Iowa, until it was merged with Land O'Lakes, Incorporated. The proof of his talent was his subsequent elevation to the presidency of Land O'Lakes, a billion-dollar-plus operation. Hofstad clearly understood the desirability of separating the functions of management and the board of directors. He repeatedly challenged management to support its rec-

ommendations to the board, particularly those related to acquisitions and new ventures.

With these changes, the 10 directors at the end of 1972 were, in order of seniority: C. M. Stanley, Hanson, Howe, R. H. Stanley, Hinkle, Smith, Cory, Hunt, Bragg, and Hofstad—two insiders and eight outsiders. It is interesting that engineering was the basic education of seven of these 10 directors, although each of these seven had, by further formal education or experience, moved beyond engineering into management, accounting, or consulting.

By 1972, we were making more effective use of the enlarged board of directors. Four board committees had been established to allow more careful review of matters submitted by management: auditing, executive development, facilities, and public policy. To accommodate meetings of these committees, quarterly board meetings were expanded to cover almost two entire days. Board members were assigned to committees with no overlap so that the committees could meet simultaneously. Stan Howe and I, along with other officers of HON INDUSTRIES, moved among the committees, serving as resource people. In these and other ways, the directors tried to discharge more effectively their responsibilities to our several publics—shareholders, members, customers, and communities—to provide appropriate policy direction and to monitor management performance.

No longer were all board meetings held in Muscatine. In 1972, for instance, only two met there. One meeting was held in Cedartown, Georgia, to inspect a new manufacturing facility of The HON Company, and one at Corry, Pennsylvania, to become familiar with the latest acquisition. During this period, we initiated the practice of inviting the spouses of directors to attend one board meeting each year. The social functions on those occasions did much to enhance the rapport of the group.

With the acquisition of Holga and Corry Jamestown, we experimented briefly with the practice of placing one director of HON INDUSTRIES on the board of each of our wholly owned subsidiaries: Austin

The 1972 board of directors and officers attending the board meeting held in Corry, Pennsylvania. Front row (left to right): Ralph Hofstad, Bill Cory, Albert Hinkle, Harold Bragg, Stan Howe, C. M. Stanley, Austin Hunt, Dick Stanley, Dan Throop Smith and Clem Hanson. Back row: Jim Arthur, president, Holga Metal Products Corp.; John Axel, vice president, administration, The HON Company; Fred Winn, secretary-treasurer, HON INDUSTRIES; and officers of Corry Jamestown Corp., Richard Fuller, president; Bill Masler, vice president, manufacturing; Marty Pfinsgraff, vice president, marketing; and Ed Thompson, comptroller.

Hunt for Corry Jamestown, William F. Cory for Prime-Mover; and Dan Throop Smith for Holga. These appointees lived reasonably close to the headquarters of the respective companies. We anticipated that this arrangement would provide a more knowledgeable director to serve as an advocate and communicator between the board of HON INDUSTRIES and the boards of the subsidiary companies. After a trial period of several years, this practice did not prove beneficial and was abandoned. We reverted to small boards of corporate officers for each of the subsidiary corporations to handle required legal functions, while the parent company's board provided broad policy direction for the subsidiaries.

CHAPTER FOURTEEN

The HON Company

GROWTH IN THE MIDDLE MARKET

Throughout the period from 1966 to 1972, office furniture manufactured and marketed by the HON Division (later The HON Company) continued to be our primary source of sales volume. Revenues increased 3.55-fold, from $9.24 million in 1965 to $32.85 million in 1972. Operating income, the bottom line used to judge profit centers, grew even more rapidly, achieving a 4.11-fold gain. Sales volume grew at an annual compounded rate of 19.9 percent, and operating income at 22.4 percent.

Accommodating this growth of sales, expansion, expansion, and more expansion became the name of the game. Factory floor space used by The HON Company's office furniture business increased 5.3-fold, from 258,000 square feet at the beginning of the period to 1,370,000 square feet at the end. New products were introduced, numerous new members were employed, and many who had been with us for a while were advanced.

By the end of the period, The HON Company was firmly established as an important factor in the broad, middle-grade office furniture market. We had broken the regional mode with respect to production as well as marketing. Once the production of office furniture and material-handling equipment were separated, The HON Company became a largely autonomous operating entity, growing less dependent on the services provided by the newly organized corporate staff of HON INDUSTRIES.

Product Development

The pace of new product introduction accelerated during the years between 1966 and 1972. By broadening our product offerings, the HON line became increasingly attractive to dealers and wholesalers. We were learning a lot about the middle market on which we concentrated. The price range between Grade A products at the top and the very cheap products at the bottom was too broad to be served by a single offering of files, desks, or chairs. Therefore, we designed and marketed products at several price points within this broad middle market.

A constant stream of new models of filing cabinets, desks, chairs, and other office furniture emerged during these years, enhancing The HON Company's ability to meet the needs of customers. Major introductions were supplemented by extensive redesign and improvement of previously introduced products to make them more functional. Redesign also reduced production costs.

These new product introductions for the middle market successfully stimulated The HON Company's sales and generated profits. However, two efforts outside this market brought us more frustration, disappointment, and experience than profit.

The VS Product Line

Since 1962, we had sought a niche in the Grade A market using the VS line offered to a limited number of dealers on a franchised basis. Ultimately, the VS offering included contemporary desks and work centers as well as the conventional desks and work centers introduced earlier. It also included a newly designed line of chairs and both conventional and contemporary files.

Despite upgrading of the initial offerings, expansion of the line, and energetic marketing under the guidance of Denny Waterman, VS acceptance remained discouragingly poor. A recasting of the VS franchise program in 1969 produced little gain.

Thus, we were finally forced to face up to the inadequacies of the VS program. The product was deficient, both in features and styling. Basically, it was no more than our Series 80 conventional and Series 70 contemporary desks, credenzas, and bookcases, plus our Series 210 files with limited modifications and cosmetic changes. Our marketing and sales approach was not well-suited to a franchised product. Territory managers, accustomed to selling to open line dealers, were not adept at selling VS products on a franchised basis.

The HON Company's reputation as a middle-market supplier did not confer on the company an appropriate credibility in the Grade A market. Obviously, the VS program was failing. We had two choices: forget the Grade A market, or develop an alternative to the VS program.

As we contemplated alternatives, we were well aware of the growing interest in the systems approach to open office design. None of The HON Company's products, including the VS line, addressed this market. We had some screens, but no panels designed to support hang-on units. The wooden partitions acquired from R.J.R. Industries in 1958 had been long discontinued. After extensive deliberation, we decided to develop and introduce a line of high-quality, systems-oriented furniture to be sold by a separate sales organization. We called it Environ 1. We believed that it would give us a toehold in both the systems and the Grade A markets.

The Environ 1 Line

Environ 1 consisted of freestanding panels in 15 standard sizes from which could be hung a variety of cabinets, shelves, and work surfaces. The line included an assortment of drawer units, storage units, tub files, and electrical accessories. Wall panels were available in a choice of paints, laminates, fabrics, and vinyls. These products, together with some of the desks, lateral files, and chairs recently introduced by The HON Company, made an attractive package. By 1971, the elements of the system had been designed, prototypes had been tested, sales literature had been prepared, and production was initiated.

We invited Bill Duval to return to the HON organization to head the marketing and sales of Environ 1. Duval, who had left Muscatine in 1963, was serving as sales manager for another firm in the office product field. He accepted our invitation and brought with him a number of salespeople who were experienced in selling Grade A office furniture. Duval put together a sales organization, including territory managers and the necessary supporting staff. He de-

Through the VS line, The HON Company hoped to develop a portion of the Grade A market for office furniture. Despite much effort, the venture proved to be a failure.

veloped sales literature that, even by to-day's standards, was good-quality and at-tractive. In early 1972, Duval gathered his sales organization in Muscatine and launched Environ 1 with great expecta-tions.

Environ 1 was scarcely under way, however, when the opportunity to acquire Corry Jamestown emerged. When negotia-tions were completed and Corry James-town became a division of HON INDUS-TRIES, we faced a difficult decision about Environ 1. Corry Jamestown, already es-tablished in the Grade A market, seemed to offer a quicker and less difficult path to ex-panding sales in the upper grade market and to be a better vehicle with which to enter the systems field. We therefore de-cided to discontinue Environ 1, much to the discomfort and displeasure of its marketing and sales staff. Duval left HON INDUSTRIES in May 1972.

We will never know where Environ 1 might have taken us. In retrospect, our de-cision to terminate this program before it got off the ground could be challenged. The termination diverted The HON Com-pany's attention from systems furniture for many years. Although HON INDUSTRIES gained an immediate sizable sales volume of Grade A furniture from Corry James-town, our progress toward systems was much slower than we had anticipated. A decade would transpire and another ac-quisition would occur before HON IN-DUSTRIES became a meaningful factor in the systems furniture market.

A Nonstarter: The Electric File

Another secondary effort became a nonstarter. In November 1964, we pur-chased the patent for an electric file, to which we made significant improvements. It was finally introduced in 1968. Perhaps the lengthy period taken to design, test, and prepare the product for market was a negative omen for the future of this in-teresting device.

The electric file consisted of a series of shelves hung on two continuous chains running over sprockets in a vertical steel housing. The chains were driven by an

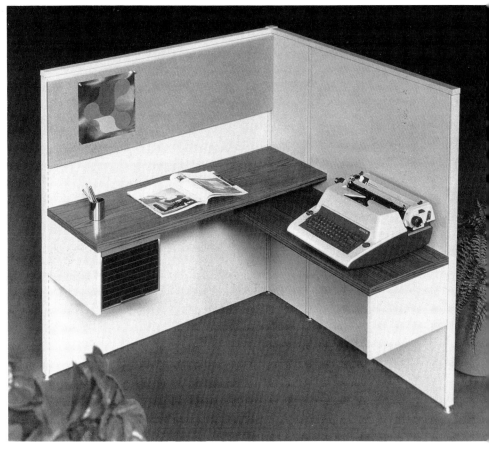

The Environ 1 line was planned to give The HON Company a toehold in both the systems and Grade A markets. Acquisi-tion of Corry Jamestown in 1972 brought an end to this product.

electric motor through a reducing mecha-nism. Access to filed material was accom-plished by rotating each tray to a horizon-tal opening in the front of the housing. An operator, seated at a stationary work sur-face at the opening, controlled shelf travel, using a self selector control to provide short-cut retrieval, designed and patented by HON INDUSTRIES.

Models in both letter and legal sizes were offered, each with a selection of 14, 16, or 18 shelves. The shelves, provided with shelf dividers, were 76 inches long and either 10 or 12 inches deep. A 14-shelf unit put filing space at the operator's finger-tips that was equivalent to that of 10 stand-ard four-drawer vertical files. Two addi-tional models were designed with configurations for filing index and tab cards of various sizes.

The electric file made sense but was difficult to sell through The HON Company's distribution channels.

We had high hopes for the electric file. We believed that it would gain customer acceptance because it conserved floor space, sped retrieval, lowered filing costs, and reduced filing clerk fatigue. We liked the product because it was a "big-ticket" item. Retail prices ranged from $3,400 to $6,200 per unit; dealer discounts were 25 percent as compared with the 40 percent then prevalent in metal case goods.

Unfortunately, our hopes were never realized. Despite the attractiveness and usefulness of our electric file, only a few of them were sold before we realized that The HON Company's distribution system was not suited to market this product effectively. Reluctantly, we dropped the electric file in November 1972.

Altogether, the product introductions made between 1966 and 1972 demonstrated the plight of those who venture something new: You win some, and you lose some. Fortunately, our batting average over the years was good. Unquestionably, the continued introduction of new products contributed greatly to the growth and profitability of The HON Company.

Production Facilities in Muscatine

Throughout the period from 1966 to 1972, escalating sales of office furniture necessitated expanded production facilities. This called for continuous and expeditious attention to the planning and construction of buildings as well as to the selection and installation of equipment. These efforts were fully as important as new product introduction and marketing. Production facilities were enlarged at the Oak Street and Geneva Plants in Muscatine, and a new plant was constructed in Cedartown, Georgia. A corporate office building was completed in Muscatine. The distribution center in Newark, New Jersey, was relocated and enlarged. These projects were not undertaken one at a time; overlapping schedules were common throughout the period.

Oak Street Plant. The Oak Street Plant remained the primary furniture production facility for The HON Company. During the fourth quarter of 1966, the two-story, 75,900-square-foot Oak Street Building Number 5 was completed. A steel receiving, storing, and processing area occupied about half of the first floor. Three truck docks and an overhead traveling crane facilitated handling of coil steel. Three cut-up lines—one new, one relocated from Oak Street Building Number 1, and one from Oak Street Building Number 3—processed the coil steel into blanks for further production.

A conveyorized file fabrication and assembly line occupied the balance of the first floor. Single-purpose press brakes for forming large parts were located close to the welding fixtures to reduce handling and storage of work in process; smaller parts fabricated elsewhere were stored nearby. Greater use was made of automatic welding equipment, much of it designed by our staff. Assembled file cases, drawers, and other parts were hung on an overhead conveyor system for a ride through the finishing system—cleaning, painting, and baking. They were removed from the conveyor on the second floor for final assembly, inspection, and packaging and were then transported via a belt conveyor to the warehouse in Building Number 4. We believed the high-speed, efficient file production line that we installed in Building Number 5 to be as fine a facility as existed anywhere in the world.

Building Number 5 also provided space on the second floor for production of insulated files. The metal elements of the insulated files were removed from the conveyor after they had passed through the finishing system for partial assembly. The insulating material was mixed and poured into the cases. After a suitable period of curing, assembly was completed and the files were packaged and transported on the conveyor to be warehoused in Building Number 4. Building Number 5 also provided 4,800 square feet of badly needed office space for The HON Company's production staff.

Warehouse space was the next problem at the Oak Street Plant. Our solution was to raze the Hawkeye Button Co. plant purchased in 1966 and construct on its site a two-story, 57,200-square-foot warehouse. This warehouse, Building Number 6, was just across Third Street from our main Building Number 4 warehouse. To link the two, a conveyor, interconnected with the one delivering products from Building Number 5, was installed on a bridge crossing the street.

By 1970, the increased sales volume of desks was threatening to outstrip our production capacity. To increase desk production capacity in Muscatine, we planned a 92,400-square-foot Building Number 7, to be located across Fourth Street, north of Buildings Number 2 and 5. It would have an overhead bridge-type connection to Building Number 5. The design of Building Number 7 took into account a future Building Number 8, the two structures to be integrated when we received permission from the City of Muscatine to close a section of Fourth Street.

For a time, it appeared that construction of Building Number 7 might be deferred if we installed a desk production line at our first branch plant in Cedartown, Georgia. This did not work out, and construction was started in December 1971. Upon completion near the end of 1972,

Building Number 7 provided a second production line for desks, together with a department for manufacturing laminated particle board tops, which, until then, had been purchased from outside sources. The desk line in Building Number 7 was used for the larger, more complex desks, credenzas, and related case goods products; the older desk line in Building Number 2 continued to produce the higher volume, lower priced furniture. Building Number 7 also provided space for chair assembly. All chair models that did not require paint were moved from the Geneva Plant, thus releasing space that was badly needed by Prime-Mover.

In 1972, on receiving authority from the City of Muscatine to close Fourth Street, we started construction on the 31,400-square-foot Building Number 8. When it was completed in 1973, Building Number 8 would become a part of the desk plant.

Oak Street Building Number 5, shown at left, enabled the start-up of a dedicated high-speed file line and the manufacture of large desks upstairs. The Hawkeye Button Building and the the Huttig Buildings, shown middle and top right, would later be incorporated into the complex.

Geneva Plant. During the period from 1966 to 1972, production of small goods, chairs, and stands continued at the Geneva Plant, which also housed the Prime-Mover operation. The only expansion at the Geneva Plant within the period was Building Number 3, a 36,000-square-foot extension completed in 1967. This extension provided some relief for both The HON Company and Prime-Mover. Further relief was provided when a part of chair assembly was moved to Building Number 7 at Oak Street in 1972.

By the end of the period, the pressures for increased space at Geneva were great. The HON Company was considering a major chair plant; Prime-Mover definitely needed more space. Something had to give. Studies were under way, weighing the various alternatives.

Our First Branch Plant: Cedartown

We had long considered the desirability of locating furniture production away from Muscatine. Several factors brought about the decision to do so. We were concerned about the maximum limit of Muscatine's work force; we were reluctant to be the employer of too great a proportion of the working population there. In addition, another manufacturing location would serve as a distribution center, thereby providing better service to our customers and reducing transportation costs of finished goods. Multiple locations would also lessen the hazards of unexpected disasters or work stoppages.

Our rapidly growing market in the southeastern United States, together with the absence of competitive manufacturing plants in that region, persuaded us to locate there. In early 1966, management brought to the board of directors a request for authorization to investigate a branch plant location in the Southeast. Agreeing that this undertaking would lessen HON's dependence on Muscatine and at the same time tap a growing Sunbelt market, the board granted authorization.

Ralph Raabe, under Stan Howe's guidance, began the search for a suitable site. After considering various alternatives, we recommended to the board the purchase of a 61,700-square-foot, one-story building located on 25 acres of land in Cedartown, Georgia. Thus, the board authorized in 1967 the purchase of the property that would become our first manufacturing facility outside of Muscatine.

Cedartown, located about 60 miles northwest of Atlanta, offered several advantages. The existence of a sizable building with adequate acreage was very attractive. A distribution system could be activated immediately, and production could be initiated in a relatively short time. Cedartown appeared to have an adequate industrial labor force. Race relations in the community and the adjacent county seemed stable; blacks and whites were working together in many plants. This was very important, considering the racial turmoil that existed in many places at that time. Finally, we received strong encouragement and considerable help from the community, largely through its Chamber of Commerce, headed by local banker W. D. Trippe. A delightful person, although something of a character, Trippe became a great booster of The HON Company.

After purchasing the building in Cedartown, we promptly established a distribution center to serve the southeastern United States. Inventory received in carload shipments from Muscatine allowed better service to customers in the area. Simultaneously, we initiated planning to modify the building, to purchase and install equipment for a file production line, and to add a 42,200-square-foot ware-

Establishment of the Cedartown, Georgia, plant was the first step made by The HON Company to decentralize its manufacturing operations. At the time, the property was also identified with a HON INDUSTRIES sign.

house, Building Number 2. The file production line, while of lesser capacity than the one just constructed in Building Number 5 at the Oak Street Plant, was designed to achieve the same level of efficiency.

Rex Bennett, as vice president of manufacturing services, was directly involved in planning the Cedartown Plant. When construction was under way, Rex and his wife, Madelene, moved to Cedartown where he assumed the responsibilities of plant manager. Modification and expansion of the building and installation of equipment proceeded rapidly. Some machinery was transferred from Muscatine; other fabricating equipment and the finishing system were new.

It was a big day in April 1969, when the first vertical file came off the Cedartown production line—on schedule and under budget. The HON Company was no longer dependent on a single production facility. It had taken a first step of what would be many steps to decentralize production across the nation. By August, the Cedartown Plant had passed the break-even point, and by year end, it was operating two shifts with output considerably above initial schedules. The additional warehouse building needed to balance production capacity was occupied by January 1970. Major credit goes to Bennett for the early and efficient operation of Cedartown.

Even before the warehouse expansion was completed, a decision was made to construct Building Number 3, a 31,700-square-foot addition to the plant, intended to house a second production line designed for desk manufacture. This addition was scheduled for completion in 1973.

A New Corporate Office

Despite the 4,800 square feet of office space provided in 1969 in Oak Street Building Number 5, the need for increased space became critical. Office as well as plant staff was expanding. Howe and I dreamed of an entirely new office building. With this in mind, in 1968 we purchased the then-unoccupied plant of the Automatic Button Company at Fourth Street and

Mulberry Avenue as a potential site. Once more we acted as an urban-renewal agency, phasing out the declining pearl button industry. The main building was razed and the area used for parking. A 5,000-square-foot building on the back of the property was retained for storage.

Urban renewal (HON style) provided the sites for plant expansions and needed parking adjacent to the Oak Street Plant. Shown here are the changes that occurred in the property at 414 East Third Street. This building ultimately became the corporate headquarters of HON INDUSTRIES.

The 1966 sales meeting brought Ed Jones (left), Max Stanley, and Philip Temple to Chicago. Temple was vice president of product engineering.

However, as pressure for office space intensified and estimates of the construction cost of our dream building escalated, we decided to take another path. In 1970, we bought an old but sound building at 414 East Third Street. It had been used at various times as a garage, a plant manufacturing overalls, and a wood-working shop. Stanley Consultants designed the remodeling and revamping of this structure to provide 15,000 square feet of fine office space, ready for occupancy in December 1970. This new office building abutted the newly constructed office of our attorneys— Stanley, Lande, Coulter & Pearce. After the creation of profit centers in 1972, this became the headquarters of HON INDUSTRIES as well as The HON Company until the latter moved into new quarters.

We also purchased and razed another old building on the corner of Third Street and Mulberry Avenue, on the far side of the law office. This space we used for additional parking. Thus, HON INDUSTRIES made a further contribution to urban renewal in an area just across the street from the impressive Muscatine County Courthouse.

People and the Organization

With the corporate reorganization of 1972, many of the same people who had been managing the production and marketing of office furniture for the middle market formed the managerial cadre of The HON Company, now a semiautonomous unit of HON INDUSTRIES. Stan Howe served as president of The HON Company as well as president and chief operating officer of HON INDUSTRIES. Ed Jones continued to head marketing, with important responsibilities held by Arthur Arnold (national field sales manager), John Van Lent (special products and promotion), Denison Waterman (franchised products), and Jerry Boulund (wholesale accounts). Rex Bennett was in charge of manufacturing. Ralph Beals managed the Oak Street Plant. Fred Winn (secretary-treasurer), Max Collins (personnel), Clare Patterson (manufacturing research), and Maurice Jones (plant engineering) were assigned to the new corporate office of HON INDUSTRIES when it was created.

CHAPTER FIFTEEN

The Prime-Mover Co.

NEW PRODUCTS FOR THE INDUSTRIAL MARKET

Prime-Mover made significant progress from 1966 to 1972, especially with respect to broadening its line of products. Sales volume increased 2.5–fold, from $1.72 million in 1965 to $4.26 million in 1972. Net operating profit also grew. The gains resulted primarily from the introduction of a line of electric-powered material-handling equipment for the industrial market.

With the separation of HON and Prime-Mover production by the end of the period, Prime-Mover had become a largely self-sufficient operating entity. This change, together with the strong entry into the industrial market, generated expectations that Prime-Mover could achieve growth rates to fulfill the expectations of top management at HON INDUSTRIES.

Product Development

From 1966 to 1972, Prime-Mover moved strongly into the industrial market with a series of electric-powered material-handling units. This action greatly lessened our dependence on the construction equipment market.

The design and marketing concepts that had been incubating in the final years of Operation Bootstrap hatched into reality with the introduction, in late 1965, of the PE-40 electric low-lift transporter (later the PX-40). With this model as a starter, 12 more electric-powered units were de-

signed, tested, and put on the market between 1966 and 1972. All of these units, with some modifications, remained in the line at least into the early 1980s.

We had cast our lot with narrow-aisle electric-powered units for the industrial market. Within this period, both of our earlier industrial market products were discontinued—the F-20 and F-40 gas engine–powered platform trucks in 1968 and 1972, respectively. During these years, only one unit designed for the construction market was introduced—the L-32 mason tender (brick and block transporter), similar to the L-36 that had been introduced in 1965.

We designed our electric material-handling equipment units to be powered by heavy-duty industrial lead acid batteries, mostly 24-volt, but in some units, 12-volt. The batteries were housed in sheet metal enclosures located and arranged to facilitate easy servicing. Batteries could be removed from either side or from overhead if a hoisting system was used. Electrical components, including 100-amp contactors and fuses, were mounted high on the trucks, away from the moisture, dirt, or corrosive materials likely to be on the floor. Controls were arranged for fast and comfortable operation, the exact configuration varying with the nature of the truck.

The drive unit designed for the PE-40 was used subsequently with only minor modifications on all of the 13 models of electric units introduced during this period. This drive unit consisted of a high torque motor driving the power wheel through a 22-to-1 reduction spur gear transmission. Braking was accomplished by disks running in oil, mounted on the motor pinion inside the transmission case. The motor, transmission castings, wheel, and gears were purchased, but other parts and the assembly were done in-house.

Lifting was accomplished by hydraulic cylinders activated by oil pressure provided by integrally mounted electric motors and gear pumps. A pressure reservoir and appropriate valves completed the hydraulic systems.

The reach truck became an important part of modern warehouse material-handling operations. The Prime-Mover model proved reliable and competitively priced.

As the electric truck product line was expanded, common design provided excellent interchangeability of parts. As would be true of all electric trucks, these first introductions were designed to provide easy access to the elements that required maintenance. They were also designed to simplify operation and to increase operating efficiency. Careful attention was given to styling in order to produce an attractive product.

The initial electric truck, the PE-40, was the most elemental of the units introduced during this period. Designed to move material stacked on a pallet, this "walkie" low-lift transporter was built so that the operator walked behind the unit and steered it manually. The unit had a lifting capacity of 4,000 pounds, a lift of four inches, and a travel speed (when empty) of three-and-one-half miles per hour. Controls for speed and lift were conveniently located on the steering post. The PE-40 was the forerunner of what became a group of nine low-lift transporters, some walkie and some rider, of varying capacities and speeds.

The PE-60 and PE-60R, introduced in 1972, each had a capacity of 6,000 pounds, a lift of six inches, and an empty travel speed of three-and-one-half miles per hour. Both were designed for pallets, and they were offered with either a 12- or 24-volt battery. The PE-60 was a walkie unit, and the PE-60R differed from it only in that it had a platform for a rider.

In 1966, the introduction of the SN-20 walkie-type counterbalanced stacker marked Prime-Mover's entry into this field, with at least eight units of this type offered later. These stackers were designed to bring the advantages of palletized handling to a small operation at a low cost and thus augment more expensive rider trucks. The outriggers permitted these trucks to lift more than their own weight; their dimensions and maneuverability made them efficient for narrow-aisle operation.

The SN-20 had a capacity of 2,000 pounds and lifts of 106 and 130 inches. Like the PE-40 transporter, a walking operator controlled and maneuvered the unit. In 1968, the SC-20 and the SC-25 expanded our line of walkie stackers. These units, although similar in many features, differed from the SN-20 in two respects. Stability was obtained by counterbalancing rather than with the use of straddle-type outriggers. Masts were tilting rather than stationary. The SC-20 had a capacity of 2,000 pounds, and the SC-25, with additional counterbalancing weight, a capacity of 2,500 pounds. Each had a lift of 106 and 130 inches.

In 1972, the line was further expanded by introduction of the SN-30 and the SC-30. These two units, with 3,000 pounds of capacity, were otherwise similar to the SN-20 and the SC-20. We identified the narrow-aisle SN series as "space-saving specialists," and the counterbalanced SC series as "workhorses of the walkies."

Facilities

For manufacturing, the 2.5-fold growth of Prime-Mover sales during these years created not only problems but opportunities. The compounded annual growth rate of just less than 14 percent required more people, more space, and more machinery—the usual situation associated with expansion. Growth, however, also provided the opportunity for improved methods and procedures, increased efficiency, and stronger staff.

Throughout the period, Prime-Mover operations remained in the Geneva Plant, sharing space with the production of chairs, small goods, and stands for The HON Company. Competition for office and manufacturing space was keen because The HON Company's production at Geneva was likewise expanding rapidly. The completion of the 36,000-square-foot Building Number 3 in 1967 was the only expansion of space during the period. Some further relief came just as the period from 1966 to 1972 was coming to an end, when assembly of chairs that did not require painting was transferred to Oak Street Building Number 7.

Well before the end of the period, the need for additional space for both The Prime-Mover Co. and The HON Company was clearly evident. One or the other needed to be removed from Geneva and

The electric order picker, which was introduced in 1969, helped the company to penetrate the warehouse segment of the material-handling equipment market.

located elsewhere. For a time, the construction of a new chair plant for The HON Company was favored. Removal of HON's production from Geneva would release ample space for Prime-Mover. As the period ended, however, emphasis shifted to the construction of a new facility for Prime-Mover. This would allow the Geneva Plant to be converted to a chair production facility for The HON Company.

A substantial expansion of machinery, tools, and equipment was required to meet increasing demands. Until 1970, the several items of equipment added had been of the conventional manually operated type. In 1970, however, Prime-Mover took a major step, purchasing its first tape-controlled machine. A used tape-controlled drilling center manufactured by the Pratt-Whitney Company was purchased for $56,000, making it by far the most expen-

Top: The Prime-Mover exhibit at the annual Material Handling Institute show displayed the full line of narrow-aisle equipment.

Bottom: Groundbreaking for the new Prime-Mover plant. From left to right: Howard Worst, Art Dahl, Stan Howe, Ron Hanson (mayor of Muscatine), Gene Waddell, George Dunker, Tom Stratton, Roy Hanson, Merv Comfort, and Dave Horney.

sive single piece of equipment yet added to Prime-Mover. In 1972, this figure was topped when Prime-Mover purchased a new $160,000 tape-controlled turret lathe. The two machines were the first of many of their type to be added in later years. These machines earned a fine return on the investments made in them, eliminating or greatly reducing the cost of tools and dies. By speeding setup times, they not only saved money, they increased the flexibility that Prime-Mover needed to shift from one part to another. In addition, they contributed to quality control.

As the volume increased, larger runs of a given product became possible, and progress was made in streamlining assembly operations. Among the other equipment added in 1972 was our first flame cutting machine used to fabricate parts from steel plate.

Management

Only one change in the roster of Prime-Mover officers occurred during this period. From the beginning, I served as chairman, Howe as president, Winn as secretary-treasurer, and Cook as assistant secretary-treasurer. Until December 15, 1970, Dahl served as vice president and general manager. When he became senior vice president of HON INDUSTRIES, he was succeeded by L. Gene Waddell.

The increasing volume of production and sales, together with the separation of Prime-Mover and The HON Company in 1972, led to a restructuring of the production organization. At the end of the period, Tom Stratton served as production manager. Reporting to him were Mervin Comfort as plant superintendent and Earl Frantz as production control supervisor.

Prime-Mover's profile was vastly changed by 1972. No longer was it dependent on powered buggies and mason tenders made for the construction industry. Prime-Mover had made a meaningful entry into the industrial market with a fleet of electric-powered material-handling trucks carefully selected to serve niches in the market that were not then occupied by the major fork-truck manufacturers. Prime-Mover had become more attractive to dealers serving the industrial market because its electric trucks were far more salable than the F-10 and F-40 flatbed units that were no longer in the product line. The potential dollar value of sales for dealers as well as for Prime-Mover had escalated substantially. Electric trucks available in 1972 ranged in list price from $1,720 to $7,645, as compared with the $1,240 list price on a Model 15–B gasoline engine–powered buggy. Moreover, the potential opportunities to expand the electric truck line were great. Our engineers were busy designing, and our model builders were at work fabricating and testing prototypes of units that would soon be in production. Productwise, Prime-Mover was making great progress.

CHAPTER SIXTEEN

Growth Through Acquisition

HOLGA AND CORRY JAMESTOWN

Up to the early 1970s, our expansion had resulted primarily from internal growth. However, two important acquisitions made in 1971 and 1972 enabled the company to gain access to segments of the office furniture market not previously reached effectively. Holga Metal Products Corp. of Van Nuys, California, gave HON INDUSTRIES a manufacturing plant and distribution center in the rapidly growing Southern California region. Corry Jamestown Corp. of Corry, Pennsylvania, put HON INDUSTRIES into the Grade A market, or, more precisely, into the contract segment of the office furniture market.

Together, these acquisitions added to our product offerings, significantly expanded our sales volume, increased our profits, and further decentralized our operations. As our experience would show however, adding companies of such size, in distant locations and with different kinds of operations, could result in frustrations and disappointments as well as benefits.

Previous Experience with Acquisitions

From almost the beginning of the company's history, the subject of acquisitions and mergers was before us. The purchase of Prime-Mover from Bell Aircraft in 1950 put us into the material-handling business. Although small, Prime-Mover quickly became a profitable and viable operation.

We also regularly considered acquisitions as a method of expanding our participation in the office furniture industry. However, our first acquisitions made—the Essington Co. in 1954 and R.J.R. Industries in 1958—proved to be disappointing. In each case, we obtained product design and inventory rather than a going business with continuing management. The costumer line from Essington produced little sales volume for us; except for a few items, it was soon dropped from our product offerings. The wood partitions acquired from R.J.R. Industries likewise generated little volume. We learned that our distribution organization was not well-suited to market them, as partitions were not then sold by office furniture dealers. They also were soon dropped from our offerings.

By contrast, the acquisition of Luxco in 1961 put us in the chair and stand business, thereby expanding our product line. It took us several years, however, to realize that the design of Luxco products, particularly seating, left something to be desired. It would be years before The HON Company developed attractive designs, efficient production, and effective marketing of chairs.

Thus, out of three acquisitions, only one could be classified as even moderately successful and, in retrospect, a good move. The other two were failures, but we did learn from them. One of the lessons was

The acquisition of Holga Metal Products Corporation in 1971 was first considered to provide manufacturing facility for The HON Company. It continued as an independent entity, however, after the purchase contract was signed.

Corry Jamestown

Acquisition of Corry Jamestown for cash in 1972 brought the company into an exciting new market.

that acquisitions were more likely to be successful if they were going businesses rather than product additions that would require different marketing or distribution.

Despite the mixed success of our early acquisitions, we continued from 1966 to 1972 to examine potential acquisitions. We did not, ourselves, actively seek out companies to acquire. Most of those coming to our attention—and there were many—could be quickly rejected as unsuitable. We were interested only in acquisitions involving product lines that could be marketed through our office furniture and material-handling equipment distribution systems. Increasingly aware of the cost, time, and damage factors inherent in serving the national market from Muscatine, we were also interested in gaining manufacturing capability for these products in eastern and western regions. Access to the Grade A market was another of our acquisition criteria.

Some of our acquisition investigations were lengthy; others were short. For instance, in 1966 it was rumored that Standard Pressed Steel Company was interested in divesting its Columbia Division, which produced office furniture at a plant in the eastern United States. This seemed a proper fit for the H-O-N Division. Seemingly, it would provide Grade A product, increased sales volume, and a manufacturing facility in a different region. A few phone calls to the company, however, revealed the rumor to be false, swiftly ending our investigation.

In 1968, we had several discussions with Joe M. Davis, president of LIT-NING Products Company of California. This company manufactured desktop accessories and other office products compatible with the HON Company line, and it had production facilities at Fresno. The discussions were not fruitful, however, as we failed to develop a mutually acceptable basis for a transaction.

Also in 1968, we considered acquisition of a Wisconsin-based organization, Duraform, Incorporated, manufacturers of metal, plywood, and concrete forms and related hardware. We looked at Duraform as an addition to Prime-Mover. Although the company was profitable and expanding, we concluded that we would have difficulty marketing the product through the Prime-Mover distribution system.

In the fall of 1970, we discussed the acquisition of the Smith Systems with Clark Smith, who visited Muscatine. Subsequently, we made a proposal to purchase Smith Systems, but this was rejected in January 1971. In retrospect, this was probably a blessing because his product was largely school-oriented, a market that would soon deteriorate.

For several months in early 1971, we carefully considered the acquisition of Globe-Wernicke, then owned by Avco, Incorporated. Globe-Wernicke manufactured a number of office products that we believed would be compatible with the HON Company line. Negotiations were serious but difficult. In April, we reached an impasse due to Avco's unacceptable demands concerning royalties and other financial matters.

Finally, in April 1971, we connected with a company that we wanted and one that we could acquire: Holga Metal Products. Only a year later, we learned about the availability of Corry Jamestown.

Acquisition of Holga Metal Products

Holga Metal Products became a wholly owned subsidiary of HON INDUSTRIES on May 21, 1971. Holga produced and marketed office furniture products for the western market, with major sales in the Los Angeles area.

We first learned of Holga some months earlier, when Thomas Maguire of Tomar Industries contacted Howe to see whether we were interested in buying Holga. Maguire had acquired Holga, along with Yawman & Erbe Manufacturing Company, a Grade A office furniture manufacturer, from Sterling Precision Corporation in October 1969. Needing funds to meet his obligations to Sterling and, perhaps, to acquire Globe-Wernicke, Maguire proposed a quick cash sale. Stan Howe and Ed Jones visited Van Nuys to look over the Holga facility with a view to its potential as a western manufacturing plant and distribution center for The HON Company. Finding that Holga had no rail siding, they concluded that it would not fit with The HON Company, so we rejected Maguire's proposal.

Some time later, Maguire defaulted on his purchase agreement, causing Sterling Precision to repossess the company. Wanting to spin off its nonfinancial subsidiaries, Sterling contacted HON INDUSTRIES. In the meantime, Ron Darnall, traffic manager for The HON Company, discovered that office furniture could be shipped from Muscatine to Van Nuys in piggyback trailers at a lower cost than by regular rail shipment. As this overcame the lack of a rail siding at the facility, we were again interested in acquiring Holga.

We revisited Van Nuys, and Jim Arthur, Holga's president, came to Muscatine to discuss the matter with officers of HON INDUSTRIES and The HON Company. Finally, on May 21, Howe and Jones traveled to Sterling's office in New York City, where in one day they completed the negotiations to acquire Holga. The HON INDUSTRIES board of directors ratified this action at its August 4th meeting. The purchase price was $850,000, plus the assumption of current and long-term liabilities of $337,595.

Profile.   Holga's product line included desks, credenzas, suspension files, shelf files, and storage cabinets, as well as drafting desks and tables. Only chairs were missing. Holga's product line was conventionally designed—heavy and sturdy.

Holga's products were marketed partly through dealers in the western states and partly by direct sales to major industrial customers, including aerospace firms and defense contractors in the Los Angeles area. Most of the products sold to local customers were picked up, uncartoned, at the shipping dock by dealers' trucks. Holga's sales force consisted of a sales manager and three salespeople in the California area.

The operations of Holga Metal Products were located in buildings at the airport in Van Nuys, California.

Holga's net sales for the four years preceding acquisition had averaged about $2.4 million per annum. Pre-tax income for this same period averaged 10.8 percent. These four-year averages indicated that Holga's volume at the time of acquisition was about 10 percent of HON INDUSTRIES' volume in 1970. We believed that pre-tax income as a percent of net sales, although acceptable, could be appreciably increased by reducing manufacturing costs. This presumably could be achieved without substantial investment.

Holga employed about 100 people, with a work force that was largely Mexican-American. The plant employees were represented by an independent union. The management structure was lean, with the office, sales, and managerial staff numbering only 15 to 18 people.

The principal officers were James Arthur as president and Dale Ivey as comptroller. Other key management staff included John Goodlad, sales manager; Dean Hayes, who supervised the plant; Carlyle (Mike) Michaelson, product design; Abner Amundson, manufacturing engineering; and Adrian Brievogel, tooling.

Facility.   Holga operated in a group of buildings located along Woodley Avenue, adjacent to the Van Nuys municipal airport. Manufacturing operations were located in two hangars of 1920s vintage and two metal buildings located on the north side of the street. The hangars showed signs of wear and tear as well as earthquake damage, but they were in usable condition. The modest offices and a warehouse were located in a modern brick structure on the south side of the street. Together, these buildings provided 75,300 square feet of floor space. The buildings were leased from three different owners, one of whom was Sterling Precision. Several smaller outlying buildings were located on the leased property. Obviously, Holga's operations were not burdened by excessive fixed charges on buildings.

The manufacturing equipment included items customary to metal furniture production: shears, press brakes, punch presses, spot welders, and a conveyorized finishing system arranged for cleaning, spray painting, drying, and baking.

The plant layout was poor, resembling a job shop operation rather than a line production. The flow of raw materials, work in process, and finished goods was unsatisfactory. Material-handling costs were excessive. Although the equipment was tolerably adequate, tooling, methods, and production control all left much to be desired. Despite these deficiencies, however, Holga was profitable.

Operations.   After acquisition, we continued the entity of Holga Metal Products, establishing a board of directors composed of Stan Howe and myself, with Howe as chairman. Jim Arthur continued as president, with Fred Winn becoming secretary-treasurer and Kermit Cook assistant secretary-treasurer.

Top priority was given to establishing a distribution center for The HON Company in one of the smaller leased buildings just east of the hangars. This center was stocked with products shipped from The HON Company's plants in Muscatine and Cedartown. Once procedures were established, The HON Company's orders could be received and processed at Van Nuys, with delivery made from the center's stock. The advantage for HON Company customers was quicker delivery and less product damage.

Meanwhile, things were humming under the command of Jim Arthur, aided by Clare Patterson of the HON INDUSTRIES staff and advised by Stan Howe. Soon after acquisition, Arthur spent several days in Muscatine for briefing on HON's ways of running a business. He spent many hours in the Oak Street Plant observing our manufacturing processes for desks and files. Arthur was a quick learner, and he returned to Van Nuys full of ideas and excited about the possibilities of revamping production methods to reduce costs and improve quality control.

Revamping the flow of material and work in process received early attention. Some new roller conveyors were installed, the finishing system's overhead conveyors were rerouted, and wall openings between adjacent buildings were broken out—probably without landlord approval. These actions streamlined the travel of a desk or a file from welding to finishing to final assembly to warehouse or shipping dock. They no longer needed to be lifted on and off a manually propelled cart for transport between the three hangars, where parts of the manufacturing were performed.

Material handling and damage to work in process was further reduced by moving the press brakes used to fabricate the larger steel parts of case goods closer to the welding areas. Labor costs were reduced by installing a used drawer welder transferred from Muscatine and a new cradle welder fabricated for Holga.

These changes in production facilities, along with improved production control and better arrangements for handling and storing raw materials, did much to improve Holga's manufacturing efficiency.

A chair assembly and packing line was set up in the warehouse area of the office building. The HON Company's Series C, E, W, and L chair lines were produced, using parts shipped from Muscatine. Some of the chairs, carrying HON labels, were transferred immediately to The HON Company's distribution center. Others bore Holga labels, serving to expand its product line.

These activities combined to boost sales and profits. In 1972, sales rose to $2.94 million, a 23 percent jump over the average of the four-year period, 1967–1970. Net profit after taxes was 7.7 percent of sales, somewhat above the corresponding 6.2 percent for HON INDUSTRIES as a whole.

Expectations. By the end of 1972, we were confident that the Holga acquisition had been a good move. Holga's sales volume was increasing and doing so on a profitable basis. Manufacturing costs were being lowered. The product line was enlarged with the addition of chairs. Other products were being improved by design changes and better quality control.

Jim Arthur was proving to be an excellent manager. His tight hands-on style of operation with a streamlined managerial staff was getting results. Arthur was a regular one-man band. He was close to everything at Holga, and his aggressiveness and enthusiasm stimulated morale. Arthur's performance underlined the crucial importance of the continuity of competent management to the success of any acquisition. This had not occurred in any of our four prior acquisitions.

The HON Company was benefiting from the distribution center located at the Holga plant. The California presence, which gave customers improved service, was helping sales of The HON Company's products in a very competitive market. The HON Company was excited about the possibility of merging Holga into its operation and converting it into a West Coast production facility for its own product lines. We assumed that the Van Nuys plant would eventually become an operation of The HON Company rather than a separate division of HON INDUSTRIES. As things developed, however, this never occurred. Many years later, Holga would be merged into one of our other divisions.

Nearly all of Holga's plant employees were Mexican-Americans. Some were U.S.-born citizens whereas others were Mexican-born, possessing authentic work permits or green cards. Because few plant workers could speak or read English, Spanish was the normal language of communication. Bilingualism was an essential qualification for supervisors. Jim Arthur, fluent in Spanish, maintained close contact with the members of his work force, enjoying their confidence and respect.

The Holga labor force was comparatively stable, and they were good workers. Wage rates were comparable with the going levels in the area—considerably lower than at Muscatine or Cedartown. Plant morale and productivity were good. Our introduction to this Mexican-American work force was educational and would serve us well in future years as the West Coast operations of HON INDUSTRIES expanded.

Acquisition of Corry Jamestown

HON INDUSTRIES had been wanting to penetrate the Grade A market, so when we learned that Corry Jamestown was for sale, we acted promptly, even though our Environ 1 program was just getting under way.

The Singer Company had acquired Corry Jamestown in 1968, at a time when its management was on a strong diversification thrust. Singer's management believed that there was synergism between office furniture and their Friden line of adding and calculating machines. But the assumed compatibility was not present. Singer found that office furniture and machines were seldom sold in packages, as they were usually marketed through separate distribution systems. Those Friden dealers who also handled office furniture already had commitments with other manufacturers. Failing in its efforts to restore Corry Jamestown's profitability, Singer management decided to dispose of its office furniture subsidiary.

Our recollections are not clear about how we first learned that Corry Jamestown might be acquired. No doubt, the virulent rumor mill of the office furniture industry first alerted us to the possibility. Awareness may have come from discussions between Howe and Leo Hooks, a former Corry

The Corry Jamestown acquisition included this substantial and underused manufacturing facility. The property included an attractive corporate headquarters (seen at right) and a large parcel of land across the highway.

Corry Jamestown office furniture installations had been regarded as solid but had fallen behind the industry in styling.

Jamestown employee, who had recently joined The HON Company. Hooks recalls that he and Howe visited Pennsylvania for a plant tour, and that Stan spent some time with Dick Fuller, Corry Jamestown's president. Howe and Hooks sensed that relations between Corry Jamestown and Singer were not happy.

Whatever the source of our information, we decided to investigate. I arranged, for January 18, 1972, in New York, an appointment with Edwin J. Graf, vice president, industrial products group, to which Corry Jamestown and Friden belonged. He confirmed that Corry Jamestown was for sale, indicating that Singer wanted to divest the property promptly. Obtaining product, financial, and other information from Singer, we began an intensive analysis and study, from which we formulated recommendations to submit to our board of directors. At its meeting in Cedartown on February 9, 1972, the board authorized management to proceed with its study leading to negotiations, taking into account the impact of an acquisition on the Environ 1 program.

Following the board meeting, we obtained more information regarding Corry Jamestown. Leo Hooks visited the Corry plant twice—in March and again in April. We concluded that we should go forward with negotiations, and, if they were successful, we could scuttle the Environ 1 program. Corry Jamestown seemed to be a bird in the hand, whereas Environ 1 was a bird in the bush, if not on the wing. Corry Jamestown offered an immediate sizable increase in sales volume and had an excellent plant. We believed that its operations could be made profitable.

March 24 was set as the date for negotiations. Howe and I flew into Chicago to meet with Singer representatives. Negotiations proceeded at an amazing pace. With return reservations to New York, Messrs. Coumo and Gabriel of Singer were apparently under instructions to wrap up a deal. Within a few hours, we had agreed that HON INDUSTRIES would purchase the tangible net assets of Corry Jamestown for book value plus $400,000, making our total cost about $9 million. This agreement was subject to final documentation as well as approval by the board of directors of HON INDUSTRIES.

July 6 was the closing date with Singer. All documents were in proper shape and were executed. A new Corry Jamestown Corp. was incorporated in Iowa to acquire the net tangible assets from Singer. The board of directors consisted of Howe, Hunt, Dahl, and myself, with Howe as chairman. An initial meeting of the new board was held in Muscatine. HON INDUSTRIES was in the Grade A market.

Profile. The Corry Jamestown Corp. had long been a nationally recognized manufacturer of metal office furniture. Entrepreneur David A. Hilstrom began in 1920 to fabricate desks and files in a small shop in Corry. As business prospered, he increased the product line and acquired additional manufacturing facilities. For many decades, Corry Jamestown ranked in the forefront of the higher quality Grade A manufacturers, along with Shaw-Walker, Steelcase, General Fireproofing, and A.S.E.

By 1972, the Corry Jamestown product line included six series of desks and credenzas, together with vertical files, bookcases, and other case goods. It also included five series of chairs. One line of desks and associated items had been designed for the Deere headquarters building in Moline, Illinois. Corry Jamestown products were heavy-duty and well-built, typical of Grade A furniture in the 1960s. For years, Corry Jamestown's advertising had featured a photograph of their plant showing a tall smokestack on which were painted the words "Steel Age," a slogan typifying Corry Jamestown products. The stack caught my eye as I entered the parking lot on my first visit to Corry.

Corry Jamestown products were marketed through dealers across the United States, with the heaviest concentration east of the Mississippi River. Products were also sold directly to major industrial and commercial accounts. Much of the product was shipped uncartoned in Corry Jamestown trucks. Showrooms were maintained on Park Avenue in New York and in the Merchandise Mart in Chicago. A company sales force, headed by a vice president, handled most of Corry Jamestown's sales to dealers and to industrial and commercial accounts. Manufacturers' representatives were used in a few western states.

In addition to manufacture of office furniture, Corry Jamestown had a contract operation that fabricated metal products for other companies. These included display cases for dress patterns for use in retail stores. Other items included stands and cabinets for various types of office machines. Customers included Xerox, IBM, and Eastman Kodak.

From a peak of $18.63 million in 1969, Corry Jamestown sales dropped to $13.8 million in 1971. This decline turned net income of $745,000 into a loss of $179,000. This loss no doubt contributed to Singer's urgency to divest a misfit.

At the end of 1971, Corry Jamestown employed 823 people. Hourly workers were represented by a strong local of the International Association of Machinists. Both the plant and management organizations appeared to be overstaffed, particularly in view of sales declines in 1970 and 1971.

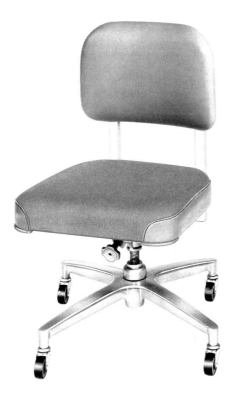

The Corry Jamestown Correlation chair.

The Corry Jamestown Doric desk with modular return.

Facilities.   At the time of acquisition, Corry Jamestown was operating three plants—two in Corry and one in Youngstown, Ohio, about 95 miles from Corry. Although Jamestown remained in the corporate name, the plant planned there was never built. The main Corry plant (Number III) was a fine, modern building of 430,000 square feet with high ceilings, located east of the Corry city limits on a 250-acre site with a rail siding. The building was constructed in 1952, with five additions made in ensuing years, the last in 1967. The corporate offices were housed in a magnificent three-story, 34,800-square-foot structure built in 1962 adjacent to the main plant. The ample space and luxurious appointments of this office were quite a contrast to the stark little room on the second floor of the original Oak Street Plant that was mine when I was president. They were even extravagant compared with HON INDUSTRIES' headquarters building in Muscatine at the time.

The productive capacity of the main plant was much too large for the level of sales in 1972. The plant layout was poor. Material handling was awkward. Manufacturing procedures were unduly time-consuming and complicated. The operation functioned more as a job shop than a production line. An enormous amount of work in process was stored on racks. But we felt there was gold to be mined through an improved organization of production.

The contract plant, known as Plant Number I, was located in the downtown district of Corry. At one time, it had been Corry Jamestown's main production facility. It was an old three-story building with 139,000 square feet of floor space. The production layout of the contract plant was typical of what had to be done in a multi-story building. It was crowded, poorly arranged, and certainly inefficient. Material handling was costly.

The third facility was the chair factory, a 22,000-square-foot building located in Youngstown. This plant used some parts manufactured in Corry. Finished goods were trucked to Corry for warehousing and shipment. As the plant was leased rather than owned and the floor space of the main plant was underused, the chair operation was an early candidate for transfer to Corry.

Operations.   We introduced few operational changes at Corry Jamestown in the months immediately following acquisition. However, we did give top priority to a study of what needed to be done to accomplish a turnaround in the company's fortunes.

We also directed close attention to an appraisal of the capabilities of senior management. After acquisition, the top management of Corry Jamestown under Singer ownership continued in office: L. Richard Fuller, president; William F. Masler,

Jr., vice president of manufacturing; Martin Pfinsgraff, vice president of marketing; and Edward S. Thompson, comptroller.

Even before completion of the acquisition, Howe and I sensed that an early replacement of the Corry Jamestown president was inevitable. Fuller, a long-time employee of the company, had assumed the presidency when Singer took over. He appeared to have little grasp of the changes needed to modernize the operation, restore sales volume, and produce an acceptable profit.

Howe and I conferred many times between the July 6 closing date and October 27, when the HON INDUSTRIES board of directors convened at Corry to review our new subsidiary. As early as September 1, I noted in my log: "Looks like we must act re Fuller." Our doubts about Fuller were confirmed during the board meeting. It became evident that Fuller was an "office" man with no hands-on contact with either manufacturing or sales. Shortly after the board meeting, the decision was made to terminate Fuller. On November 10 his resignation was accepted.

On November 30, Howe and I were again in Corry to announce the transfer of Fuller's duties and to stimulate the Corry Jamestown organization. During the visit I made separate presentations to the senior executives, the office staff, the shop supervisors, and the union Bargaining Committee.

Howe, as chairman of the Corry Jamestown board, assumed most of the responsibilities of the presidency, designating Masler as vice president of operations. Pfinsgraff continued as vice president of marketing, and Thompson as comptroller. Dahl became vice president. Fred Winn served as secretary-treasurer and Kermit Cook as assistant treasurer and assistant secretary.

We left Corry hoping that the organization had been given a new lease on life and that substantial improvement would be forthcoming. Masler worked closely with Howe. The existing Marketing Committee was continued, and a Production Committee was established. Arrangements were made for Rex Bennett to spend about 40 percent of his time at Corry to introduce better production methods.

Expectations. Our expectations concerning Corry Jamestown were different from those at Holga. We knew that we had a turnaround situation, but we believed that we could manage it in short order. We viewed Corry Jamestown's main plant as large enough to accommodate the needs of a considerably expanded sales volume. We thought sales volume could be increased rapidly through new product introduction and stimulated sales effort. We were confident that manufacturing costs could be substantially reduced through improved methods and modern equipment. We expected Corry Jamestown to serve as the vehicle for our early entrance into the market for systems furniture—enough so that The HON Company promptly dropped its Environ 1 program.

All of these expectations would come about, we believed, once we had strengthened the Corry Jamestown management. It appeared that the major obstacle to overcome was the lethargy that had gripped Corry Jamestown in the latter years of the Hilstrom regime and during the period of Singer ownership.

The acquisition put us into the Grade A market, but our hopes for rapid progress toward attainment of a major position in systems furniture turned out to be overly optimistic. We acquired a going business and a fine physical facility; however, achievement of a desired level of profit would prove to be extremely elusive.

PART FIVE

ANOTHER SURGE OF GROWTH, 1973-1985

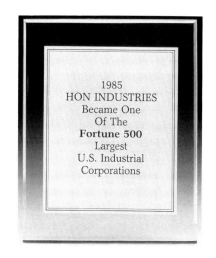

1985
HON INDUSTRIES
Became One
Of The
Fortune 500
Largest
U.S. Industrial
Corporations

This limited edition memento was made to commemorate the occasion of HON INDUSTRIES joining the Fortune 500.

At the time of his death in 1984, Max Stanley had written *The HON Story* from conception up to 1972, with plans to carry the account into the 1980s. Writing from the point of view of an active participant, he vividly described his experiences in launching a new manufacturing enterprise and guiding it to a position of leadership in American industry.

The Home-O-Nize Co., the firm he founded in 1944, overcame severe difficulties in its early years only because of Stanley's persistence and personal financial commitment. This paid off, as Home-O-Nize became a million-dollar company, in terms of annual sales, in 1953, a scant six years after starting manufacturing operations. Exciting growth characterized the ensuing decades, as sales surpassed the $10 million mark in 1965 and reached nearly $50 million in 1972. HON INDUSTRIES, the name adopted in 1968, was a major factor in the office furniture industry, and, through The Prime-Mover Co., occupied a small but profitable niche in the material-handling equipment business.

In his account, Max Stanley pointed to the manufacturing and marketing strengths that were responsible for HON's achievement of a position of leadership in metal office furniture for the middle market. Clearly, what occurred on the factory floor was crucial. Over the years, Stan Howe and his team of engineers and technicians designed and installed some of the most advanced manufacturing methods, processes, and equipment used in American industry, enabling HON to produce high-quality goods in large volume at low unit cost.

Rex Bennett, one of the key early members of this team, later explained how this happened: "In the atmosphere that existed at HON, we were always looking for a better way. We met once a week and just brainstormed. One idea bred another. That's essentially the way we put in so many of the manufacturing ideas that made HON a success." In the perspective of time, we can see that the men of Muscatine were installing

141

in their factories in the 1950s and 1960s many of the elements of efficient mass production for which Japanese industry later gained fame.

Stan Howe remembered well the words of one of his professors at the Harvard Business School in the late 1940s—that more than 90 percent of what goes on inside a factory is unnecessary. To reduce material-handling costs to a minimum, production was planned to allow a direct flow of material over the shortest distances possible. Deadline production of parts and components as they were needed for assembly into finished products minimized the costs of carrying inventories of work in process. This was the HON version of the "just-in-time" system.

Product engineers and manufacturing engineers worked together closely to reduce production costs by simplifying the manufacture of the product as much as possible. Clare Patterson, who joined Home-O-Nize as an industrial engineer in 1957, later recalled: "I had a desk about five feet away from the head of the product engineering group. As he designed things, he slid them over to me, and I looked at them from a tooling and production standpoint. By the time he had designed a product, we knew exactly what the equipment needs would be."

Vertical integration was a basic element of the HON system of mass production. Instead of just assembling components produced by other firms, HON workers, starting with coils of steel and other basic materials, performed virtually all the manufacturing operation needed to turn out finished products. The people at HON knew their own needs better than could any outside specialists, and they had the manufacturing know-how to devise ways to improve the quality and lower the costs of almost every component that went into a HON product.

The organization of a system of mass production required the development of a system of mass distribution. Not only did HON manufacture quality products at low cost; it also made it easy for customers to buy those products.

In the late 1950s, Home-O-Nize made an important marketing innovation with the initiation of sales through wholesalers on a regular basis. This gave the company a lead over its competitors in penetrating the middle market for office furniture. Low production costs provided the key to this marketing breakthrough by making wholesaling profitable for both the wholesaler and the manufacturer. With a larger volume of sales in the 1960s, the company made the transition from manufacturers' representatives to a company sales force, organizing a corps of territory managers who sold HON products throughout the country. Through sales to Sears, initiated in 1964, the company gained greater access to the small business and home markets for office furniture.

Max Stanley had planned the major theme of the next section of his book to be the company's diversification into wood office furniture and the contract segment of the industry. Success in these ventures, along with continued dominance of the middle market for metal office furniture, resulted in phenomenal growth in the

1970s and 1980s. The entry of HON INDUSTRIES into the Fortune 500 in 1985 was an event that undoubtedly would have given great satisfaction to founder Max Stanley.

The perspective now changes to that of the outside observer using company records and interviews with many of the participants to put together a historical account of the years from 1973 to 1985. Chapter 17 provides an overview of corporate developments. Chapter 18 focuses on developments at The HON Company, the corporation's largest division. Chapter 19 covers the entry of HON INDUSTRIES into the contract segment of the office furniture industry through a series of acquisitions in the 1970s and 1980s. And chapter 20 discusses the activities of HON INDUSTRIES outside of the company's principal business of office furniture.

CHAPTER SEVENTEEN

HON INDUSTRIES

A GROWING AND PROFITABLE ENTERPRISE

I t had taken HON INDUSTRIES 28 years to reach an annual sales level of $49 million, but only 13 more years to attain $473 million. A nearly tenfold increase in sales between 1972 and 1985 propelled HON INDUSTRIES into the Fortune 500. That this was a profitable as well as a growing company is indicated by some of the measures used to compare HON with other members of this select group of the nation's manufacturing corporations. HON INDUSTRIES ranked number 478 in sales, 481 in assets, 446 in stockholders' equity, and 413 in size of labor force in 1985, but the company was number 149 in net income as a percent of sales and number 51 in net income as a percent of equity in that year. Over the 10 years up to 1985, total return to HON's investors was 80th best among the Fortune 500.

Strategies of Growth

Throughout these years, office furniture accounted for more than 90 percent of the revenues of HON INDUSTRIES. As in earlier periods, the engine of growth for the office furniture industry was the expansion of the office and the increase in the white-collar work force in American business. The most visible manifestation of this was the boom in office construction, with one authority estimating that more than one-third of all the office space ever built

in the history of the United States was built from 1975 to 1985. During these years, white-collar employment was increasing at a compound annual rate of 3 percent. Each white-collar worker who joined the employment rolls created the need for additional investment in the form of furniture as well as office space and office machines. In addition, office managers increasingly recognized the importance of the office environment to maintaining and improving efficiency and productivity. This encouraged an increase in capital investment per office worker and in the unit value of the office work station, providing a further stimulus to sales of office furniture.

Diversification into Wood Furniture.
Traditionally, the office furniture industry was divided into two segments from the point of view of materials—metal and wood—with metal accounting for the dominant share of industry sales. HON's rise to prominence in the office furniture industry in earlier periods had rested on the development of expertise in manufacturing and marketing conventional metal office furniture. However, in the late 1960s, changes in the use of materials were beginning to occur in the industry as combinations of metal and wood, as well as plastic, were being increasingly used in the same product. Thus, the Strategic Plan of HON INDUSTRIES for 1969 stated: "We

are not, by policy, limiting ourselves to metal office furniture."

HON INDUSTRIES was not unprepared to deal with the new trend that emerged in the 1970s, as sales of wood office furniture in the United States began to grow more rapidly than did those of metal products. Wood had many attributes that appealed to users of office furniture. However, a powerful stimulus to wood's gain in market share was the increased cost of steel resulting from the sharp advance in energy prices in the mid-1970s. As Max Stanley explained in a memorandum to Stan Howe in late 1975, diversification into wood furniture would afford the company "a partial protection against high costs of steel and high costs and low availability of energy."

A strategy of growth for HON INDUSTRIES would now include development of a position in the wood sector of the office furniture industry. The acquisition of Norman Bates Incorporated in 1974 gave HON INDUSTRIES its first experience in wood furniture. Three years later, purchase of the assets of Murphy-Miller, Incorporated, put The HON Company firmly into wood seating for the middle market. About the same time, The HON Company began producing wood desks in Muscatine.

The Move into the Contract Segment.

While The HON Company maintained dominance of the middle market during the 1970s and 1980s, HON INDUSTRIES was also seeking to develop a strong position in the contract segment of the office furniture industry. To attain this goal, the company used a strategy of acquiring existing companies with a position in that area.

Max Stanley described in Chapter 16 the first steps in carrying out this strategy — the acquisition of Holga Metal Products in 1971 and Corry Jamestown in 1972. The acquisition in 1980 of Hiebert, Inc., brought into HON INDUSTRIES one of the nation's leading producers of high-quality wood and systems furniture. A year later, the J. K. Rishel Furniture Company, an old established manufacturer of high-quality wood furniture, became a part of HON INDUSTRIES.

After the internal merger of Norman Bates and Holga into Corry Jamestown in 1982, HON INDUSTRIES would carry out its strategy of growth in office furniture through three nationwide operating companies. The HON Company continued to focus on the middle market, offering through multiple distribution channels a broad line of medium-priced metal and wood office furniture, conventional and systems. Corry Jamestown represented HON INDUSTRIES in the contract segment of the office furniture market, with the original Corry organization and Holga emphasizing metal furniture. Hiebert, including the former Rishel plant in North Carolina, produced and marketed top-quality wood open plan office systems as well as freestanding wood furniture. In 1984, HON INDUSTRIES established Rishel's operation in Pennsylvania as a separate operating company because of its concentrated sales to the United States government. (In 1986, Hiebert and Corry would be merged into one nationwide operating unit to represent HON INDUSTRIES in the contract segment of the office furniture market.)

Diversities. Although HON INDUSTRIES had become one of the nation's largest office furniture manufacturers, the company from the beginning held interests in other types of business. The establishment of Prime-Mover in 1950 had carried Home-O-Nize into the manufacture of material-handling equipment even before the company began to produce office furniture. In 1981, HON INDUSTRIES moved into another area with the acquisition of Heatilator, a leading manufacturer of metal fireplaces. In 1983, HON INDUSTRIES made the first step in the acquisition of Ring King Visibles, Incorporated, a leading manufacturer of filing products for computer diskettes and microfilm.

Guides to Decision Making

Out of the company's experience evolved a set of basic objectives that guided decision making. In the strategic planning process that began in the late 1960s, the objectives provided standards against which to judge the current situation and proposed future actions. Furthermore, as one recent Strategic Plan explained, HON INDUSTRIES would "strive for a high standard of excellence in all things that it does in the achievement" of those objectives.

HON INDUSTRIES would attain *high standards of profitability.* Among these standards was operating income of not less than 25 percent of total assets employed and a net return after taxes of at least 20 percent of equity. An additional goal was to earn a profit after taxes of 6 percent or more of net sales. *Economic soundness* ensured the protection of the shareholders' investment. Long-term debt would be used to gain leverage, but it would be limited to a level that represented 20 to 40 percent of permanent capital. *A sound growth pattern* would double the size of HON INDUSTRIES every four or five years, but this expansion would have to be within the company's financial and managerial capabilities.

All of these objectives, stated in financial terms, were intertwined with the goals of being a *good place to work* and a *good corporate citizen.* Profits provided not only the return on investment desired by shareholders but also the funds needed for the kind of growth that would provide opportunity and economic security for members. A growing business, soundly financed, was in a position to generate a steady stream of new products and better product value—advantageous not only to HON but also to the dealers who handled the company's products and the customers who used them.

A New Structure of Management

Business historians have observed that structure follows strategy in the business world. A strategy of growth usually results in not only a larger but also a more complex business firm. Thus, a new structure of management has to be created if the corporation is to continue to be managed efficiently. This is what happened to HON INDUSTRIES in the early 1970s.

After the rapid growth of HON INDUSTRIES in the 1960s, the time had come to separate the production of office furniture and material-handling equipment. The acquisition of Holga and Corry Jamestown made imperative a change in the organizational structure of HON INDUSTRIES. In Chapter 13, Max Stanley explained how HON in the early 1970s began the transition from "one big family" to a modern multidivisional, decentralized corporate structure, with the creation of profit centers or operating companies to conduct all of the firm's manufacturing and marketing.

When the new structure of management was implemented in the early 1970s, there were four operating companies—The HON Company, The Prime-Mover Co., Holga Metal Products Corp., and Corry Jamestown Corp. When Norman Bates and Hiebert were acquired, in 1974 and 1980 respectively, they also became profit centers. Each company had an executive vice president—later designated as president—who was chief operating officer, reporting to the president of HON INDUSTRIES, who served as chief executive officer of each of the profit centers.

The corporate office of HON INDUSTRIES established overall policy, coordi-

Strategic planning had long been an important aspect of the company's success. The first corporate-wide strategic planning session coordinating all the divisions of the corporation was held in 1978. Officers and key department heads as well as most of the division presidents attended.

nated the work of the operating companies, and appraised the results. The corporate staff supplied a variety of services and consultation to the operating companies. Some of these were mandatory, such as accounting, auditing, legal services, risk management, safety, and purchase of members' health insurance policies. In other cases, operating companies could elect to use the services provided by the corporate office. These included advertising and publicity, management recruiting and training, manufacturing engineering, product or company acquisitions, development of data processing, and organization of systems and procedures. Operating companies were billed to cover all costs of providing these services. In spite of far-reaching responsibilities, expenses of the corporate office were limited to less than 1 percent of consolidated net sales.

As the structure evolved over the years, the operating companies assumed increasing responsibility for developing and implementing their own strategies of growth. In the late 1960s, HON INDUS-TRIES had installed a long-range strategic planning process, which became one of the company's most important management tools. A five-year plan, updated and extended periodically, was used as a guide to all major operating decisions. These plans not only diagnosed problems in the existing business that needed to be treated, but, even more importantly, they defined future opportunities to be pursued. From the start, the process was based on the assumption that workable plans could be most effectively developed by the people responsible for putting them into effect. Thus, management at the level of the operating company, rather than a corporate planning staff, became the key element in the preparation of strategic growth plans within the guidelines of the basic objectives of the corporation.

A Reorganization of Management

The fruits of the strategy of growth in the 1970s led to another change in management structure at HON INDUS-TRIES, whose annual sales exceeded $200

million by 1980. Six chief operating officers and four vice presidents in charge of functions at corporate headquarters were reporting directly to the president of HON INDUSTRIES, who also served as the chief executive officer of each operating company. It became imperative to relieve the burden that this situation had come to impose on the effective functioning of the office of the president.

The solution to this problem was to reorganize the parent company staff under fewer officers and to merge the office furniture companies into fewer entities. Thus, in 1982 the officers in charge of most of the corporate functions, including the vice presidents of finance, personnel, and manufacturing research, began to report to the senior vice president. The senior vice president and the secretary of the corporation became the only corporate officers to report to the president. As a result of the internal merger of Holga and Norman Bates into Corry Jamestown, also in 1982, the number of operating companies in the office furniture field was reduced to three—The HON Company, Corry Jamestown, Corp., and Hiebert. J. K. Rishel Furniture Co., purchased in 1982, temporarily became a part of Hiebert, although the Williamsport plant was established as a separate division two years later. (Another internal merger, that of Corry Jamestown and Hiebert in late 1986, created a new organization called the CorryHiebert Corporation.

Managing HON INDUSTRIES

For many years, Max Stanley as chairman and chief executive officer and Stan Howe as president and chief operating officer worked together closely as a top-level decision-making team. However, while Stanley continued to be involved with the business of HON INDUSTRIES, his attention turned increasingly to the work of the Stanley Foundation and other civic activities during the 1970s. Thus, Howe came to assume greater responsibility for directing corporate affairs. As a reflection of this development, the board of directors officially named Stan Howe as chief executive officer in 1979. After the sudden death of Max Stanley in 1984, what had for so many years been a shared burden of responsibility now belonged solely to Stan Howe, who became chairman as well as president.

As HON INDUSTRIES grew in size and complexity, the system of management that Stanley and Howe had encouraged over the years became even more important to the firm's continuing success. As Stanley explained in Chapter 7, a combination of necessity and philosophy had created a results-oriented style of management within the growing organization. A participative approach to decision making was characteristic, with committees playing an important role in discussion and communication. However, the accountability of the individual manager was emphasized at all levels, thereby avoiding the kind of politicizing so prevalent in large bureaucratic organizations. To avoid the development of excessive layers of

management, HON INDUSTRIES continued to use a moderately broad span of control, with the functions of each management position continually evaluated.

A management development program helped to assure that through selection and training, the long-range management needs of HON INDUSTRIES and the operating companies would be fulfilled. This plan was designed to identify potential management candidates from within the corporation as well as to determine the development techniques that best fit the needs of both the individual and the corporation. But when necessary, the company was not reluctant to recruit top executives from the outside.

The Headquarters Staff. When Art Dahl retired in 1981, Mike Derry succeeded him as senior vice president. John Axel, who had been vice president of administration at The HON Company, was appointed in 1978 to the newly created position of vice

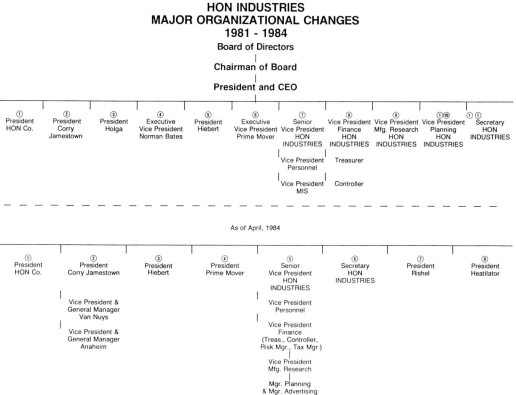

HON INDUSTRIES major organizational changes, 1981–1984.

Art Dahl (above) retired in 1981 after serving with the company from its beginnings. Dahl had a firm grasp of management as well as of manufacturing. R. Michael Derry (below) brought a strong financial management background with him when he joined the company to replace Dahl.

president of finance at HON INDUSTRIES. Max Collins continued as vice president of personnel, as did Clare Patterson as vice president of manufacturing research. Herb Williamson served as vice president of planning from 1973 until his death in 1981. Jim Goughenour was vice president of management information services from 1979 until 1982, when he was transferred to The HON Company. Fred Winn continued as secretary-treasurer until his retirement in 1976. He was succeeded by Bruce Jolly, who held the position until 1979. Bob Carl, who had long served as assistant to the president, then became secretary and Carol Schallert treasurer. The latter was succeeded by Bill Snydacker in 1980. Donald Swanson was controller from 1976 to 1979. Mel McMains, who had joined HON INDUSTRIES as internal auditor in 1979, became controller in 1980.

Board of Directors

HON INDUSTRIES continued the tradition of an outside board whose members played an important role in making strategy decisions. The board regularly reviewed the long-range plans of the parent company and the subsidiaries. Score Card was a practice initiated during this period, whereby once a year, the president of each operating company made a progress report to the board regarding implementation of his company's strategic plan. Committees continued to be used to facilitate the transaction of the board's business. Quarterly meetings were held in Muscatine and at other company facilities.

As the activity of corporate raiders escalated in the late 1970s and early 1980s, the board gave special attention to the development of tactics to be used in the event of a hostile takeover attempt. Seeing the wreckage of corporations that had been the victims of industrial pirates, Max Stanley had determined that such a fate would not befall the company to which he had contributed so much of his effort. The board adopted his position that it was in the best interests of the shareholders of HON INDUSTRIES not to be unfairly subject to sudden complex offers to buy that perhaps would subject them to unequal treatment.

Directors sought advice from representatives of leading investment banking and law firms. One action that was taken was to increase to three years and stagger the terms of the directors. Also, the articles of incorporation were amended to require approval of a "super majority" for certain takeover offers.

The board lost three members because of death during this period, including two founders—Chairman Max Stanley in 1984 and Director Emeritus Clem Hanson in 1985—as well as Dan Throop Smith in 1982. Albert Hinkle resigned in 1977 after serving for 12 years. J. Harold Bragg, who had been a board member since 1971, resigned in 1979 when he became president of The HON Company. Members elected earlier who continued as directors during this period included Stan Howe, Richard H. Stanley, William F. Cory, Austin T. Hunt, Jr., and Ralph P. Hofstad.

A number of new members joined the board during these years, bringing fresh perspectives. In 1977, William N. Letson, partner in the law firm of Letson, Griffith, Woodall & Lavelle and former general counsel of the Westinghouse Corporation, became a director. The following year, Eleanor M. Birch, associate professor of business administration at the University of Iowa—later associate dean of the College of Business Administration—was elected. Four new members joined in 1980: David F. Wentworth, administrative partner in the certified public accounting firm of McGladrey Hendrickson & Company; Michael S. Plunkett, vice president of industrial relations and personnel at Deere & Company; Thomas M. Shive, president of Fisher Controls Company; and Herman J. Schmidt, retired vice chairman and a director of Mobil Oil Corporation. The latter was also a director of several other leading corporations, including H. J. Heinz Company, NL Industries, Inc., Kaiser Cement Corporation, MAPCO, Inc., and C.I.T. Financial Corporation. Two men served for relatively short periods of time: Charles A. Hanson, senior vice president, Deere & Company, was a director from 1976 to 1980, and Morris L. Neuville, a management consultant, from 1977 to 1980.

With the death of Max Stanley, Stan Howe became chairman of the board of directors. The size of the board increased slightly, from 10 in 1972 to 11 in 1985, although there had been as many as 13 directors in 1980 and 1981.

The 11 directors at the end of 1985, in order of seniority, were Howe, R. Stanley, Cory, Hunt, Hofstad, Letson, Birch, Wentworth, Plunkett, Shive, and Schmidt. This was truly an outside board; only Chairman Howe was a member of management.

Corporate Planes, Incorporated

By the end of the 1970s, the need of executives and staff to visit the company's many locations and major customers around the country generated a considerable volume of air travel. However, it did not appear that the amount of travel by HON personnel alone justified investment in a private plane at that time.

The solution was the formation in 1980 of Corporate Planes, Inc., a joint venture with Stanley Consultants, whose personnel also did a considerable amount of air travel. Corporate Planes then bought a new Cheyenne turboprop craft. HON and Stanley Consultants shared the use of the plane equally until 1985, when the latter firm reduced its ownership of Corporate Planes to 10 percent.

The corporate plane quickly came to play an important role in the management of a corporation that in 1985 operated 17 plants in nine states from coast to coast, many in communities that could not be reached from Muscatine by direct commercial flights. By enabling top executives to travel to these far-flung locations more easily and quickly, and with less stress, the corporate plane contributed to the productivity of management.

Finance

The strong financial position of HON INDUSTRIES facilitated the funding of acquisitions as well as new construction, increased accounts receivable, and larger inventories that accompanied the expanding

Officers of HON INDUSTRIES, from left to right: John W. Axel, vice president, finance; Carol J. Schallert, treasurer (1979); and Melvin L. McMains, controller.

Robert L. Carl (right), secretary, and Clare A. Patterson (left), vice president, manufacturing research.

Max A. Collins (left), vice president, personnel, and Herbert C. Williamson, Jr. (right), vice president, planning.

James F. Goughenour (left), vice president, management information services, and William F. Snydacker (right), treasurer.

sales of these years. Retained earnings, which rose from $10 million in 1972 to $110 million in 1985, continued to be the major source of financing, supplemented by a moderate amount of long-term debt. In line with long-standing policy, short-term debt was to be used only for short-term purposes.

No new issues of stock were made during this period. In fact, the company regularly made treasury purchases of outstanding common stock, primarily for use in the member stock purchase program, to be discussed later.

The program of retiring the company's 6.5 percent cumulative preferred stock was completed as the result of action taken in 1985. The board of directors authorized the redemption of all the remaining outstanding shares of HON INDUSTRIES preferred stock at par value, with no further dividends to be paid.

With the growth of the equity base, long-term debt as a proportion of HON IN-DUSTRIES' permanent capital (long-term debt plus equity) declined significantly. According to company policy, long-term debt was to constitute between 20 and 40 percent of permanent capital. Long-term debt in 1973 was not far below the top limit. By the mid-1980s, long-term debt stood at just over 20 percent of permanent capital.

Moreover, the method of borrowing changed dramatically. In 1973, the term loan from Prudential still accounted for much of the company's long-term debt, supplemented by a line of credit from the Northern Trust Co. of Chicago, the company's lead bank. As interest rates rose in the 1970s and 1980s, HON INDUSTRIES kept borrowing costs under control by an increased use of industrial revenue bonds to finance plant expansion. The first of these came in 1974, with an issue of $1 million for partial funding of the Prime-Mover plant in Muscatine and one of $750,000 for equipping The HON Company's leased plant at Richmond, Virginia. In contrast to the 8 percent interest on the Prudential loan at that time, tax-exempt bonds, authorized by local industrial development agencies and sold to banks and insurance companies, carried an interest rate of 6 percent. Other industrial revenue bond issues came in ensuing years:

- 1978—$3.5 million: plant expansion, Cedartown, Georgia.
- 1978—$1 million: plant expansion, Geneva Plant, Muscatine.
- 1979—$8.5 million: plant expansion and equipment, Cedartown; Owensboro, Kentucky; Geneva Plant, Muscatine.
- 1981—$4.3 million: assumed with Heatilator acquisition, Mt. Pleasant, Iowa.
- 1982—$3.7 million: plant expansion, Heatilator, Mt. Pleasant.
- 1982—$1.25 million: plant expansion, Owensboro.
- 1984—$5.58 million: equipment, South Gate, California.
- 1985—$8 million: plant, Sulphur Springs, Texas.

In addition, an agreement was negotiated with the U.S. government in 1984 for an urban development action grant of $2.2 million, the proceeds of which were used to equip the The HON Company's South Gate Plant in the Los Angeles area.

Reflecting the growing national presence of HON INDUSTRIES, the company in 1977 selected Ernst & Ernst (later Ernst & Whinney) as its auditors. This national firm, which had offices convenient to HON facilities in seven states, replaced McGladrey, Hansen, Dunn & Co. of nearby Davenport.

Investor Return. The company's shareholders continued to fare well. As indicated earlier, HON INDUSTRIES stood number 80 among the Fortune 500 in total return to investors over the 10 years up to 1985. Dividend payments increased almost ninefold between 1972 and 1985, an annual payment of 7 cents per share rising to 60 cents (taking into account stock splits). Taking the longer view, HON INDUSTRIES had a record of making 124 consecutive quarterly common stock dividends by the end of 1985. Cash dividends from a single share issued by Home-O-Nize in its first public offering in 1946 totaled more than $10,600 by 1985. Such were the rewards for the purchasers of a

Edward E. Jones (left), senior vice president; Arthur E. Dahl (middle), senior vice president; and Stanley M. Howe (right), president.

security that state regulators had once required to be stamped SPECULATIVE STOCK.

The company continued its policy of cultivating an improved market for HON INDUSTRIES' common stock. Stock splits of 2-for-1 in 1973, 3-for-2 in 1977, and 2-for-1 in 1979 increased the number of shares available to investors and kept the per-share price at a popular level. In 1983, HON INDUSTRIES became a part of the National Market System of the National Association of Securities Dealers Automated Quotations (NASDAQ). By offering investors continuous data on transactions and encouraging more newspapers to carry daily quotations, the listing helped to increase the volume of trading and thus the visibility of the company's stock to the investing public.

Providing meaningful information about the company also contributed to investor interest and confidence. The Annual Report for 1982 was rated Best in Its Industry by the National Association of Investment Clubs and selected for a Merit Award by *Financial World* magazine, as was the Annual Report for the following year.

These actions, as well as the growing dividends based on rising earnings, contributed to a strong performance of share prices in the market. Share prices advanced from a range of 3⅞ to 5⅞ in 1976 (adjusted for subsequent stock splits) to 17¼ to 31¼ in 1985.

Albert H. Hinkle (left), a partner with Ernst & Ernst, served on the board from 1965 until 1977. J. Harold Bragg (right) was vice president of Lennox Industries and general manager of the Marshalltown Division when he joined the HON INDUSTRIES board in 1971. He was chairman of the board and chief executive officer of Winnebago Industries before he accepted the position of president of The HON Company.

In spite of a steady growth in the number of outside stockholders, people closely associated with HON INDUSTRIES and its subsidiaries continued to hold an important stake in the company's fortunes. In the mid-1980s, more than one-half of the company's outstanding shares were held by officers, directors, and present or former members, together with their families and the trusts they had established.

Member Relationships

Max Stanley and Stan Howe had always recognized that success in building a profitable and growing business depended on having adequate numbers of competent and well-motivated people at all levels in the organization. Despite a significant increase in the number of members between the early 1970s and mid-1980s, there was no basic change in the policies developed earlier to make HON a good place to work.

Treating people with fairness and dignity remained a basic premise of management in dealing with members. No class system was allowed to develop within the company. Present in the plant and in the office was a kind of permissiveness that allowed a member to say something besides "yes" to his or her boss. The personal desires of individuals were taken into account and accommodated wherever possible. The company was constructive and firm when mistakes were made, not abusive or vindictive toward the individual.

However, top management recognized that personal relationships might sometimes be difficult to preserve in the context of a large organization. Thus, in the mid-1970s, HON INDUSTRIES resolved to limit the size of manufacturing plants so that personal contact with members would not be lost.

In an effort to reduce some of the traditional distinction in industry between factory and office workers, the management of The HON Company decided to experiment with a plan to replace hourly remuneration with a salary basis of payment for members who worked in the plant. The first test of the plan was made at the Richmond Plant soon after its opening in 1975. All members were paid by the week; no one had to punch a clock. However, plant management soon discovered that workers resented being questioned about their absences. Thus, a noble experiment in innovative labor relations was abandoned.

HON INDUSTRIES continued the long-established policy of providing members with wages and benefits that were competitive for the communities and industries in which the company operated. No less important was the program of growth that offered challenge, opportunity, and job security to the individual member. This included appraisal reviews, counsel, and development programs (both in-house training and education reimbursement plans), with encouragement to members to seek greater opportunity through transfer or promotion.

At regularly scheduled meetings, top management continued to inform members in the factory and in the office about the company, its progress, goals, problems, and current condition. Members not only listened, but they also had an opportunity to express their views to management, thereby contributing to the individual's sense of participation in the company.

HON INDUSTRIES' profit-sharing and stock-purchase programs, initiated earlier, were designed to give members an added opportunity to share in the company's success, beyond steady employment and perhaps promotion. The total value of the profit-sharing retirement fund, into which one-half of each member's share of profits was paid, increased nearly tenfold between 1973 and 1985, from $6.4 million to $63.96 million.

Offerings of stock, made to members at 90 percent of market value, were regularly oversubscribed. Purchases were facilitated with a payroll deduction plan. During this period, members purchased the following numbers of shares (not adjusted for later splits): 1974, 31,118 shares; 1975, 48,880 shares; 1979, 45,000 shares; 1983, 29,639 shares; and 1985, 47,895 shares.

HON INDUSTRIES was no less aware of the importance of the physical well-being of members. The company continued to emphasize safety on the factory floor. As the average age of members increased, the company recognized in the mid-1980s that some individuals might be doing jobs that required a physical activity level beyond their capability. Thus, management sought to address the needs of these older members by automating jobs where feasible or by transferring individuals to other tasks.

The philosophy of employment at HON had always reached beyond regular working hours. The Activities Committees, to which members volunteered their services, continued to organize the many social functions that contributed to a sense of community among HON members and their families. These activities helped members to realize that one of the factors that made HON a good place to work was the people they worked with.

The annual picnic continued to be held in Muscatine, attracting several thousand members and their families each year. Despite inclement weather, 2,300 attended

Clem Hanson added the excitement to the enterprise that kept people working and enthusiastic long after the company might otherwise have closed its doors. He helped tide it over until better times finally arrived.

The Public Policy Committee of the board of directors in 1981. Seated: Eleanor M. Birch (left) and Thomas M. Shive. Standing: Herman J. Schmidt (left) and Michael S. Plunkett.

The Auditing Committee of
the board of directors in
1981: David F. Wentworth
(left), William F. Cory
(standing), and Austin T.
Hunt.

The Strategy Committee of
the board of directors in
1981. Seated: William P.
Hofstad (left) and William
N. Letson. Standing: Dan
Throop Smith (left) and
Richard H. Stanley.

the 1977 picnic at Flaming Prairie Recreation Area. As reported in the October 1977 *On Target,* "The rides were very popular and there was always a long line of children and adults waiting to ride the ferris wheel. Other rides were swings, tub-of-fun, cards, and moon walk. Much pop, ice cream, cotton candy, and sno-cones was consumed." Mid-winter festivities included Christmas parties for the adults and for children, an adult dance, and a teen-ager dance (to which sons and daughters of members could bring a friend). The committee also organized excursions to Chicago for football games and shopping.

Sports were also popular among the men and women of HON. Over the years, teams represented the company in local competition in Muscatine in a wide range of sports, including basketball, trap shooting, bowling, softball, tennis, and golf.

The high degree of continuity of employment persisted, with many veteran members at the company's locations. Each year the company held an Annual Recognition Dinner to honor members who had attained 10, 15, 20, 25, 30, and 35 years of service. Each person so honored received a HON pin, with a different stone for each five years, as well as a cash gift. The Founders Club, launched in 1977, was created to honor not only Max Stanley but also all members of the original companies with 25 years of continuous service. Each member received 10 shares of HON INDUSTRIES common stock on induction into the club.

With the establishment of branch plants, the activities long established at Muscatine were introduced at other company locations as well. Cedartown held its first annual picnic in 1969. According to a report of the affair held in September 1978, "old-fashioned Southern Barbecue was the main attraction at lunch. More than a few diets temporarily fell by the wayside as seconds were disbursed liberally." Richmond's first picnic was organized in August 1976, with about 120 members and guests participating in volleyball, bingo, egg tossing, shuffleboard, and other activities. Christmas parties, recognition dinners, sports teams, and other activities were also introduced in these plants.

HON INDUSTRIES in the Community

Max Stanley explained in Chapter 12 the reasons for his determination that HON should always be a good corporate citizen. Providing employment for the work force was a significant act in itself. This was especially true for a community like Muscatine, where the growing number of jobs at the company's factories replaced many of those lost as a result of the decline of the old button manufacturing industry

However, Max Stanley and Stan Howe believed that there was more to corporate citizenship than this. They recognized that a corporation's reputation was an invaluable and permanent business asset. Thus, they spelled out a set of rules to ensure that the company observed the highest standards of integrity in the conduct of its relationships with customers, suppliers, members, local communities, and the general public. Like other citizens, the company had the obligation to comply with all applicable laws and regulations.

While profits were the cornerstone on which all other corporate activities necessarily were based, Stanley and Howe believed that the modern business corporation had an obligation to contribute to society in other ways as well. From the mid-1960s, the company had allocated 1 percent of the previous year's pre-tax earnings for contributions to civic, health, and charitable organizations. Then, in 1985, the HON INDUSTRIES Charitable Foundation was incorporated to carry out this re-

sponsibility. The trustees, Stan Howe, Mike Derry, and Max Collins, were charged with the responsibility of distributing to worthy causes each year the income from an endowment provided by HON INDUSTRIES.

However, the philanthropic activities of the corporate office have not constituted the whole of HON's exercise of social and civic responsibility. The company also has always encouraged members to participate actively in civic life.

Few individuals have taken the responsibilities of citizenship more seriously than have HON's leaders. The Prologue reviewed the many civic and philanthropic interests of founder Max Stanley, including world peace, higher education, local economic development, and art collecting. Stan Howe has provided leadership in the community through a number of organizations, including the Muscatine Community Health Foundation, the Muscatine Development Corporation, the Muscatine Chamber of Commerce, the Rotary Club, the Boy Scout Advisory Council, and the Wesley United Methodist Church. He has long been a member of the Iowa Wesleyan College Board of Trustees and a member of the Visiting Committee of the University of Iowa's College of Business Administration. Active in national and regional business organizations, he has served as a member of the board of directors of the National Association of Manufacturers, the Iowa Manufacturers Association, and the Business and Institutional Furniture Manufacturers Association.

Stan Howe and C. M. Stanley served as the Executive Committee of the board of directors in 1981.

CHAPTER EIGHTEEN

The HON Company

NATIONAL LEADERSHIP INTO THE 1980S

The HON Company, largest of the operating units of HON INDUSTRIES, grew in a phenomenal manner in the 1970s. Revenues increased more than four-fold from 1972 to 1979. Even while sales growth slowed as a result of the recessions in the national economy during the early 1980s, The HON Company was putting new capacity in place. Thus, when the economy turned up, the company's revenues exploded, rising 2.5-fold from 1982 to 1985. Over the period from 1972 to 1985, sales increased 12-fold and profits almost that much. Much of this growth was the result of internal expansion, although the acquisition of Murphy-Miller in 1977 added a new dimension to The HON Company's capabilities.

The continuing expansion of the office and the white-collar work force in American business may have fueled the demand for the products of The HON Company. But it was the strategies developed by Stan Howe, Ed Jones, and their colleagues that made possible the emergence of the company as a leader in the industry. Engineering and manufacturing know-how maintained the company's position as a low-cost producer of a comprehensive line of quality office furniture. Sales to wholesalers made HON products available to many retailers in different segments of the broad middle market for office furniture. Financial strength supported continuing in-

vestment to expand operations and to improve productivity.

Management

With the implementation of the new corporate structure of HON INDUSTRIES in 1972–1973, The HON Company became a profit center, with performance measured by the company's return on assets and on sales. To carry out its mission, the company quickly developed a management structure of its own. The position of chief operating officer was created, at first carrying the title of executive vice president and then, in 1977, president. The managers in charge of manufacturing, marketing, sales, and administration reported to the chief operating officer, who in turn reported to Stan Howe, who served as chief executive officer of each of the operating companies. In line with HON INDUSTRIES' long-standing emphasis on a participative management style, committees were organized within The HON Company to discuss and communicate decisions regarding marketing, manufacturing, administration, product development, data processing, and other activities.

Ed Jones became the first chief operating officer of The HON Company, designated executive vice president in 1973 and president in 1977. After attending Pennsylvania State College and Carnegie Institute of Technology, Jones pursued a career in industrial marketing before joining Home-O-Nize in 1963 as sales manager. He became vice president of the H-O-N Division in 1964. Jones developed many of the marketing and sales strategies that contributed to the success of The HON Company in penetrating the middle market for office furniture in the 1960s and 1970s. Seeing the advantages of selling office furniture through company salespeople rather than through manufacturers' representatives, Jones expanded the company's sales force of territorial managers. He played an active role in trade associations in the office products field.

When Jones expressed the wish to retire in 1979, Harold Bragg succeeded him as president of The HON Company. Bragg, an engineering graduate of the University of Missouri, had 30 years of managerial experience with Lennox Industries before becoming chairman and chief executive officer of Winnebago Industries in 1977. His contributions as president of the Iowa Manufacturers Association initially brought him to the attention of Max Stanley, who recruited him as a member of the board of directors of HON INDUSTRIES in 1971. When Bragg unexpectedly resigned from his position with Winnebago in 1979, Stanley and Howe invited him to serve as interim president of The HON Company while a search was made for a successor to Ed Jones.

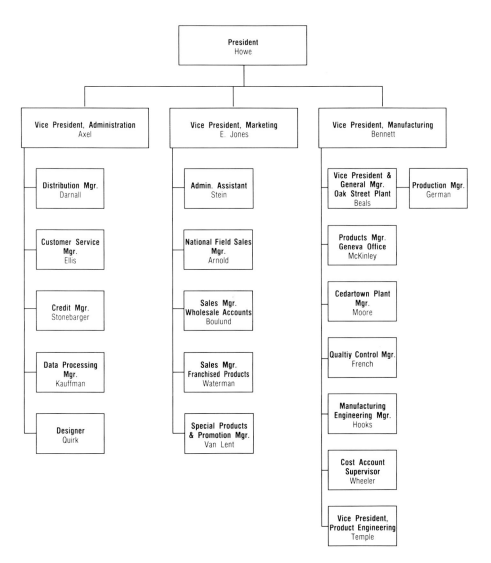

Organization chart of The HON Company, January 1, 1973.

Executives of The HON Company in 1983. Foreground: Ralph Beals (left), vice president, manufacturing services, and Walt Connor, vice president and general manager, Murphy-Miller Co. Middle row (left to right): Chuck Washington, vice president and general manager, Oak Street Plant Number 1; Ron Jones, president; Cliff Brown, vice president, seating group; and Jim Fuhlman, vice president and general manager, Cedartown Plant. Standing (left to right): Jim Johnson, vice president, sales; Harry Matthews, vice president and general manager, Richmond Plant; Lee Maurath, vice president, engineering services; and Jim Goughenour, vice president, distribution services.

As a result of that search, Ron Jones became president of The HON Company in 1983. A graduate of Central Methodist College and with graduate training in business at Southern Methodist University, he served in a number of executive positions with Hoover International Corporation before joining The HON Company.

Under these chief operating officers, a number of very capable executives managed the various functions that made The HON Company grow so phenomenally. Rex Bennett had joined Home-O-Nize in 1955. As vice president of manufacturing, he organized The HON Company's new manufacturing facilities at Cedartown and then at Richmond. He served as president of Holga from 1977 until his retirement in 1980. Bennett continued to contribute to HON INDUSTRIES as a consultant, assisting with the management

of the property in South Gate, California.

Ralph Beals, with HON since 1961, became vice president and general manager of the Oak Street plant in 1972, vice president of case goods in 1978, and vice president of special projects in 1983. Lee Maurath, with The HON Company since 1968, was appointed vice president of engineering in 1981 and vice president of case goods in 1983. Robert McKinley served as vice president and general manager of the Geneva Plant from 1978 until his retirement in 1982. He was succeeded by Cliff Brown, who was appointed as vice president of all of The HON Company's seating operations in 1983.

The following people served during this period as vice presidents and/or general managers of The HON Company's plants: Charles Washington, Oak Street Plant Number 1; Don Blevins, Oak Street Plant Number 2; Ken Meyerholz, Geneva Plant; Jim Fuhlman, Cedartown Plant; Harry Matthews, Richmond Plant; John McGlinn, South Gate Plant; Jim Drum, Modular Systems Plant; and Walt Connor (until his retirement in 1984) and Tom Dossenbach, the Murphy-Miller Plant at Owensboro.

On the sales side, Denison R. Waterman, who joined The HON Company in 1965, was vice president of sales from 1977 to 1980. He was succeeded by James F. Johnson. Wayne Buchanan served as vice president of marketing from 1977 to 1980.

John Axel was The HON Company's vice president of administration from 1972 to 1978, when he moved to HON INDUSTRIES as vice president of finance. Richard H. German served as vice president of administration at The HON Company from 1978 until 1982, when he was transferred to Heatilator as vice president of manufacturing and later to Corry Jamestown.

Product Development

Attainment of The HON Company's objective of being a truly broad line manufacturer of office furniture for the middle market required holding an important position in all significant product categories. In the 1950s, Home-O-Nize, The HON Company's predecessor, had become a major producer of metal filing cabinets. In the next decade, the company expanded into production of metal desks and seating products. The HON Company maintained its leadership in metal office furniture and, in the 1970s, began to diversify into wood office furniture and then, in the 1980s, into open plan modular systems furniture.

In product development, management of The HON Company defined as an objective the introduction of at least two new products per year, each with a minimum sales volume of $1 million. As in earlier periods, the strategy of The HON Company was to identify existing products that fit well-defined market needs and to make them better, less costly, and more readily available. To reach the many segments of the broad middle market, individual product lines were usually modified to provide additional price points.

Metal Furniture. Annual unit sales of vertical files, which had earlier played such an important role in The HON Company's growth, tripled between the early 1970s and mid-1980s, despite recurring predictions of the imminent arrival of the paperless office. The HON Company's share of this market almost doubled from 1972 to 1985. As lateral files grew in popularity, the company increasingly emphasized that type of storage device. Emergence of the electronic office generated the growth of work surfaces for video display terminals and other products, but unit sales of The HON Company's metal desks increased threefold during these years, and market share doubled.

The HON Company continued to make impressive gains in metal seating products. Unit sales of these products grew more than sixfold from 1973 to 1985. Ergonomics and adjustability were receiving increased attention in this market, and the European influence emphasized the element of styling in the design of new lines of chairs.

Murphy-Miller was acquired in 1977 to provide an entry into the wood seating market for The HON Company. Here, Murphy-Miller executives tour the drying yard at the plant with Denny Waterman, vice president, sales of The HON Company. Pictured from left to right are: Dan Lauterwasser, product manager; Walt Connor, general manager; Waterman; and Harold Nall, customer service manager.

Diversifying into Wood Office Furniture

The HON Company's rise to prominence had rested primarily on its success in manufacturing and marketing metal office furniture, but by the second half of the 1970s, the firm was ready to diversify into wood furniture through both internal expansion and acquisition. In 1978, The HON Company started producing wood desks at new facilities in Muscatine—Oak Street Plant Number 2. A year earlier, the purchase of the assets of Murphy-Miller, Inc., had put The HON Company into wood seating in a significant way.

Murphy-Miller seating products such as these served a wide range of needs in the middle market. The company had developed a sound reputation for quality when it was acquired.

Acquisition of the Murphy-Miller Company.

Murphy-Miller was founded in 1945 in Owensboro, Kentucky. When the Kroehler Manufacturing Company, which had owned the Owensboro company since 1963, decided to put its subsidiary on the block, HON saw an opportunity to diversify into wood seating. With the acquisition of a product line that was well-regarded in the marketplace, HON could apply its know-how in mass production and mass distribution to improve the volume and efficiency of the Murphy-Miller operation.

In 1977, HON INDUSTRIES, as the parent company, purchased the assets of Murphy-Miller for $2.72 million in cash. A new corporation, the Murphy-Miller Co., was organized to operate as a division of The HON Company. The HON Company's marketing organization quickly added Murphy-Miller wood chairs to the lines of office furniture sold through the company's multiple distribution channels.

Open Plan Systems Furniture

Introduced in the United States in the late 1960s, open plan office furniture sys-

tems grew in popularity as office designers came to understand the advantages in flexibility of arrangement and efficiency in use of space that these systems offered. Industry figures showed that sales of open plan systems were growing in the late 1970s and early 1980s at a much faster pace than those of conventional office furniture, with predictions of an increased share of the market in the future.

The HON Company early became aware of the potential of this rapidly expanding market. As Max Stanley recounted in Chapter 14, the Environ 1 line was planned in the early 1970s to give the company a toehold in the new systems market. However, Environ 1 was also perceived as an effort to establish The HON Company's presence in the Grade A market. Thus, when HON INDUSTRIES acquired Corry Jamestown, already established in Grade A where the major potential for open plan systems furniture then existed, The HON Company abandoned Environ 1.

Historically, innovations in office furniture usually started in the premium-priced range. After acceptance there, they were adapted for the middle market. By the early 1980s, there was some evidence that the middle market was ready for the development of systems, as leading producers of open plan furniture were becoming more price competitive. More and more, dealers were becoming active with this type of product.

Thirty months of planning at The HON Company led in 1982 to the organization of the HON Systems Group. The new product line consisted of a simplified open office panel system specifically designed and priced for the middle market.

By the mid-1980s, The HON Company was making significant progress with its line of modular furniture, although systems still accounted for only a small portion of the company's total sales.

Reaching Customers

The size and scope of The HON Company's marketing network dwarfed that of its competitors in the middle market. To make it easy for users of office furniture to buy HON products, the company had early developed the strategy of selling through multiple distribution channels to reach many segments of the market.

HON maintained a strong position with major wholesalers, who continued to be a vital link between the company and the office furniture dealers who served the middle market. The number of wholesaling locations across the United States and Canada served by The HON Company nearly doubled during this period, helping the firm to retain its position as the nation's leading supplier of office furniture to wholesalers.

By the early 1980s, large dealers were accounting for a growing proportion of industry sales. Thus, The HON Company began to formulate plans to put increased emphasis on this distribution channel. In 1983, the company initiated the *Team Up With HON* program, which provided travel awards to dealers who purchased in large volume. Greater penetration of the large dealers at the upper end of the middle market seemed to be crucial to the company's hopes to expand its sales of systems furniture.

An important part of The HON Company's growth in the 1970s consisted of sales to the small business and home markets, reached through Sears and other large retail chains since 1964. However, a new situation was evolving in the early 1980s. The growth potential of this market encouraged new types of mass merchandisers to seek supplies of goods that could be offered at lower prices. Buyers in this segment were influenced primarily by price, secondly by service. To strengthen its position at the lower end of the middle market, the company introduced a low-priced Promotables line of products in the early 1980s.

The introduction of the HON Systems Group in 1982 challenged the HON Company management to devise a strategy to reach the middle market with the new systems furniture, because the company's existing channels of distribution did not appear ready to handle that type of office furniture. Thus, specialized salespeople were put into the field to develop ap-

proaches to this segment of the market for systems furniture.

In the early 1980s, the U.S. government became, for the first time, an important customer of The HON Company. Stimulated by the downturn in the commercial market for office furniture during the recession of those years, The HON Company was at the same time encouraged to seek government contracts as the result of contract simplification procedures then being implemented by the General Services Administration (GSA). The first big order—for 50,000 filing cabinets—included shipments to U.S. government installations in such diverse and remote locations as Sri Lanka and Upper Volta. In the mid-1980s, The HON Company was building on the experience gained in filling these GSA contracts by putting increased emphasis on seeking business from other government agencies, on the state, local, and federal levels.

Expansion of Production in Muscatine

Oak Street Plant. The expansion of the Oak Street Plant in 1972 represented the largest single addition to company facilities ever made up to that time. Yet, this "mother plant" continued to be expanded to meet the growing demand for HON office furniture. In 1973, the closing of a city street enabled the company to construct a 31,400-square-foot addition to this facility, thereby integrating The HON Company's manufacturing facilities in downtown Muscatine into one plant. The following year, finished goods storage capacity at the Oak Street facility was enlarged by leasing a newly constructed 60,000-square-foot warehouse nearby.

With production at the Oak Street Plant running near capacity, HON INDUSTRIES in 1976 purchased the buildings and land of the Huttig Manufacturing Co., adjacent to the Oak Street facility. Temporarily, part of the former Huttig factory provided additional warehousing for finished goods. Two years later, the main building of the Huttig plant became The HON Company's Oak Street Plant Number 2, used to produce wood desks. In 1981, The HON Company completed a new 39,000-square-foot warehouse addition at Oak Street, which connected two warehouses formerly separated by a street.

Growth also generated the need for additional office space. The remodeling of one of the buildings acquired from the Huttig firm into architecturally attractive and functionally efficient office space received community commendation. The HON Company staff moved into the facility in early 1980. New computer facilities were provided in the renovated structure.

Geneva Plant.   With the completion of the transfer of Prime-Mover production to a new facility in Muscatine in early 1976, the way was clear for The HON Company's growing metal seating operation to occupy the entire premises of the Geneva Plant. Here, the company planned to create one of the most efficient chair manufacturing facilities in the office furniture industry. Like other operations of The HON Company, this plant would be vertically integrated, producing such components as foam cushions, plywood parts, and chair bases, which many chair manufacturers purchased from outside sources. A complete chrome plating department was installed in 1977 and a tubing mill three years later. The plant was designated as a shipping point and contained warehousing for all products made there.

The success of The HON Company in the metal chair market soon created a need for expanded production facilities. Thus, in mid-1979, construction was started on an addition to the Geneva Plant, doubling the size of the facility. A two-story addition was constructed to provide office space for all personnel required to support the plant operations. In the meantime, the plant, which had been leased since 1956, was purchased in 1978.

Modular Furniture.   When the HON Systems Group launched its line of open plan furniture in 1982, manufacturing operations were carried out in a leased facility in South Muscatine. In late 1982, the Group moved production to new facilities adjacent to the Prime-Mover Plant. The new location provided substantially improved manufacturing capabilities.

A Strategy of Branch Plants

The strategy of producing goods near regional marketplaces turned out to be an important factor in the rapid growth of The HON Company. Max Stanley and Stan Howe believed that once an efficient production level of files and desks had been achieved at a location, more was to be gained by locating manufacturing and distribution facilities nearer to customers. Established in 1969, Cedartown had become The HON Company's first manufacturing facility outside Muscatine. In the ensuing years, other plants were established in Virginia, California, and Texas.

Expansion at Cedartown.   Almost as soon as production started at the Cedartown Plant, it was clear that The HON Company had successfully transferred the elements of its system of mass production from Oak Street to a new environment in Georgia. Thus, the decision was made to expand. When the new building was completed in 1973, almost doubling the facility, a second production line began to turn out more filing cabinets. Expansion continued, with manufacturing and warehousing space doubling again by 1980. In the mid-1980s, Cedartown was producing six major lines of metal case goods products on four production lines.

In the 1980s, desks were produced at a rate of one every 60 seconds at Oak Street Plant Number 1.

Richmond. In the early 1970s, The HON Company began to look for a suitable location for a manufacturing facility to serve the northeastern states. In this populous market area, the company's sales penetration was somewhat lower than in other regions. Executives considered many potential sites. But they always had to keep in mind the need for access to a supply of natural gas, which was restricted by federal government regulations as a result of the energy crisis that started in 1973.

The decision in 1974 to lease a 200,000-square-foot factory building at Chester, Virginia, along Interstate 95 near Richmond, served both goals. This location enabled The Hon Company to place manufacturing facilities close to a vast customer base in the Northeast. The plant, formerly occupied by a manufacturer of medicine cabinets, was assured of an adequate allocation of natural gas.

Thanks in large part to the experience with branch plant management gained at Cedartown, there were minimal problems in starting up the operation at Richmond. Even before the new plant opened its doors, the company began to assemble a labor force prepared to implement all of the elements of the HON manufacturing system. The state of Virginia furnished instructors to teach mathematics and the use of measuring instruments. The company provided an indoctrination program of HON's practices and policies. All of this paid off handsomely by assuring a high-quality work force to start operations.

The HON Company's new Richmond Plant began production in late 1975, with the first shipment of goods made in early 1976. Within a year, two shifts were producing suspension files and other products on two production lines.

In 1980, HON transferred the distribution function for the Eastern Region from Edison, New Jersey, to the Richmond Plant. Management had learned that distribution centers could be operated most effectively in connection with manufacturing plants. In addition, because the company's over-the-road truck fleet, initiated in mid-1978, reduced costs as well as in-transit time, goods could be shipped to most points in the northeastern market as quickly and economically from Richmond as from the more expensive distribution operation that had been located within the New York metropolitan area.

Los Angeles. For some years, The HON Company had considered establishing a plant in California to produce office furniture for the middle market on the West Coast, one of the largest and fastest growing regions of the country. Indeed, this had been a factor in the Holga acquisition, although Holga never became a part of The HON Company.

In the early 1980s, company executives were investigating potential sites in Southern California when they became aware of the availability of the vacated Firestone South Gate manufacturing complex in the Los Angeles metropolitan area. What made the property particularly attractive to a manufacturer of office furniture was the possession of air emission rights for the volatile organic compounds involved in painting operations.

In April 1976, the governor of Virginia officiated at the opening of The HON Company plant at Richmond. From left to right: Rex Bennett, who started up the facility; a plant member; Carroll Waller; Stan Howe; Governor Mills Godwin; and Ed Jones.

In 1981, HON INDUSTRIES purchased this huge facility at South Gate, with more than 1.6 million square feet of buildings situated on 52 acres. Because The HON Company could use only 500,000 square feet of plant on about 18 acres of land for manufacturing and distribution, much of the remainder of the property was leased out. Subsequently, HON INDUSTRIES sold at a profit the property not being used in its own operation.

The first step in the use of the new property was to establish a distribution center. The HON Company already had a distribution center as an adjunct at the Holga Plant, but that small facility was able to provide only limited service to customers. The relocation of the distribution center to South Gate, in the heart of the Los Angeles metropolitan area, stimulated a substantial increase in business.

The South Gate Plant began production of suspension files on a dedicated file line in early 1982, marking The HON Company's first manufacturing on the West Coast. Production gains of 35 percent were recorded in each of the first two years of operation.

Installation of a second major production line increased manufacturing capacity in late 1984. This was a high-capacity line with the flexibility to make a wide variety of steel office furniture products, including suspension and nonsuspension files, lateral files, desks, and bookcases. This flexible production line enabled The HON Company to fill its West Coast customer needs more efficiently. The company not only achieved a significant savings in freight compared with the cost of shipping a variety of goods from other plants, but it also gained a greater capability to ship orders for diverse products complete and on time.

Texas.   With manufacturing established on the West Coast, The HON Company proceeded to search for another plant site in the growing Sunbelt. This led to the purchase of a 110-acre site at Sulphur Springs, Texas, on Interstate 30 about 75 miles east of Dallas. Ground-breaking ceremonies were held in late 1985, with construction to begin in early 1986. The HON Company planned a distribution facility to be in operation at Sulphur Springs by the end of 1986 and a production line by mid-1987.

The Los Angeles–South Gate Plant. The white-roofed area at the upper left-hand portion of the facility is used by The HON Company.

Owensboro. In the meantime, top management at Muscatine was providing the capital, technical assistance, and moral support for Walt Connor and his colleagues at Owensboro to implement a major reorganization of wood seating production at the Murphy-Miller Plant. HON INDUSTRIES made a major investment in more sophisticated machinery and buildings. With the help of Clare Patterson's expertise in manufacturing engineering, work flows were rearranged to move production toward the in-line manufacturing system. A predryer system soon paid for itself through facilitating a reduction of wood inventory. A new 36,000-square-foot mill building was completed in 1982, ahead of schedule and at a lower cost than originally estimated.

The company also transferred to Owensboro the concept of HON as a good place to work. For example, "fly-wheel" production was introduced to build chairs for inventory when sales were slow. This helped to minimize the sharp seasonal swings in employment that had previously characterized Murphy-Miller operations. Investment in a new warehouse made fly-wheel production possible at Owensboro.

Nevertheless, workers at the Murphy-Miller plant continued to be represented by the International Union of Upholsters, as they had under previous ownership. A bitter strike occurred in the spring of 1979 when local union leaders challenged the right of management to reorganize the final assembly line operations. In the aftermath of the 13-day strike, the National Labor Relations Board ruled in favor of management with respect to charges of unfair labor practices filed by the union. Despite the acrimony surrounding the events of the strike, labor relations at the Owensboro plant improved significantly during the ensuing years.

Mobilizing for Growth in the 1980s

A small decline in sales in 1982, occasioned by a recession in the national economy, resulted in a significant decline in profits. Over two decades of yearly earnings growth at The HON Company came to a halt. This shocking experience directed the attention of top management to a series of problems that had been created by the rapid expansion of the company's operations in the 1970s.

By the early 1980s, The HON Company had become not only considerably larger in size, but also a much more complex operation. Products were being manufactured at five geographical locations and distributed through a number of different channels. Yet, many of the ways of doing business had been created for a considerably smaller company with a limited product offering made at a single manufacturing location. It was clear that many opportunities for future growth in office furniture existed. However, exploiting these opportunities required the development of new and more effective ways of mobilizing The HON Company's human and material resources.

Growth in size and complexity of a business almost always increases the dangers of losing touch with the customer. To preserve the HON tradition of making it easy for the customer to buy the company's products, the company began in the early 1980s to implement a restructuring of management and a major reorganization of its marketing and distribution efforts. The first moves were planned during the administration of Harold Bragg. But it was the responsibility of Ron Jones to put The HON Company back on track.

Traditionally, The HON Company had emphasized a broad span of executive control to improve communication and to avoid excessive layers of bureaucratic management. As in the case of so many rapidly growing companies, decision making had remained highly centralized in the senior headquarters staff. A major reorganization of management structure drove decision making down to levels closer to the marketplace. Two operational groups were formed—Seating and Case Goods—each headed by a vice president who was responsible for all plant operations in his particular product area. Strategic, stand-alone business units were created to focus on meeting customer needs in specific segments of the market. General managers of regional manufacturing and distribution facilities were assigned broader responsibilities to serve their markets more effectively, particularly in developing ways to meet customer needs in their regions. With increased computer power available at lower cost, the company sought to decentralize some of its data processing hardware to regional locations.

Central to The HON Company's strategy of growth for the 1980s was a series of actions taken to improve the perception and reality of service, so important to maintaining of leadership in the increasingly competitive middle market. High priority was assigned to development of new management information systems to meet the customer service objectives of the company, including complete, on-time shipment of orders. The customer service group was restructured to move this function from the company's headquarters to regional distribution centers, bringing this important function close to the customer. Initiation of a simplified discount structure and freight policy for shipments from all distribution locations made it easier for customers to do business with HON. Special efforts were made to assure damage-free shipments in order to differentiate The HON Company from many of its competitors. Implementation of improved methods of handling a large number of stockkeeping units reflected the company's perception that a changing market would in the future require a greater range of products, models, and variations in order to meet customer needs.

To continue to be easy to do business with required the development of new ways to satisfy the needs and anticipate the wants of customers. Traditionally, The HON Company had been more sales than marketing oriented. Now, marketing specialists who were experts on the various distribution channels would be responsible for gathering and analyzing market information, determining the needs of customers, and keeping track of the competition.

To meet the varying needs of different types of customers, a reorganization of the field sales force emphasized customer classes rather than product categories. Greater use of consultative selling techniques would improve the ability of the territory manager to solve customer problems.

Serving the National Market

By the mid-1980s, almost one-half of The HON Company's office furniture was being produced outside of Muscatine. With the completion of the Sulphur Springs facility, the company would have factories and distribution centers in six states. Manufacturing facilities outside of Muscatine were no longer perceived as "branch plants." Each plant was an entity in itself. The HON Company was truly a national enterprise, with the ability to provide excellent service to all major market areas in the United States.

The HON Company's attainment of a position of national leadership in the middle market for office furniture was a result of its highly efficient manufacturing operations, the breadth of its product line, and its vast distribution network. These would continue to be major strengths. The changes implemented in the 1980s would contribute to the company's continuing profitable growth in a new economic environment.

CHAPTER NINETEEN

Diversification into the Contract Segment of the Office Furniture Industry

As successful as The HON Company was in penetrating the broad middle market for office furniture, it was apparent that the continuing rapid growth of HON INDUSTRIES would require successful entry into the contract segment of the market. The office furniture industry included many segments served by different distribution channels, with significantly different buying influences and varying quality and price levels. Max Stanley and Stan Howe believed that no one office furniture company could serve all segments of the office furniture market well. Certainly, the experience with the VS line had demonstrated that success in the premium segment could not be attained through marketing doctored up products that were too similar to those of The HON Company. Rather than try to develop the products and resources internally, Stanley and Howe determined to carry out a strategy of diversification through a series of acquisitions that would position HON INDUSTRIES in the contract segment of the office furniture industry.

The first steps toward this strategy were the purchases of Holga in 1971 and Corry Jamestown in 1972. Both of these companies produced metal office furniture. The 1974 acquisition of the Norman Bates firm of Anaheim, California, gave HON INDUSTRIES its first experience in the wood furniture field. Hiebert, Inc., of Carson, California, acquired in 1980, enabled the

corporation to establish a strong position in high-quality office systems and wood furniture. The following year, purchase of the J. K. Rishel Furniture Co. provided the Hiebert subsidiary with eastern facilities for the manufacture of high-quality wood furniture.

Corry Jamestown

As Max Stanley described in chapter 16, expectations were high when HON INDUSTRIES acquired Corry Jamestown Corp. in 1972. He and Stan Howe firmly believed that this move would enable them to carry out their strategy of diversifying into the contract segment of the office furniture industry. They recognized that they had a turnaround situation on their hands, but they were confident that a strengthened Corry management would quickly find ways to increase sales volume and reduce manufacturing costs. Events, however, proved that bringing Corry's profitability up to HON standards would take considerably more time to achieve than initially anticipated. HON INDUSTRIES' experience in trying to turn Corry Jamestown around illustrates the difficulties so often encountered in changing the ingrained ideas, attitudes, and methods of doing business held by people within an established organization.

169

*Officers of Corry James-
town Corp. in 1983 (standing, left to right): Bruce
Kanter, vice president and
general manager, Van Nuys
Plant; Roland Guhl, Jr.,
vice president, operations;
Gerald L. Rosen, vice
president and general
manager, Anaheim Plant;
(seated) Vincent J. Danesi,
Jr., vice president, marketing; Samuel C. Clarke,
president; and Philip A.
Temple, vice president,
product engineering.*

*The Corry Jamestown 1000
system was a popular and
durable design. It is still in
production.*

Finding the right leadership to make
things happen at Corry Jamestown was no
easy matter. After Richard Fuller was terminated as president in 1972, Stan Howe assumed most of the responsibilities of that
office. William Masler, as executive vice
president, was put in charge of operations.
In 1978, Samuel Clarke was appointed
president. Masler left within a year. When
Clarke resigned to take another position in
1984, Nigel M. Ferrey became president.

It was known that previous owners
had lagged in modernizing the company's
manufacturing processes as well as in introducing new products. Some of the best industrial brains from Muscatine, including
Stan Howe, Clare Patterson, Rex Bennett,
and Ralph Beals, put in time at Corry over
the years in an effort to demonstrate to the
people there how things could be improved. Office furniture for the contract
segment of the market was not as standardized as were the products for the middle
market; therefore, not all of the elements of
the HON system of mass production could
be transferred. Yet much needed to be

done to raise the level of productivity in the Corry plant.

Perhaps the most serious challenge to top management at Corry Jamestown was to find a way to deal with labor relations. Workers had long been represented by the International Association of Machinists. Under previous ownership, a confrontational, "we-they" style of relationships had evolved between management and the union. As a result, the attitudes of both supervisors and the union workers on the line created serious barriers to the efforts of HON INDUSTRIES to implement more efficient manufacturing methods.

A nine-week strike called by the union in 1975 was costly but resulted in a contract containing a wage settlement of only 3 cents more than the initial company offer. A shorter strike occurred in 1978, when the union membership rejected a proposed contract agreement reached by management and the union's bargaining committee. But in a second vote, taken two weeks later, the rank and file accepted the package of wages and benefits as originally submitted.

To provide motivation for increased output from the labor force at Corry, the company introduced the Improshare Plan in early 1978. Under this program the fruits of improvements in productivity in the plant were to be shared equally between workers and the company. Other methods, including a work simplification program, were used to encourage employee involvement in their work. A formal written appraisal procedure covering both hourly employees and manufacturing supervisors was established. Efforts were made to improve communications between management and the rank and file in the factory at Corry.

When acquired, Corry Jamestown included a Contract Division that specialized in the custom manufacture of special cabinetry and stands for other manufacturers. This proved to be a marginal operation. Sale of the Contract Division in 1979 allowed Corry Jamestown management to concentrate on the company's primary business, the production and sale of high-quality office furniture.

In marketing and product development, management was slowly changing the image of Corry Jamestown from that of being a somewhat stodgy manufacturer of good-quality, solid metal case goods and seating to a supplier of conventional and systems furniture attractive to designers and architects. In addition to a new emphasis on design of the products manufactured in its own plant, Corry began to import seating from three European seating manufacturers.

Holga Metal Products

When Holga was purchased in 1971, the management of HON INDUSTRIES assumed that the new acquisition would become the West Coast manufacturing facility for The HON Company. Indeed, one of their first steps had been to move the West Coast distribution center for The HON Company's products to Van Nuys. However, Holga retained a separate identity for a decade as a producer of metal office furniture, largely for the California market. It was clear that Holga reached segments of the market different from those served by The HON Company and used different dealer channels. Holga proved to be a profitable operation, with its sales expanding even faster than those of The HON Company for several years during the 1970s.

Corry Jamestown installations showed the ability of the company's designers and craftspeople to put glamour into metal furniture.

The Holga 4000 series contemporary desk, shown here, was attractive and popular.

Jim Arthur remained Holga's president until he retired in 1977, operating in much the same manner as before the acquisition by HON INDUSTRIES. He continued to emphasize prompt delivery and meeting the special needs of customers, thereby commanding a premium price for his products. Much of the success of the business during those years rested on Arthur's method of providing excellent service to dealers and customers. In addition to desks, seating, and traditional office files, Holga manufactured specialty files for state and local governments and drafting furniture for aerospace firms. The market remained largely the Los Angeles, San Diego, and San Francisco metropolitan areas, where, Arthur believed, the company could sell all that it could make. Major improvements in manufacturing methods were made with stimulation as well as capital from corporate headquarters in Muscatine. But the factory at Van Nuys was still not a HON-style production line operation because of the broad range of products manufactured and the limited volume of each.

When Rex Bennett became president of Holga in 1977, his principal task was to plan and manage a major new manufac- turing facility at Van Nuys. New equipment as well as added floor space would contribute to a significant expansion of productive capacity. During his three years at Holga, Bennett also began to build a management team for the larger scale of operations planned by HON INDUSTRIES. His efforts resulted in an increase in production capacity and improved manufacturing efficiency in a plant that continued to produce a wide range of products. After his retirement in 1980, Bennett continued to provide service to HON INDUSTRIES as a consultant on the South Gate facility.

At the same time, an expanded sales and marketing department implemented a campaign to extend Holga's sales through the western states. Dealers were appointed in secondary markets in California, Arizona, and Nevada, not previously covered, and distribution was strengthened in the northwest states.

Member Relationships. Many of the elements of the HON approach to member relationships were transferred from Muscatine to the Van Nuys facility and its predominantly Hispanic work force. Recognition dinners were begun in 1973 to honor members with five or more years of service. A Christmas party held each year at the plant included a buffet luncheon and gifts for members' children. The annual family picnic was an important morale builder. A member pension plan was implemented in 1974. A year-end bonus, begun by previous owners, was continued. Quality circles were started in 1981 to allow more and better member input and participation in the direction of the company.

Workers at the Van Nuys plant had long been represented by the Holga Employees Association. In a spirited campaign conducted in 1979, the United Steel Workers tried to become the bargaining agent for the Holga workers, but in the election, the Holga Employees Association won by a large margin.

Norman Bates Inc.

Already strongly established in the metal office furniture field, HON INDUSTRIES began to move up the learning curve in the field of wood office furniture with the acquisition of Norman Bates Inc., in 1974. Norman Bates, with long experience in wood furniture, had formed the company bearing his name in 1972. With a product line composed primarily of high-quality wood desks and seating, he had attained a sales volume of about $1 million by 1974. The modern leased plant located in Anaheim, California, had a much larger production capability. However, the principal objective of the acquisition, made with 2,667 shares of the company's common stock, was to enable HON INDUSTRIES to acquire skills in the design and manufacture of wood office furniture.

In contrast to the experience with Holga, the Bates operation was unprofitable from the time of purchase to the closing of the plant in 1984. Because the purpose of the acquisition had been to learn about making wood furniture, the losses could be charged as "tuition," or a learning cost.

As in the case of Corry Jamestown, HON INDUSTRIES experienced some difficulty in putting together an appropriate management team at Norman Bates. Bates remained as executive vice president when his firm became a unit of HON INDUSTRIES. When Bates resigned in 1977, John Grant became general manager of the Anaheim operation for a short time. Later in the same year, Gerald Rosen was appointed general manager, and in 1979, he was designated executive vice president of Norman Bates.

HON INDUSTRIES made many efforts to expand the sales of Norman Bates products. Soon after acquisition, Corry Jamestown took on the sales function for Norman Bates products outside of the latter's established base in Southern California. Another marketing channel was added in 1981 when Holga began to sell wood desks manufactured at the Bates plant. In the same year, a new sales staff was organized, and territory managers were named to work with manufacturers' representatives in key cities throughout the West and Southwest. In spite of these marketing efforts and the introduction of a number of new products, sales of the Norman Bates division never reached a profitable level.

Bates had recognized the carpenters' union as collective bargaining agent for the factory work force. Shortly after the acquisition, HON INDUSTRIES negotiated a two-and-one-half year contract. After this contract expired in 1978, workers at the Norman Bates plant sought to have their union decertified. The National Labor Relations Board granted the request after an election.

Hiebert, Inc.

In the late 1970s, Norman Bates was providing HON INDUSTRIES with some needed experience in wood technology. At the same time, Corry Jamestown was beginning to develop a position in systems furniture. However, it was apparent that an acquisition would accelerate the move to establish HON INDUSTRIES as a major participant in the growing contract segment of the market for wood and systems furniture. This led in 1980 to the purchase of Hiebert, Inc., of Carson, California, for 642,500 shares of HON INDUSTRIES stock. With $18 million in annual sales, Hiebert had an outstanding product line

Hiebert case goods were as famous for their quality as for their innovative design.

Hiebert wood furniture made a definitive statement about the stature and success of its owner. Hiebert stylists had captured a modern, yet solid feeling in its design.

and a tremendous potential for growth. HON INDUSTRIES had the resources to finance and manage this growth.

The phenomenal success of Hiebert in the 1970s rested primarily on the design and marketing skills of Jay Timmons. With experience as a manufacturers' representative in the office furniture field, Timmons, along with two other local investors, purchased Hiebert, a small and struggling maker of wood office furniture, in 1965. Timmons early spotted the potential of open plan office furniture, creating systems of finely designed wood furniture and panels. He also recognized the changes that were occurring in the marketing of this office furniture. No longer was the dealer the only key figure. Increasingly, the architect or designer specified the manufacturer who would supply the furniture. The manufacturer then negotiated the sale directly with the customer. The distinctive "look" of Hiebert systems and furniture was found increasingly in the offices of many of America's leading corporations.

The next step in the strategy of HON INDUSTRIES was to designate the Louisburg, North Carolina, plant of the J. K. Rishel Furniture Co.—acquired in 1982— as Hiebert's eastern manufacturing facility. With strategically located plants in California and North Carolina, Hiebert could provide faster deliveries and better service to customers while reducing freight costs. However, it soon became clear that integrating the Louisburg facility into its own operations was simply beyond the capability of Hiebert's management.

After HON INDUSTRIES acquired Hiebert, Timmons and Albert A. Kaufman continued as president and vice president, respectively. Although Hiebert maintained a rapid pace of growth for the next several years, it was becoming clear that growth was creating a number of operational problems at Carson. A management style that had contributed so importantly to Hiebert's earlier success now became a source of weakness in operating a considerably larger company.

The expiration of Timmons' employment contract in 1984 led to the appointment of Richard D. Major as Hiebert's pres-

ident. With experience in the architectural and design sector of the office furniture industry, Major was charged with the responsibility for making important changes in the structure and operations of Hiebert. Timmons remained semiactive in the business as vice chairman.

J. K. Rishel Furniture Company

Although the primary purpose of the acquisition of the J. K. Rishel Furniture Co. for 475,000 shares of HON INDUSTRIES stock was to provide an eastern manufacturing facility for Hiebert, Rishel was destined to play its own role within HON INDUSTRIES. Rishel, founded in 1857, was one of the largest suppliers of wood furniture to the federal government. With plants in Williamsport, Pennsylvania, and in Louisburg, North Carolina, the company manufactured an extensive array of office, dining room, and bedroom furniture for the government. Rishel was well-known for the premium quality wood desk line used in U.S. embassies around the world. Rishel also manufactured wood furniture and components on a contract basis for other furniture manufacturers.

After the acquisition in 1982, Rishel for a time became Hiebert East, Inc. Richard E. Mellish, who had been the principal owner of the J. K. Rishel Furniture Co., remained in charge of operations in the two former Rishel plants, becoming a vice president of Hiebert. Rishel continued to manufacture for the General Services Administration of the federal government in the Williamsport plant.

However, Hiebert executives at Carson saw little synergy between their own operations and the government contract work that was performed at Williamsport. Thus, in 1984 the Rishel Division was established to operate the plant in Williamsport, with the Louisburg facility remaining a part of Hiebert. As a separate business within HON INDUSTRIES, Rishel would specialize in the government contract work that it had been doing before the acquisition. Richard Mellish was appointed president of the division.

Officers of Hiebert, Inc., in 1983 from left to right: (standing) Richard E. Mellish, vice president; William C. Shutt, vice president, manufacturing; Albert A. Kaufman, vice president; (seated) Lee M. Allen, vice president, marketing; and Jay K. Timmons, president.

Rishel furniture is used extensively at higher levels of the federal government. This desk is located in a special press briefing room for members of Congress.

Toward a New Corry Jamestown

Rishel traditional furniture adapts to modern computerized offices as easily as more contemporary designs. Its hand-rubbed finish and hand-selected walnut veneers were important in its success.

This Rishel furniture is typical of the furniture purchased by the Justice Department.

In 1982, HON INDUSTRIES merged Holga and Norman Bates into Corry Jamestown. The Bates facility at Anaheim, producing only a small volume, was closed two years later. The Holga plant at Van Nuys became the western production facility of Corry Jamestown. Holga products, along with those of Corry Jamestown, were to be marketed through the latter's national sales and distribution system. However, the Holga Products Group, manufactured at Van Nuys, continued to be sold by a separate sales force in the western states. A unified product development program was instituted.

In the early and mid-1980s, Corry Jamestown received several awards from industry sources for the design of its product lines. More and larger showrooms were being opened in major cities across the country. The sales organization was strengthened with the addition of professionals skilled in selling to the design and corporate communities. Corry's computer-aided design system, introduced in 1985, specified Corry Jamestown products in the plan view drawings that office designers created for their customers, thereby providing assistance in the selling process. The dealer system was expanded, and many new national accounts were added.

A major decision contributing to the enhancement of Corry Jamestown's position in the contract segment was to move the company's headquarters from Corry, Pennsylvania, to the Dallas–Fort Worth metropolitan area. All marketing and product development functions as well as general administration were relocated to the office complex of Las Colinas in Irving. The move contributed significantly to an improvement in Corry Jamestown's national presence and strengthened the company's position in growing Sunbelt markets.

From this new location, Corry Jamestown management could more effectively project an image of the company as a leading manufacturer of high-quality, high-style furniture for the offices of America's top business corporations. Close proximity to a major airport facilitated the visit of important customers, dealers, and specifiers to the company's headquarters. The amenities of a major metropolitan area appealed to professional people, making it easier to recruit key management personnel, especially in marketing and product development.

Toward a New Hiebert

To mobilize Hiebert's resources for growth in the 1980s, HON INDUSTRIES had to replace the informal, entrepreneurial style of making and carrying out decisions with a more formal management structure. By 1985, progress was being made in implementing a long list of major changes.

Many of the tools of management common in other units of HON INDUSTRIES were being installed at Hiebert: the use of budgets, a cost accounting system to support pricing decisions, and the use of standard practice instructions and basic decision documents. Ordering and billing procedures had to be reorganized. Documentation of the design features of each individual item produced in the plant was being developed to make it easy for customers to reorder.

To improve productivity, the manufacturing layout at Carson was changed. To deal with problems of finish, so important in high-quality wood furniture, a new finishing system was installed. Preventive maintenance programs, previously lacking, were implemented. Quality was to be sought not by doing something over until it was right but by solving problems in order to perform the operation correctly the first time. While these basic changes were being made, Hiebert's senior managers contacted specifiers and customers to listen to their views of Hiebert and to resolve their outstanding problems.

A change in distribution channels was an important element of Hiebert's strategy of growth for the 1980s. Selling major systems projects and major corporate standards programs required a marketing effort directed toward professional specifiers in architectural and design firms, large dealers, and end users. Instead of the commissioned factory representatives and the personal selling efforts of Jay Timmons on

which Hiebert had relied, the company began in 1983 to recruit a company-employed sales force. Although a direct sales force was to Hiebert's long-run advantage, salaries and travel expenses increased dramatically at a time when the efforts of the sales staff were being diluted by the operational and clerical problems that accompanied a growth of sales. Also important to Hiebert's marketing efforts, new showrooms were opened in major cities around the country, and older ones were redesigned.

With 60 percent of the total U.S. office furniture market located east of the Mississippi River, long-run strategy made the Louisburg, North Carolina, plant the primary candidate for Hiebert's future growth. However, converting the former Rishel facility from the manufacture of products for the General Services Administration to the production of the Hiebert product line imposed a heavy burden on management. Nonetheless, by 1985, with the plant transformed into a well-run operation and a new management team in place, Louisburg accounted for nearly one-third of Hiebert's total production.

In 1985, HON INDUSTRIES had four divisions in the office furniture industry. The HON Company held a dominant position in the middle market. Rishel was a leading producer of wood furniture for the federal government. Corry Jamestown and Hiebert were gaining in their drive to penetrate the market for high-quality systems and conventional office furniture. Corry and Hiebert would be merged in late 1986, further contributing to the strength of HON INDUSTRIES in the contract segment of the office furniture industry.

The Corry Jamestown 2000 series of case goods met the needs of open space plan and conventional offices when it was introduced. It has continued to do so into the 1990s. Versatile, attractive, easy to reconfigure, it proved to be the workhorse of Corry Jamestown systems furniture.

CHAPTER TWENTY

Investments in Diversities

PRIME-MOVER, HEATILATOR, AND RING KING VISIBLES

For most of its history, HON INDUS-TRIES had been involved in two undertakings: material-handling equipment and what became the corporation's principal business of office furniture. From its original line of motorized wheelbarrows for contractors, Prime-Mover diversified into electric transporters and narrow-aisle electric lift trucks for industrial uses in the 1960s. These came to constitute the principal product lines in the 1970s and 1980s.

Max Stanley had long talked about a third diversity to which HON INDUSTRIES could apply its expertise. This would not only contribute to growth but would afford protection in the event that the markets for office furniture and material-handling equipment plateaued. In 1981, Heatilator Inc., a leading manufacturer of metal fireplaces, became the third diversity. Although the new subsidiary was in the home building products industry, HON INDUSTRIES could apply its skills in metal fabricating to the operation.

For some years, HON INDUSTRIES had considered diversifying into the field of office supplies, which were marketed through many of the wholesalers and dealers who sold HON office furniture. Indeed, the first products that Home-O-Nize manufactured for the office had been small goods like card files. In 1983, HON INDUSTRIES began the acquisition of Ring King Visibles, Inc., a leader in the manufac-

ture of products to file computer diskettes and other computer output. (The acquisition was scheduled to be completed in 1988.)

The Prime-Mover Co.

Prime-Mover's entry into the industrial truck market in the 1960s had generated expectations that this semiautonomous unit could attain growth rates comparable with the overall achievement of HON INDUSTRIES. However, for most of this period, the sales growth of Prime-Mover's material-handling equipment did not match the record attained by HON in office furniture. Prime-Mover's sales increased slowly in the 1970s and declined in the early 1980s. Not until the mid-1980s did sales begin to move ahead rapidly.

Manufacturing. It had become apparent in the early 1970s that there was insufficient space for both The HON Company and Prime-Mover at the Geneva Plant. Thus, construction of a new factory and office for Prime-Mover began in 1974 and was completed the following year. The facility, located on the eastern outskirts of Muscatine, contained 150,000 square feet, a production space two and one-half times that of the old Prime-Mover plant. Transfer of Prime-Mover operations from Geneva to the new plant was spread over several months, resulting in minimum disruption of production.

The plant was laid out, tooled, and equipped for the "batch" type of manufacturing needed to produce a line of relatively low-volume products. Vertical integration was developed where cost advantages justified the investment. Improving plant productivity was emphasized through increased material, manpower, and machine use. The engineering staff produced efficient designs that were economical to manufacture. As in other operations of HON INDUSTRIES, the management at Prime-Mover directed careful attention to the control of indirect costs.

Products. Production of electric industrial trucks had begun in 1966 with a relatively simple low-lift pallet truck that soon became Prime-Mover's leading product line. By the early 1970s, Prime-Mover was offering a variety of models of the operator-led and stand-on rider types, ranging up to 4,000 pounds of lifting capacity and 18 feet in stacking height. A stream of ever more sophisticated models emerged during the ensuing decade and a half, offering higher capacity and increased speed to enable users to reduce their material-handling costs.

Prime-Mover pursued a strategy of seeking niches in the market. The company made a specialty of meeting the needs of specific users of walkie-type or stand-up electric trucks, especially in designing trucks to operate in the narrow aisles of warehouses and factories. Rather than designing products to be the lowest priced in the market, Prime-Mover emphasized quality, performance, reliability, simplicity of operation, and service to the user, including availability of replacement parts. Indeed, the company's pricing policy was intended to reflect and promote the high-quality image of its products.

Throughout these years, efforts were continued to improve product quality by upgrading component specifications. As product requirements became more complex, the capability of the engineering department was expanded in the areas of theoretical analysis, design, testing, and prototype construction.

Heatilator fireplaces represent a "third diversity" to which HON INDUSTRIES could apply its expertise.

In order to keep tolerances close and costs down, Prime-Mover used state-of-the-art manufacturing equipment. This programmed cutting device, which uses flames to make close tolerance cuts in plate steel, is a typical example.

The RR40 reach truck incorporated aviation hydraulics to increase its dependability.

Prime-Mover continued to produce motorized wheelbarrows for handling concrete and other bulk materials. But the markets for this original product line were not growing and accounted for only a small proportion of the division's total sales in the mid-1980s. In an effort to improve its position in the markets for construction equipment, the company developed gasoline- and diesel-powered articulated front-end loaders as well as rough-terrain forklifts in the late 1970s and early 1980s.

In the same way that HON INDUSTRIES was expanding its position in the office furniture industry through purchase of existing companies, so too did The Prime-Mover Co. consider acquisition as a method of more rapid growth. One proposed acquisition was aborted, but another succeeded in enlarging Prime-Mover's product line.

In 1976, HON INDUSTRIES signed a letter of intent to purchase the assets of the White Material Handling Company, a division of the White Motor Corporation. The White firm manufactured conventional gasoline-, diesel-, and electrically powered forklifts in medium-to-large capacity, which were operated from a seated position. The White product lines were seen to be very compatible with Prime-Mover's smaller electrically powered trucks that were operated from a walking or a stand-up rider position. The plan was to move the equipment and inventory used in the manufacture of the White Material Handling products to Prime-Mover's plant in Muscatine. However, the negotiations were terminated when further studies indicated that the acquisition would not contribute as favorably to Prime-Mover's operations as originally expected.

A more modest acquisition that did take place was that of the Oakes Mfg. Company, made in 1980 for 39,997 shares of HON INDUSTRIES stock. Located in Oakes, North Dakota, this small firm had been founded in 1978 to produce a line of skid steer front-end loaders for the farm market. The Oakes line of skid steer loaders complemented Prime-Mover's existing line of articulated-type front-end loaders. Although the agricultural markets served by farm equipment dealers soon declined sharply, Prime-Mover found the skid steer loaders to have applications in its markets for construction and industrial equipment.

Channels of Distribution. Prime-Mover continued to market products nationwide through two separate dealer channels. Industrial trucks were sold through material-handling equipment dealers, and sales of equipment for handling construction materials were made through construction equipment dealers. Dealers were aided in their selling efforts by an organization of company sales representatives working in the field. Over the years, Prime-Mover regularly conducted factory schools for dealer personnel in both sales and service.

A decline in sales that occurred in the early 1980s stimulated Prime-Mover to develop ways to increase national account volume. Thus, the company expanded its sales to large food wholesalers and other corporations with extensive warehouse operations. Field service backup was being expanded, with technical experts deployed to enhance Prime-Mover's relationship with key customers and fleet users.

A significant new source of growth in the 1980s was the program to sell to original equipment manufacturers (the OEM sales program). In 1983, Prime-Mover concluded an agreement with Clark Equipment Company that called for Prime-Mover to manufacture a specified number of specialized electric trucks for Clark to sell under its own brand name. This type of business came to account for a sizable portion of Prime-Mover's total sales volume.

Management. Gene Waddell became general manager in 1970, was promoted to executive vice president in 1974, and was elected president in 1981. Roy Hansen has been vice president of national accounts, and Gerry Kirkland vice president of marketing and sales. Dennis Wolfs was employed as vice president of manufacturing in 1980. In the same year, Fred Noller was advanced to the position of vice president of engineering.

Heatilator Inc.

In 1981, HON INDUSTRIES purchased the assets of the Heatilator Fireplace Division of Vega Industries, thereby establishing a position in the home building products industry. The price for adding this third diversity was $377,000 in cash and the assumption of Heatilator's debt.

Heatilator, founded in 1927, was one of the oldest and best-known brand names in fabricated metal fireplaces. The company's Mark C, a heat-circulating steel form used by masons to build fireplaces, held a commanding share of that market for several decades. However, in 1966–1967, development of the zero-clearance fireplace, which could be installed on and against combustible surfaces, made the manufactured fireplace easier and less costly to install. Heatilator introduced its Mark 123 version in 1968. By making fireplaces affordable for more people, the zero-clearance product greatly expanded the market.

Thus, Heatilator shifted its resources to the manufacture and marketing of zero-clearance fireplaces in the early 1970s. Rising oil prices starting in 1973 increased the popularity of wood burning in fireplaces

The Prime-Mover management team (from left to right): Roy Hansen, vice president, sales; Gene Waddell, president; Fred Noller, vice president, engineering; and Dennis Wolfs, vice president, manufacturing.

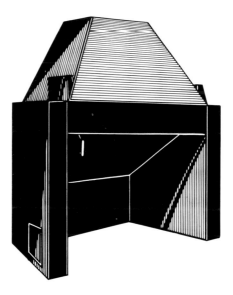

The Mark C Heatilator masonry form was the first heat-circulating fireplace of its kind.

and stoves as an alternative form of energy. As a result, the company's plant located in Mount Pleasant, Iowa, was soon running three shifts, seven days a week, unable to make all the fireplaces that could be sold. This led to the establishment of a second factory at Centerville, Iowa, in the mid-1970s.

However, a slowdown in housing starts in 1979 occasioned by rising interest rates caused a sharp decline in fireplace sales. The increased competition resulting from overcapacity in the industry soon revealed serious weaknesses in Heatilator's position, evidenced by a declining market share. The basic problem was Heatilator's obsolete product design. The market had passed the company by. As sales declined, losses mounted. Heatilator, in serious financial trouble, was unable to secure additional funds to develop and market a new line of fireplaces. With the untimely death of the principal owner of Vega Industries, Heatilator's corporate life was in jeopardy unless a new owner could be found.

For HON INDUSTRIES, acquisition of Heatilator would bring into the corporate fold a company which was widely recognized in its field of factory-built fireplaces, thus providing Max Stanley's third diversity. It appeared that HON INDUSTRIES could supply the elements needed to turn Heatilator's fortunes around: financing to underwrite a much needed new product line and expertise in metal fabricating to improve productivity in the manufacturing process.

A new corporation, Heatilator Inc., was organized as a wholly owned subsidiary of HON INDUSTRIES. Bob Day, formerly president of the Heatilator Division of Vega Industries, remained as president of Heatilator Inc. Bob Burns became president when Day retired at the end of 1985. Rick German, vice president of administration of The HON Company and former manager of the plants at Cedartown and Richmond, was transferred to Heatilator as vice president of manufacturing soon after the acquisition.

Manufacturing. The first step in the turnaround was to consolidate manufacturing operations in the main plant at Mount Pleasant. Thus, the Centerville factory was closed and sold. Also, the company's central offices were moved from Des Moines to Mount Pleasant. These actions to scale down facilities along with staff helped to trim overhead costs.

Manufacturing operations were streamlined at Mount Pleasant with the redesign of the plant layout as well as the installation of new equipment such as numerically controlled punch presses. Attention to material handling and control of inventory were only the most apparent applications of HON's expertise in metal fabricating. All of these changes in manufacturing methods contributed to a significant reduction in production costs.

The Work Force. A new approach to labor relations was an integral part of the effort of HON INDUSTRIES to make significant improvements in the efficiency of operations at Heatilator. With the goal of developing and maintaining a quality work force in the Heatilator plant, many of the principles and practices of member relations developed at Muscatine were transferred to Mount Pleasant.

Top priority was assigned to regularizing employment in the Heatilator plant. In the past, Heatilator had adjusted to seasonal variations in sales by sharp swings in the size of the labor force. This resulted in the loss of many of the most productive, highly skilled workers as well as the need for constant training of new members. Heatilator now implemented a plan to smooth out production by scheduling vacations, taking physical inventory, and producing for fly-wheel inventories during the months of slow sales, and using overtime when sales were strong. In addition, the company intensified its efforts to develop a greater market share in the Sunbelt states where sales were less seasonal.

One of the principal changes in the compensation package was installation of a profit-sharing and retirement plan at Heatilator with the same basic features that distinguished the plan in use at The HON Company, HON INDUSTRIES, and The Prime-Mover Co.

In line with the HON tradition that members were to be valued for their ideas about improving the work process, Heatilator developed a "task force" approach to problem-solving. Groups of managers and workers made major contributions to solving manufacturing problems in the areas of cost reduction, method improvement, quality improvement, shipping damage, improved service, and inventory reduction.

Products. In the meantime, Heatilator was launching a multipronged program of new product development. At first, the emphasis was placed on development of a line of highly energy-efficient zero-clearance fireplaces, positioned at different price points for different segments of the market. Then, as consumer preference shifted away from efficiency of operation toward demand for a unit that looked like a masonry fireplace, Heatilator introduced a Designer series of decorator zero-clearance fireplaces including two corner units and a see-through unit that fit between two rooms. Heatilator also looked back toward its original line—masonry fireplace products—bringing out an improved Mark C masonry form.

A fire test tower and laboratory, completed in 1984, were vital to Heatilator's product development program. Up to this time, Heatilator had used the test facilities at Auburn University. But the advantages of external test services were outweighed by the disadvantages, including timeliness, assurance of confidentiality, and ability to test competitive products.

An acquisition also served to strengthen Heatilator's product development efforts. In 1985, the division purchased the assets of Arrow Tualatin, Incorporated, a small manufacturer of fireplace inserts and woodburning stoves. Located in Tualatin, Oregon, Arrow had grown out of local heating and cooling and sheet metal businesses into the manufacture of stoves and fireplace inserts in the late 1970s. Because a large portion of Arrow's market was then located in the Pacific Northwest, Heatilator continued to operate the plant in Oregon, planning eventually to produce also in Mount Pleasant. By adding new lines,

the acquisition strengthened Heatilator's competitive position, giving the company one of the most complete lines of wood-burning products in the industry.

Marketing. Strengthening Heatilator's competitive position also called for an expansion of the division's marketing efforts. Traditionally, Heatilator fireplaces had moved through a two-step channel of distribution. The factory sold to more than 250 building material and fireplace distributors throughout the United States and Canada, each of whom sold in turn to between 10 and 500 dealers. These dealers then sold Heatilator products to installers, whether builders of multiunit housing or do-it-yourselfers working on their own homes.

As a result of the strong competition that existed in the fireplace industry in the early 1980s, Heatilator and other manufacturers began selling directly to dealers, accelerating a shift from two-step to one-step distribution. In addition, Heatilator was expanding its national accounts business with major building material outlets, such as Wickes, Lowe's, and Payless Cashways, thereby reaching more of both the do-it-yourself and the builder markets.

Officers of Heatilator Inc., in 1983 (from left to right): Richard H. German, vice president, manufacturing; Robert L. Day, president; and Earnest A. Sulaski, vice president, research and development.

Part of the process of the Heatilator turnaround was member involvement. Here, plant members show T-shirts they earned for suggestions or performance.

Bob Burns (right) became president of Heatilator Inc., in 1985. Here, he is shown with home builders. Burns worked hard to bring the company's products into line with what its principal customers were asking for.

Craig Drake, president of Ring King Visibles, Inc., watches as Layton Zbornik, draftsman, displays a new product on a computer-assisted design system.

Ring King Visibles, Inc.

In 1983, HON INDUSTRIES purchased 35 percent of the outstanding common stock of Ring King Visibles, Inc. Ring King, located in Muscatine, manufactured and marketed office products for personal computers and word processors. This acquisition represented the first step of a move by HON INDUSTRIES into the office supplies field.

Ring King Visibles was an outgrowth of a local office supply dealership. In 1963, Byron and Martha Massey, the owners, began to manufacture visible record products then used in looseleaf binder format. Sales by direct mail and through a small network of specialized office supply dealers grew slowly through the 1960s.

In the early 1970s, the Masseys adapted their visible record equipment for the filing of microfiche. As the first to provide a systematic way for users to file these small pieces of film, they found an overwhelming response to their introduction of this new product line to a distribution channel of microfilm equipment dealers. Sales doubled in 1971, and then doubled again in 1972. Ring King was spun off as a separate corporation.

What turned out to be an even more exciting growth opportunity appeared in the mid-1970s when IBM introduced small computers with removable memory disks to be known as floppy diskettes. Ring King made modifications to accommodate these new floppy diskettes into its filing systems, not realizing how large an impact the microcomputer would have in the next decade.

After the retirement of the Masseys in 1978, a new management team—including their grandson, Craig Drake—took over. With the explosive growth of microcomputers in the early 1980s, Ring King's sales of floppy diskette storage devices took off.

However, in 1982 the company faced a familiar problem for rapidly growing enterprises—the need for more capital to fund high-paced growth. With profits not sufficient to fund the needed expansion, Ring King Visibles increased its debt load to the maximum that the company could carry. At this point, management decided to sell equity in the company to raise additional capital for expansion. Many different plans were considered, with continued control of Ring King a prime consideration. This led to the initial agreement with HON INDUS-TRIES in 1983.

From the point of view of HON IN-DUSTRIES, a stake in the ownership of Ring King Visibles provided an opportunity to diversify into the related field of office supplies. At the same time, HON INDUS-TRIES understood the channels of distribution and method of selling the products being offered by Ring King. The small company had much to offer in terms of a well-known and highly respected name in its line of computer-related products. Acquisition of Ring King by HON INDUS-TRIES would fit into the growing trend of horizontal consolidation in the office products industry, as several of Ring King's competitors had been acquired by larger corporations. In addition, a motivated, young management was in place and had proved its competence in building and operating the enterprise, a factor of particular importance to HON INDUSTRIES.

In short, Ring King Visibles had unusually good growth opportunities. HON could supply the elements essential to fulfill those opportunities—capital and a strong position with wholesalers and other agents in the distribution system for these products.

After the initial agreement, John Axel, vice president of finance at HON INDUS-TRIES, took a seat on Ring King's board of directors. A healthy climate of cooperation quickly developed between HON INDUS-TRIES and Ring King Visibles, with the two companies routinely sharing data and expertise. Ring King and The HON Company undertook the manufacture of components for each other.

As the relationship proved to be a beneficial one, in 1984 HON INDUSTRIES acquired for $910,000 a block of Ring King 9 percent convertible preferred stock, which, if converted, would give HON a controlling interest. (This option was exercised in 1986, giving HON INDUSTRIES ownership of 56 percent of Ring King's equity, with an agreement to acquire full ownership by 1988.)

In addition to its principal business of office furniture, HON INDUSTRIES had developed a position in the manufacture of material-handling equipment as well as a presence in the metal fireplace industry. However, although Prime-Mover and Heatilator contributed some diversification to the corporation's overall operations, these two diversities accounted in the mid-1980s for only about a tenth of the total sales of HON INDUSTRIES. The steps taken in the early 1980s to acquire Ring King Visibles represented a move to diversify into a field more closely related to office furniture.

Ring King's Sound-write acoustical covers reduce office noise made by impact printers.

Epilogue

This history has shown how a small business grew over four decades into one of the leaders of American industry, joining the ranks of the Fortune 500 in 1985. From small beginnings, the company that became HON INDUSTRIES developed into a viable and thriving business, attaining annual sales of nearly $500 million and providing jobs for more than 5,300 men and women in nine states in the mid-1980s.

No single factor adequately explains the success of HON INDUSTRIES. It helped, of course, to be in the right place at the right time. A major development in the American economy during the post–World War II decades was the rapid growth of a white-collar work force, which meant continually expanding demand for office furniture as well as office space. But other companies already established in the office furniture industry were not able to capitalize on the growth opportunities generated by these broad trends. This history helps to explain how HON INDUSTRIES became one of the leaders of a rapidly growing but highly competitive industry that served the needs of a growing segment of the American work force.

In the early years, Home-O-Nize had to struggle simply to survive, threatened as it was by a number of problems. Only Stanley's strong motivation to succeed in manufacturing kept the new company alive. At a crucial time, badly needed funds came out of his own financial resources and those of others whom he persuaded to invest. Home-O-Nize slowly gained a foothold in industry—first in contracting work, then in producing Prime-Movers, and finally in beginning to manufacture products for the office.

Not the least of Max Stanley's achievements was his ability to persuade talented individuals to work for Home-O-Nize, especially during the period when the success of the company was not assured. Among these men was Stanley M. Howe, who would succeed to the presidency of The Home-O-Nize Co. in 1964 and to the chairmanship of HON INDUSTRIES in 1984.

After studying engineering at Iowa State University and business administration at Harvard, Howe began work as a production engineer at the fledgling plant in 1948. His decision to take this job with what, at the time, could have been viewed only as a highly risky venture stemmed from his confidence in Max Stanley, his boyhood Sunday school teacher and scout master. With a depth of knowledge in the engineering, financial, and marketing areas as well as an ability to place the small detail in the context of the larger picture, Howe assumed more and more of the leadership role in HON's rise to prominence in the business world. For many years, Stanley and Howe served as the executive committee of the board of directors, working closely together, as one executive later observed, "like father and son, only better."

Out of the circumstances of HON's origins and development emerged a unique set of strengths. Superior engineering and manufacturing know-how enabled the company to produce a large volume of quality products at low cost. Pioneering in the distribution of office furniture through wholesalers gave Home-O-Nize a lead over its competitors in penetrating the broad middle market. A strategy of branch plants provided manufacturing and distribution facilities that efficiently served the national market for office furniture.

A viable and profitable enterprise possessed the financial strength to put new productive capacity in place, thereby continually keeping ahead of the growing demand generated by the increase of the office work force in America. With multiple channels of distribution, the company reached several different segments of the office furniture market. Once the enterprise had gained a dominant position in the middle market for office furniture, HON INDUSTRIES began to diversify into the contract segment of the industry. By the mid-1980s, HON INDUSTRIES, through its operating units, had developed a special position in the industry as a manufacturer of wood and metal office furniture, both conventional and systems, with products sold to most segments of the market.

Early in the company's history, Max Stanley, Stan Howe, and their associates developed a set of business objectives that continued to serve as a guide to corporate decision making. They determined that their firm would attain high standards of profitability, would be economically sound, and would follow a sound growth pattern. In order to attract and retain competent and well-motivated people at all levels, they made certain that HON was a good place to work. Also, they recognized that being a good corporate citizen was essential to success in the modern business world. These goals represented more than mere wishes; the leaders of HON carefully defined their objectives and fashioned a management structure through which the goals could be achieved. And finally, these objectives could be achieved only by effectively meeting the needs of customers.

In assessing the factors bearing on success in the business world, a noted economist once pointed to the various kinds of situations that called for different approaches to decision making. There were some situations, to use economist John Jewkes's words, "where probably conservatism and caution pay best," and there were others "where imagination and daring produce the best results." The most successful business decision makers seem to know instinctively which approach to follow in each situation. Perhaps this same observation was expressed in another way when a retired top executive of the corporation commented that he could never quite decide during his years with the company whether Max Stanley and Stan Howe were "conservative gamblers" or "gambling conservatives" in guiding HON INDUSTRIES to a prominent position in the American business world.

At the 1981 Annual Meeting, the "Pioneer Shareholders" were honored. These early investors had held shares for more than 26 years and had received, at the time, all 104 consecutive quarterly common stock dividends paid by the company through March 1, 1981. One original share held by a Pioneer had grown to 1,944 shares in 1981. Accumulated cash dividends from that single share were then more than $5,500. By the late 1980s, that share had grown to 3,888 with annual cash dividends from that single share at more than $2,300.

Appendix

Appendix Table 1. HON INDUSTRIES:
Consolidated Data, Sales, Earnings, and Members, 1947–1985

Year	Sales	Net Income			Members	Year	Sales	Net Income			Members
	$(000)	$1,000	% Sales	% Equity	(Year End)		$(000)	$1,000	% Sales	% Equity	(Year End)
1947	90	−30	n.m.			1966	13,682	875	6.4	20.4	676
1948	420	40	9.5			1967	16,228	1,061	6.5	20.8	607
1949	323	−30	n.m.			1968	18,289	1,307	7.1	21.7	656
1950	610	−24	n.m.			1969	25,087	1,758	7.0	24.0	868
						1970	24,178	1,761	7.3	16.5	755
1951	1,009	−38	n.m.			1971	28,635	1,883	6.6	15.8	933
1952	987	24	2.4			1972	49,319	3,035	6.2	21.0	1,871
1953	1,436	37	2.6			1973	71,139	4,645	6.5	28.4	2,202
1954	1,720	62	3.6			1974	89,172	5,068	5.7	24.8	2,193
1955	2,117	103	4.9			1975	85,215	5,658	6.6	22.6	2,033
1956	2,784	103	3.7	19.2	217	1976	104,400	7,499	7.2	24.7	2,159
1957	2,975	65	2.2	10.8	193	1977	142,850	10,956	7.7	29.5	3,024
1958	3,313	51	1.5	7.6	226	1978	183,394	14,914	8.1	32.0	3,149
1959	4,359	121	2.8	15.4	248	1979	198,741	17,641	8.9	31.0	2,961
1960	4,365	150	3.4	16.1	236	1980	201,846	15,186	7.5	22.2	3,600
1961	5,767	262	4.5	21.3	307	1981	280,657	19,050	6.8	23.6	4,314
1962	7,175	357	5.0	19.4	340	1982	283,167	11,172	3.9	12.3	4,806
1963	7,273	369	5.1	17.6	346	1983	352,600	15,669	4.4	15.6	4,748
1964	8,919	546	6.1	21.2	424	1984	396,691	16,772	4.2	15.4	5,348
1965	10,962	766	7.0	24.9	521	1985	473,292	26,024	5.5	22.3	5,375

Appendix Table 2   HON INDUSTRIES:

Net sales and net income, 1948–1986

Year	Net Sales	Net Income
1956	2,784,141	103,115
1957*	2,975,000	64,982
1958*	3,313,000	51,331
1959	4,358,747	121,040
1960	4,364,622	150,484
1961	5,766,948	261,594
1962	7,175,083	356,755
1963	7,273,013	368,848
1964	8,919,138	546,310
1965	10,961,915	765,898
1966	13,682,268	875,449
1967	16,227,863	1,060,866
1968	18,288,659	1,307,105
1969	25,087,198	1,758,451
1970*	24,178,150	1,769,853
1971	28,634,604	1,883,088
1972	49,318,676	3,034,996
1973	71,139,164	4,645,351
1974	89,172,400	5,067,537
1975*	85,215,431	5,658,424
1976	104,400,500	7,499,600
1977	142,850,000	10,956,000
1978	183,394,000	14,914,000
1979	198,741,000	17,641,000
1980*	201,846,000	15,186,000
1981	280,657,000	19,050,000
1982*	283,167,000	11,172,000
1983	352,600,000	15,669,000
1984	396,691,000	16,772,000
1985	473,292,000	26,024,000
1986	503,575,000	29,254,000

* Year of decline in sales and/or earnings.

Appendix Table 3   HON INDUSTRIES:
Common stock history

Year	Common Stock Shares Outstanding (2)	Common Stock Dividends (1)	Common Stock Cash Dividends/Shares(3)
1956	14,698,800	19,209	.002
1957	13,984,704	27,721	.002
1958	10,131,728	24,771	.002
1959	14,469,408	32,539	.002
1960	15,125,256	45,282	.003
1961	15,887,736	58,530	.004
1962	16,259,040	80,697	.005
1963	16,472,232	103,280	.006
1964	17,984,664	135,614	.008
1965	18,004,392	172,722	.010
1966	19,357,200	261,818	.013
1967	19,507,392	284,121	.015
1968	19,507,392	353,573	.018
1969	19,507,392	430,788	.022
1970	20,634,738	520,440	.025
1971	20,601,672	523,458	.025
1972	20,625,360	545,308	.027
1973	20,619,360	739,074	.036
1974	20,806,068	1,034,546	.050
1975	21,115,348	1,214,621	.058
1976	21,115,348	1,689,228	.080
1977	20,947,136	2,312,123	.110
1978	20,929,512	3,664,191	.175
1979	20,559,170	4,799,737	.230
1980	21,402,572	4,939,541	.240
1981	21,194,200	5,538,117	.260
1982	22,001,830	5,969,717	.280
1983	22,061,128	6,177,044	.280
1984	21,690,090	6,136,627	.280
1985	20,804,132	6,410,454	.300

(1) Dividends shown in year declared.

(2) Stock outstanding at year-end adjusted for splits and stock dividends less treasury shares.

(3) Dividends shown in year paid – adjusted for splits and stock dividends.

Appendix Table 4   HON INDUSTRIES:

Progression of one original share of common stock

Record or Distribution Date	Cost	Splits/Stock Dividend	# Shares (Rounded)	Basis (Rounded)
3/22/44	$100		1	$100
12/31/57		10 for 1	10	$ 10
11/01/62		5 for 1	50	$ 2
11/16/64		5% Stock Dividend	52	$ 1.923
11/17/66		5% Stock Dividend	54	$ 1.852
4/27/68		3 for 1	162	$ .617
4/18/69		2 for 1	324	$ .309
4/27/73		2 for 1	648	$ .154
4/29/77		3 for 2	972	$ .103
3/16/79		2 for 1	1,944	$ .051

Index